The
Moral
Society

JOHN
DAVID
GARCIA

The Moral Society

a rational
alternative
to death

THE JULIAN PRESS, INC.
NEW YORK, 1971

to
The Children
that they may prevail

CONTENTS

PART TWO   OBSERVATION

CONTENTS   ix

PART THREE   EXPERIMENTATION

CONTENTS

PART FOUR   SUMMATION

PREFACE

The human race is on the verge of suicide. It is my purpose to show that this is the case and to present a rational alternative to death. This is, therefore, a plan and a justification for human survival. I say "justification" because survival is not an end in itself. It will be shown that happiness without purpose and security without awareness are self-defeating goals that must be abandoned if human evolution is to continue.

Evolution is not only the key to human survival; it is the avatar of the meaning of life. Noble efforts to show that this is the case were made by Francis Bacon, Spinoza, Goethe, H. G. Wells, Teilhard de Chardin, Julian Huxley and others. However, these efforts failed to show little more than a goal toward which man could and should evolve. Purpose without method cannot be sustained. I shall, therefore, speak of a way to achieve the goals of these men.

The context of this book is the context of political, scientific and technical reality. The book should accordingly be judged on the same basis as any scientific theory—on how well it works. I make no claims to novelty or originality. What is presented is a synthesis of common knowledge in the form of a plan for ethical action. It will be shown that ethical action is the only end and that human survival is its logical consequence.

Eventually a single pattern will emerge which unifies ethics, science, evolution and socio-political action.

The book is simply written. Very little technical or scientific terminology is used. I have tried to make the *gestalt* of unified human experience explain the individual complexities. Therefore, no part of the book stands alone; a person wishing to understand fully any part must try to understand all parts until the *gestalt* is complete. The best way to perceive the pattern is to read through the book quickly without getting "bogged down" in details.

The book is divided into four mutually-supporting parts. Part One lays the philosophical basis for the plan in Part Three. Part Two specifies current conditions, constraints and the dangers of not implementing the plan. Part Four integrates the entire book. The Glossary is included as an aid to the reader because many words are used in a highly specific sense. It was decided not to footnote statements of fact unless the facts were of an esoteric nature. This was done to be brief and not give the deceptive appearance of "scholarliness" to what is primarily a book of speculation. However, all statements of fact can be documented and are supported by the Bibliography.

Whatever errors are in the book are solely my responsibility; the virtues I owe to many persons. I would, therefore, like to express my gratitude to those who have had a direct, immediate influence on my work. Foremost among these is my friend Humberto Fernandez-Moran. Our infrequent but always stimulating conversations during the last year were among the principal reasons why this book was written. My friend Sandra Hass served as editor, gadfly and typist on the manuscript. I owe much to her. I wish to acknowledge gratefully the abundant feedback from Frank M. Graves and many others on the early drafts of the manuscript. Finally, I would like to thank my beloved wife Bernice, who has been my personal catalyst.

John David Garcia

Washington, D.C.
July, 1970

We are given to boasting of our age being an age of Science! And if we are thinking merely of the dawn compared to the darkness that went before, up to a point we are justified. Something enormous has been born in the universe with our discoveries and our methods of research. Something has been started which, I am convinced, will now never stop. Yet though we may exalt research and derive enormous benefit from it, with what pettiness of spirit, poverty of means and general haphazardness do we pursue truth in the world today! Have we ever given serious thought to the predicament we are in?

—Pierre Teilhard de Chardin
THE PHENOMENON OF MAN

INTRODUCTION

The moral issue to be resolved is whether happiness in the absence of awareness is good. Ultimate goals have no basis in logic. The only meaning life has is the meaning we choose to give it. The only ultimate goal that is compatible with human survival is the continued expansion of awareness. Awareness subsumes the ability to predict and control the total environment. If man is to prevail, he must make a *deliberate* choice to expand awareness as an end in itself and not as a means to an end. Mankind has always had two and only two goals: to expand awareness or to expand happiness. All human desires are variations on these two prime desires. The two goals are not mutually exclusive; they are interrelated in many complex ways.

The development of the human species has resulted mainly from man's desire to be happy. While there was Darwinian competition, man could not be happy without becoming aware. If he did not grow in awareness, he was quickly made unhappy by competition from other animals, men and/or by the forces of nature in general. Therefore, man became increasingly aware as a means of being happy.

Man became aware, in part, by building machines which enabled him to predict and control ever greater aspects of his total environment.

In the broad sense of the word, tools, language, clothing, computers, and drugs are all machines. The process for creating and using machines is technology.

Technology has advanced to the point where a decreasing number of persons can create and operate all the necessary machines for making an increasing number of men happy. In the near future it will be possible for all men to be happy without necessarily being aware. This would be the case in a completely automated society where all machines are operated, maintained, and even created by other machines. That this is possible is shown by the exponential growth in computer technology.

The basic technology already exists for making super-computers in which the logic and memory units are packed with a density approaching and perhaps exceeding that of the human brain. Such computers could completely control an automated society, even though they might not be as creative as some human beings. This is not a vision of the distant future. A completely automated society might be created in twenty years; however, it would probably be ungovernable.

Under our current social structure, a nation in which everyone had unlimited leisure time would result in chaos. The chaos already being wrought by the youth in the democracies is, in part, a direct result of excess leisure time without creative purpose. The central problem facing the human race is, therefore, how to bring about a realignment in values so that a common, creative purpose may replace the obsolete goal of happiness. The only adequate substitute seems to be the direct pursuit of awareness.

Happiness and awareness can be causes and effects of each other. In the past, happiness was the prime goal and awareness was the prime effect. Today we must make awareness the prime goal and happiness will be the prime effect. If we do not, the pursuit of happiness without creative purpose will destroy the human race.

In our highly-automated society it has become possible for most persons to survive and reproduce independently of their awareness. Deleterious mutations are a constant and possibly unavoidable process of nature. Unless something is done to reduce the deleterious mutations that decrease awareness, the human race will become so degenerate that it will become extinct. This will occur because the genetic potential for awareness will disappear before the capability to reproduce disappears. The result will be a society of intellectually degenerate human beings who are completely dependent on an inherited, self-sustaining technology that they can no longer understand or control. By the time the machinery broke down, humanity could be too degenerate to care for itself. Genetic decay is the inevitable consequence of structuring a society solely to make men happy.

Of course, this is a long-term danger, which most persons think is secondary to such immediate problems as pollution, war, and over-population. These latter problems have the same basis as genetic decay. Man's problems all stem from hedonism—the pursuit of happiness without awareness.

We have pollution because societies are structured to maximize happiness, not awareness. Pollution can only be stopped by making many persons somewhat unhappy and a few persons very unhappy. Pollution is, at this time, only a minor irritant. Therefore, most persons, in effect, prefer pollution to more expensive machines and/or restricted freedom. The problem is that by the time pollution becomes sufficiently irritating so that people will seriously wish to stop it, it may have begun an irreversible process which will destroy the human race and perhaps the entire biosphere.

War is an analogous and even more dangerous process. We have wars, in part, because most nations, particularly the leaders, are more concerned with happiness—usually their own—than with expanding awareness for themselves and others. The hedonistic structure of nations makes it possible for unethical men to achieve a monopoly of power by promising ever greater happiness to their people, who have been conditioned to want and expect nothing but happiness out of life. These unethical men control highly-automated, increasingly-lethal weapon systems that can destroy civilization and perhaps the human race.

Compounding the problems of pollution and war is over-population. Excess human beings are rapidly depleting the natural resources and producing increasing amounts of pollution. Every new person partakes of technological advancements that have the stated purpose of making persons happy by giving them more leisure time and consumer goods. These "advancements" cause an ever-increasing depletion of resources and an overwhelming amount of pollution. The shortage of resources causes increasing international competition and this causes even greater tension and danger of war.

The pursuit of happiness without awareness is, therefore, likely to destroy the human race by war, pollution, genetic decay, or the gradual depletion of resources until it is no longer possible to maintain an expanding civilization. The latter would represent a gradual extinction of a humanity that no longer had the resources to continue its evolution.

Those who value and desire human survival must perceive the danger and join in a determined, common effort to restructure world culture so that the expansion of awareness becomes the central goal of mankind. Once this is accepted, then the methods for achieving the goal may be derived logically and scientifically. Methods can always be modified by reason; only ultimate goals are beyond reason. In order to see that ever-expanding awareness is the only goal that is compatible with human survival, it is necessary that man perceive himself in an evolutionary perspective.

From chaotic energy evolved matter; from matter evolved life; from life evolved man. Man is evolving toward ever-greater mind. Mind is that effect of energy, matter and life which creates awareness. Awareness is reflected in the mind's ability to predict and control the total environment. The total environment includes all forms and combinations of energy, matter, life, and mind; the total environment includes the self. The highest form of awareness is creation. The greater the awareness of any mind, the greater is its potential to create. The highest form of creation is mind as an effect of itself.

To create is to cause the formation of new relationships that increase awareness. That mind creates by organizing matter and life into new patterns is self-evident. Once mind begins to organize energy, matter and life as a means of extending itself, then mind becomes less an effect of life and more an effect of itself. An extrapolation of this process implies that, asymptotically, it should become possible for mind to produce the entire spiral of creation from itself, thereby creating energy from thought, matter from energy, life from matter, and ever-greater mind from itself until mind becomes an effect of itself. Thus the mind evolves forever toward pure thought, always getting closer but never reaching it. This is the ever-ascending, infinite spiral of evolution that has no beginning or end. Those who choose to ascend the spiral of evolution will be a part of an infinitely-growing awareness within an infinitely-expanding universe.

The one common denominator in evolution is ever-greater awareness through increasing complexity. Chaotic energy becomes elementary particles. The elementary particles increase their collective complexity by organizing into more complex systems of particles. These complex particles join to form atoms. The atoms join to form molecules. The molecules become increasingly complex until new complexity results from giant organic molecules joining to form cells. The cells then become increasingly complex until further complexity can only occur by further joining. At this point, multicellular animals—the metazoa—come into being. The metazoa continue to develop and grow in complexity and awareness until man, the first metazoan aware of its own awareness, evolves. Awareness of awareness produces a new type of evolution; awareness catalyzes itself by becoming increasingly an effect of itself.

Once man became aware of his own awareness, he began to evolve psychosocially by acquiring knowledge and building machines to predict and control the total environment. As this process continued, he became increasingly dependent on collective human knowledge and machines until he has almost stopped evolving biologically. Indeed, he may be degenerating biologically. Today man is a *gestalt* of men, collective knowledge and machines. Each part of the *gestalt* is essential to the totality of man.

An extrapolation of evolutionary trends in general, and human evolution in particular, indicates that mankind is about to undergo another evolutionary joining in which the whole becomes more aware than the sum of the parts. Similarly, a metazoan is more aware than any group of individual cells. However, the human joining will not be a biological occurrence in which the elements lose their individuality. The existing evolutionary patterns indicate that the human joining will be a psychosocial process in which men, machines, and collective knowledge become a single super-organism in which each person remains free and individualized. The awareness of each person will become part of the collective awareness of all persons. The collective awareness of all persons will amplify the individual awareness of each person until each man possesses all human knowledge. This new organism (the Moral Society) would have the same relationship to a man as a man has to a cell. The collective awareness produced by the billions of cells that make up a human body enabled man to spread his awareness over the Earth; the collective awareness of the billions of persons who make up the Moral Society should enable mankind to spread his awareness throughout the Universe. The purpose of this book is to begin the creation of the Moral Society.

The world is dominated by unethical men who have rejected the principles of life (awareness) and embraced the principles of death (happiness without awareness). The ethics of life are the pursuit of awareness for ourselves and others. Ethical men and women who value awareness must join together in a common cause. There can be no compromise with unethical men. They must be removed from power before they destroy the human race.

The actions to be taken are:

1 All ethical persons must join together in a determined effort to create the Moral Society.
2 Withdraw all support from the political bureaucracies that are dominated by unethical men.
3 Teach the ethics of life widely and effectively.
4 Form an ethical political party to promote ethical candidates.
5 Create an Ethical State.
6 Expand the Ethical State to include all men who wish to join it.
7 Create the Moral Society.

Ethical ends can only be achieved by ethical means. The prime ethic of life is *each person must do his best to expand total awareness*. This book is an effort to teach the prime ethic as clearly and effectively as possible. Whoever can teach it better is ethically bound to do so.

The
Moral
Society

PART ONE

speculation

a man's reach should exceed his grasp

—Robert Browning

Speculation is not science, but it is a necessary first step in the scientific process. In the following three chapters, known facts about evolution are formulated into a coherent pattern that explains the past and predicts the future. This is speculation. These speculations on evolution lead to the manifestation of an overall pattern. But the pattern, like any manifestation no matter how clear and logical, may still be in error. Any statement concerning cause and effect relationships may be in error. Every description, hypothesis, theory and strategy in this book may be erroneous. We can never be absolutely certain when we are right. It is usually easier to discover our errors. In the end, a person who is honest with himself always has doubts.

It will be shown that: 1) it is unethical to be certain; 2) it is ethical to doubt; and 3) inaction is unethical. The problem each person must solve for himself is how to act ethically when the future outcome of every act is uncertain. The concepts of "evolution" and "ethics" are inextricably intertwined. Understanding one is a precondition to understanding the other. To see that this is the case, it is first necessary to understand the concept of "awareness."

1

THE
GAME OF
LIFE

AWARENESS

To be aware is to know, to understand, to perceive directly. Awareness implies the ability to predict and control. Our "total awareness" is measured by the extent to which we can predict and control our total environment—physical, biological and psychosocial.

To predict our total environment is to be able to imagine events—physical, biological, and psychosocial—correctly before we have directly perceived them. The ability to predict is fundamental to the structure of mind. An entity totally incapable of prediction would be incapable of seeing the patterns tying its perceptions together. It would perceive neither a past nor a future, but would exist only in the present in a state of continuous destruction.

"Control" refers to the directed causal formation of a predicted set of events. Control, in turn, is essential to prediction. An entity totally devoid of the ability to control would be incapable of prediction because it could not direct itself. It would be deprived of "feedback."

"Feedback" means perception of the consequences of our actions. In order to have feedback, there must be action, i.e., "prediction and control," particularly control of ourselves. Feedback is essential to test the validity of our predictions and the nature of our perceptions. No entity can be aware or survive without feedback.

"Awareness," therefore, subsumes the notions "intelligence," "knowledge," and "consciousness." To be intelligent is to be aware. To increase our knowledge is to increase our awareness. To expand our awareness is to expand our consciousness. "Awareness" is a concept that we can define only asymptotically, obtaining better and better descriptions as we become ever more totally aware, but never completely capturing the full meaning of the term. The concept of "awareness" will at first be indistinguishable from the more limited notion of "intelligence," and will tend to empasize the more tractable and specific definition of "ability to predict and control the total environment." The reader must at first use his imaginaton to complete the *gestalt* that forms the total pattern of awareness. In Chapter 2 a distinction between intelligence and awareness will be established.*

Our total awareness reflects the total sum of our knowledge and consequently our ability to predict and control every aspect of our total environment. "Knowledge" is information that either enables us to predict and control or tells us what it is that we can neither predict nor control. Awareness can be narrow or it can be broad. Awareness is narrow when knowledge is limited primarily to a few aspects of the total environment. Awareness is broad when knowledge is divided approximately equally among many aspects of the total environment. A person with narrow awareness will be called a "specialist." A person with broad awareness will be called a "generalist." The total individual sum of knowledge of a specialist and a generalist may in some sense be equal, but their ability to

* For a brief discussion of "awareness" and the specific sense in which other concepts are used, see the Glossary.

predict and control the *total* environment will probably be quite different.

There does not seem to be any logical reason for believing that one type of knowledge is more important than another. It seems reasonable to assume that it is just as important to predict and control one aspect of the environment as another. Each quantum of knowledge is, therefore, equal in value to every other quantum of knowledge. What seems to make the differences in total awareness is not so much the total sum of the knowledge quanta as their arrangement.

The total environment has many dimensions. At this point in human evolution the total environment seems to be logically divisible into three primary dimensions—the physical, the biological and the psychosocial. For most of us, it is easy to think in three dimensions. The physical universe, as we know it, seems in fact to be logically divisible into four orthogonal dimensions (the three dimensions of space and the dimension of time). The total environment is, therefore, probably divisible into many more dimensions than three. It may in fact have infinitely many orthogonal dimensions.

As the circle is to the sphere, so is the sphere to the four-dimensional hypersphere. By analyzing circles we obtain some insights into the nature of spheres. By analyzing spheres we obtain some insights into the nature of hyperspheres. By analyzing the total environment in three dimensions we may obtain some insights into the true infinite hyperdimensional nature of total awareness.

TOTAL AWARENESS

Keeping in mind that total awareness probably has infinitely many orthogonal dimensions, we assume total awareness to be an entity in three-dimensional noospace, i.e., mind space. The units of measurement in noospace are the quanta of knowledge and information.

We assume that knowledge is quantized in noospace just as energy is quantized in physical space. A quantum of knowledge is the minimum amount of information that will enable a person to alter his state of total awareness in order that he may predict and control some aspect(s) of his total environment which previously had, to him, been unpredictable and uncontrollable. Knowledge is, therefore, transferred or acquired in discrete quanta. When we have acquired a critical mass of relevant information, we have knowledge where before we had none. Subjectively this may be understood as insight or direct perception of a *gestalt* in noospace. Of course, information itself is probably also quantized but that need not concern us in this discussion.

Broad awareness in noospace is represented by a body tending toward sphericity, i.e., a generalist who has increased his knowledge in all directions equally. Narrow awareness is represented in noospace by a body tending toward ellipsoidicity, i.e., a specialist who has increased his knowledge in a particular direction at the cost of knowledge in other directions. This situation is illustrated in the figure opposite.

Positive quantities along each axis represent information and knowledge about what can be predicted and controlled, i.e., positive knowledge. Negative quantities along each axis represent information and knowledge about what cannot yet be predicted and controlled, i.e., negative knowledge. Every time we learn how to predict and control new aspects of the environment we also learn of other aspects of the environment that we cannot yet predict and control. Our total awareness reflects both that which we know and that which we know that we know not. Therefore, knowledge is probably symmetric.

Positive feedback enables us to acquire positive knowledge. Negative feedback enables us to acquire negative knowledge. We learn just as much from negative feedback as from positive feedback.

A point in noospace that does not lie on any of the axes represents a composite of two or more orthogonal components of awareness. For example, knowledge of biophysics represents a combination of physical knowledge and biological knowledge. Knowledge of biophysical psychology represents a combination of physical, biological and psychosocial knowledge. Most persons are psychosocial specialists as in Fig. 1(a). They have considerable knowledge of how to get along with others and of how to predict and control some aspects of human behavior. However, very few persons have comparable knowledge of the physical and biological environment. Most artists, politicians and salesmen are ex-

FIGURE 1 *Generalists and Specialists*

Graphical Representation of Total Awareness
in Three-dimensional Noospace for a
Specialist (a), and a Generalist (b)

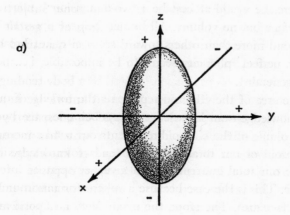

Specialist, narrow awareness
(Ellipsoidal)

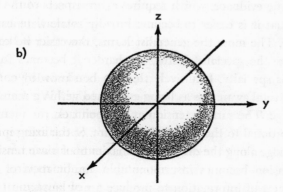

Generalist, broad awareness
(Spherical)

x – dimension measures physical information and knowledge
y – dimension measures biological information and knowledge
z – dimension measures psychosocial information and knowledge

amples of psychosocial specialists. However, only generalists seem to be truly creative* in the psychosocial environment.

Almost all the points in noospace are composite points. No human being appears to be totally lacking in any of the components of knowledge. If he were, he would at best be a two-dimensional, unaware creature with a surface but no volume. All human beings appear to be ellipsoidal. Some tend more than others toward sphericity, i.e., broad awareness. However, perfect sphericity seems to be impossible, i.e., no one is ever a perfect generalist.

The surface area of the ellipsoid represents the totality of our information and knowledge—our knowledge always being less than our information. The volume of the ellipsoid represents our total awareness. The more the ellipsoid of our total awareness tends toward sphericity, the greater will be our total awareness for a given amount of information and knowledge. This is the case because a sphere has maximum volume for a given surface area. Therefore, the maximization of total awareness implies becoming broadly aware as opposed to being narrowly aware. Since all knowledge is probably equal, it is probably just as easy to become broadly aware as narrowly aware.

There is some evidence, which requires arguments beyond the scope of this book, that it is easier to become broadly aware than to become narrowly aware. The more the generalist learns, the easier it becomes to learn. The more the specialist learns, the harder it becomes for him to learn within his specialty. Intuitively this can be shown by considering the ellipsoid of total awareness as being contained within a membrane of liquid knowledge. The surface tension at any point on the membrane is inversely proportional to the radius of curvature. Specializing implies extending knowledge along the direction of maximum surface tension until the surface tension becomes insurmountable, i.e., it requires an ever-increasing amount of information to produce a new quantum of knowledge. Most persons seem to have reached their limit in psychosocial specialization. Generalizing implies always extending knowledge along the direction of minimum surface tension in order to maintain a spherical shape. This means that a generalist will try to integrate simultaneously

* To be creative is to organize the environment into new patterns which increase awareness. Creativity is the highest form of awareness.

all of science, art, history, philosophy, and anything else that might be considered knowledge in order to form an ever-expanding, coherent model of the universe. He will never learn one thing to the future exclusion of everything else. His intelligence will determine the volume of his awareness—not the shape. The shape of the ellipsoid of awareness is a function of ethics, as will be shown later in this chapter.

Figure 2 illustrates the notion that no one is ever a complete specialist or a generalist. A sphere is a special case of an ellipsoid. Therefore, generalists and specialists exist on a continuum; each is an approximation to the other. The complete generalizing generalist is represented by an expanding sphere. The specializing specialist is represented by an elongating ellipsoid. The complete specialist is represented by a degenerate ellipsoid, i.e., a line. Specialization makes a person tend toward one-dimensionality and zero total awareness, even when the one-dimensional knowledge becomes infinite.

Awareness starts as a point, i.e., a sphere with zero diameter, at the intersection of all the orthogonal axes in noospace. The earlier a person specializes, the more one-dimensional he will tend to be. A totally ignorant person is a person with no knowledge. He is a degenerate generalist represented by a sphere of zero diameter. He, like the perfect specialist, has zero total awareness. The sphere and the ellipsoid, the point and the line represent the geometric boundaries of generalists and specialists, ignorance and knowledge, total awareness and the absence of awareness. Awareness, however, can be real or it can be imaginary.*

Illusions of knowledge, i.e., the subjective belief that we have knowledge (positive or negative) when we have none, are represented by imaginary quantities along orthogonal imaginary axes that correspond to the real axes in noospace. Illusions of awareness result from imaginary knowledge. The totality of our real plus our imaginary knowledge is represented by our total complex awareness which, by extension of our current three-dimensional model of real awareness, exists in six-dimensional, complex noospace.

Imaginary awareness cancels out real awareness. The greater the im-

* "Imaginary" in this context refers to illusions and not to the creative component of intelligence. Illusions of knowledge are measured with "imaginary" numbers instead of "real" numbers.

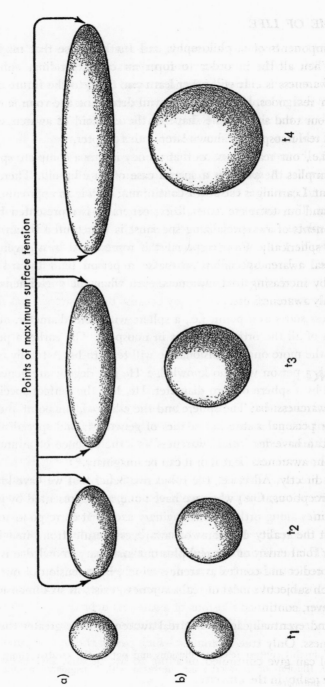

Points of maximum surface tension

FIGURE 2 *Expansion of Awareness*

Illustration of two idealized generalists (spheres at time t_1) increasing their knowledge in equal amounts at times (t_2, t_3 and t_4). (a) specializes; (b) generalizes. The one who specializes becomes more totally aware than the one who specializes. Both maintain equal surface areas, but not equal volumes. (b) has a rapidly increasing total awareness relative to (a).

aginary components of our awareness, the less our total real awareness will be. When all the imaginary components are zero, then our total complex awareness is entirely real and is equal to the real volume of the ellipsoid in real noospace. When the imaginary components are not zero, then our total awareness is less than or equal to the volume of the ellipsoid in real noospace minus the volume of the ellipsoid in imaginary noospace, i.e., our real minus our imaginary awareness. Negative total awareness implies the inability to learn in many or all aspects of the total environment. Learning is the acquisition of real knowledge.

To expand our total awareness, therefore, means to expand only the real components of awareness in such a way that our total real awareness is growing spherically. From now on the word "awareness" will refer only to "real awareness" unless otherwise indicated. It will be shown that only by increasing total awareness can the quality of life be improved. Only awareness can give us joy because only awareness has meaning.

MEANING

Only awareness has meaning, because only awareness is beyond doubt. Our personal awareness is the only part of the universe about which we can have no logical doubts. We can have doubts about the reality of our awareness, but not about the awareness itself, because we perceive it directly. All cause and effect relationships are in doubt, but not our perceptions. Only the causes of our perceptions and awareness are uncertain.

We test the reality of our awareness by attempting to predict and control our total environment. Imaginary awareness which does not enable us to predict and control is an illusion of awareness. It is possible to find as much subjective meaning in imaginary awareness as in real awareness. However, continued illusions of awareness deprive any organism of feedback and eventually lead to its destruction. Only real awareness is true awareness. Only true awareness which passes the test of prediction and control can give continued meaning to life because awareness may be the only reality in the universe.

Some existentialists have asserted that life is basically meaningless and absurd, but that each individual life can be made meaningful through purposeful action.* Which purposes should be pursued and why are questions which existentialism has not adequately answered.

There is an inexorable determinism which underlies all human activity. We can sometimes do as we will, but we can never will as we will. Each of us is born of parents and in a place he did not choose and is thereby totally a product of a heredity and an environment that he does not control. Our every thought, every emotion, and every action can be traced to causes beyond our control. Therefore, how can purpose give meaning to life when our purposes are not truly our own?

An answer to this question might be that "own-ness of purpose" is not a precondition to meaning. However, becoming aware implies eventually realizing that our actions are always determined by causes outside ourselves. It is difficult to conceive of a person finding the life of a puppet on a string meaningful simply because the life is full of action and purpose. It seems that for purpose to give meaning to life, there must be an element of free choice. But our choices are themselves determined by factors outside of ourselves.

There are, of course, many metaphysical arguments, pro and con, concerning determinism.† It seems, however, that the basic dilemma of determinism cannot be resolved by logical analysis. Instead, each person who seeks a meaningful life must make a conscious choice whether or not to play the "Game of Life."

THE GAME OF LIFE

"The Game of Life" is an attempt to make the contradictory notions of determinism and free will compatible with each other by looking at our life, not in terms of cause and effect relationships, but in terms of a game which expands awareness whenever we play it. The concern is not with what causes us to seek awareness, but what attitudes and rules of

* See J. P. Sartre, *Being and Nothingness*; also the writings of Albert Camus, particularly *The Myth of Sisyphus* and *The Rebel*.
† Taylor, Richard, *Metaphysics*.

behavior can enhance the expansion of awareness. Life is, therefore, simply a game in which we try to win ever-greater awareness. We do not make up the rules of the Game, but we must follow them if we are to win.

The "Game of Life" is a game in which we are the pieces as well as the players. As pieces, we are totally in the control of a cosmic force* which completely determines our lives. As players we are part of the cosmic force and, in turn, partially control ourselves and others, i.e., we cause events even though something outside ourselves causes us to cause them. The stakes of the Game are an ever-expanding total awareness for each player and the human race.†

The rules of the Game are as follows:

1 Each player must assume that he has free will and is totally responsible for his actions.
2 The sole purpose and goal of each player must be to expand total awareness as best he can.
3 Each player must start the expansion of total awareness with himself.
4 Each player must direct his every action toward winning the Game.
5 If a person plays the Game, he wins.
6 If a person refuses to play the Game, he loses.

As each player becomes ever more totally aware, he asymptotically becomes less a piece in the Game and more purely a player. Eventually all players are united as an ever-increasing part of the cosmic force. In other words, the more aware a player becomes, the more events he will cause until eventually all players begin to interact and asymptotically begin jointly to cause all events.

A determinist may say that he plays the Game of Life only because of the environmental and genetic forces that have acted upon him. An

---

* The "cosmic force" subsumes all natural laws; it is the cause of all events.
† The Human Race (man, mankind, humanity, etc.) is considered as a dynamic entity that is continuously changing. It is not limited to *Homo sapiens*, but includes our pre-*sapiens*, sentient ancestors and whatever our species is still to become. "Sentient" refers to any entity aware of its own awareness.

advocate of "free will" may say that the Game of Life is not really a game to him but represents the way he "chooses" to live. The important thing is that both players know the rules of the Game. They are aware of being aware and of the possibility of becoming more aware. They can ignore whatever it is that causes them to play the Game. They need only concern themselves with winning.

Assuming that the rules of the Game of Life are clear, it is still not clear why anyone should choose to play the Game. Indeed, as we look around, we see the overwhelming majority of our fellow men doing everything in their power to avoid the Game. Is it not, after all, obvious that the purpose of life is to be happy? Deferring a discussion of "happiness," we address ourselves to the following propositions: *The Game of Life is the fundamental matrix on which the pattern of all evolution is woven. To refuse to play the Game is to avoid reality and to become extinct.*

EVOLUTION

The entire pattern of evolution consists of chaotic energy becoming matter, elementary matter becoming atoms, atoms joining to form molecules, molecules becoming increasingly complex and organized until they become self-replicating, and life continues as unified matter increasingly predicting and controlling its environment. The life forms in turn become increasingly organized and complex; those species better able to predict and control their environment supplant the lesser species until man—the first known life form aware of its own awareness*—appears and begins to supplant all other species. Man is, in effect, becoming a new phylum,† fanning out into the ecosystem, filling the niches of one species after another. Man is, therefore, riding the crest of a wave of ever-expanding awareness leading from chaos to matter to life to mind.

---

* The dolphin and other cetaceans may also be aware of their own awareness; but as will be shown later, this is not likely.

† A phylum is a group of life forms that have unique structural similarities which differentiate them from all other life forms. What makes man unique is the fact that he is aware of his own awareness.

Evolution, although directional, seems to proceed by a process of random trial and error. The basic pattern has been to create ever more-aware species from less-aware species. Because the more aware could better predict and control their environment, they would supplant the less aware wherever there was drastic environmental change or competition for resources. When there was no competition, the less-aware species such as plants, usually served to support the more-aware species, such as animals. Humanity began and has developed by the same process. Entire subspecies of men have been ruthlessly exterminated by their more-aware cousins. Only man deliberately destroys his competitors. Such was probably the case between the European Neanderthal man and Cro-Magnon man.* The pattern has been repeated in cultural development. When civilizations failed to expand their total awareness at a greater rate than rival cultures, they were overwhelmed.

Sometimes the conquered and the conquerors interacted synergistically so that the new resulting civilization was more totally aware than the previous two combined. Such was the case when the semi-barbaric but dynamic Hellenes conquered the more refined but stagnating Minoan civilization. The result was classical Greece. The influence of Greece persisted and spread throughout humanity. This is analogous to a benign mutation giving higher fitness† to those to whom it is transmitted.

Sometimes the conquerors and the conquered interacted anergistically and the resulting civilization was less totally aware than either of the previous two. Such was the case in the Turkish conquest of the Arab civilization. In this case the new civilization, the Ottoman Empire, had no constructive influence on the human race and its effects were localized and soon dissipated when it in turn was destroyed by a superior civilization—Europe. The Ottoman Empire was analogous to a deleterious mutation that decreases the fitness of those to whom it is transmitted.

Evolution is a blind and clumsy force, not a carefully thought-out

---

* The non-European Neanderthal-like men seem to have been much less specialized and appear to have been "assimilated" into the mainstream of human evolution rather than "decimated."

† "Fitness" means "the potential for producing progeny."

plan. Evolution drives matter toward mind by a random groping process that tests each clumsy attempt at greater awareness against other attempts. The more aware survive at the price of extinction for the less aware. Man is no longer significantly tested by other species; *he tests himself*. In so doing he has, until now, imitated the groping, clumsy quality of the evolutionary force; man has been unaware of what he has been doing to himself. Today man must deliberately and consciously test himself or he will bring about his own extinction by submitting blindly to the random and increasingly dangerous testing process of the evolutionary force. Evolution is a creative force that can also destroy. Similarly, light enables us to see but too much light can blind us. The electromagnetic analogy may be carried further.

Small amounts of hard electromagnetic radiation, such as X-rays and gamma-rays, will cause both benign and deleterious mutations. As radiation increases, the price for the few benign mutations is a much faster increasing number of deleterious mutations. Very large amounts of radiation completely destroy the organism without providing any benefit. The evolutionary process not only uses radiation, but is analogous to an ever-increasing source of radiation which is constantly increasing the rate of evolutionary change until it is on the brink of becoming lethal. If not brought under control, evolution can completely destroy the biosphere instead of improving it.

Man in the last one hundred years has evolved to the point where, as Julian Huxley put it, "He has become evolution conscious of itself." If he does not master that which caused him, he will be destroyed by it. Man, driven by the unreasoning need for security* and personal power† has played the Game of Life as blindly as evolution has created him. He is now at the point where he must deliberately play the Game or be destroyed by his need for security and personal power.

The need for security and the need for personal power are evolutionary mechanisms that drive man toward greater awareness. Security and

---

* "Security" is a subjective state of mind that consists in having or readily obtaining all that one believes one needs and not fearing the loss of what one already has.

† "Personal power" is control over the environment used solely to enhance personal security.

personal power are means to an end, not ends in themselves. Until very recent times, it was not possible for the vast majority of mankind to be secure or have personal power unless they were increasing their awareness. Natural selection and competition forced men to face reality and to play the Game of Life. The greatest source of insecurity is an unpredictable and uncontrollable environment. In the past, if men did not increase their awareness, they were quickly destroyed by negative feedback, i.e., the testing† of other species, other men, and natural forces in general.

Man, by turning security and personal power into ultimate goals, is bringing about his own extinction by avoiding reality. Reality includes what we can neither predict nor control. An illusion of reality is an illusion of awareness. Man has an innate need to be aware. Increasingly men are finding security by avoiding reality, i.e., by acquiring imaginary awareness. They do this by deliberately destroying their negative feedback. They delude themselves into believing that they are aware when they are not because negative feedback makes most persons insecure. They then deliberately sink into matter through hedonism (the pursuit of pleasure in the absence of awareness). Man is no longer forced to play the Game of Life. He must now play it deliberately. By insulating himself from minor testing (i.e., feedback and readjustment) through bureaucracy,* man is causing the evolutionary force to build up a dangerous overload of testing potential within himself.

Man's personal power has evolved to the point where he can either 1) completely destroy all his competitors and, in the process, himself; or 2) bring about the mind-numbing security of life and pleasure in the absence of awareness. The pattern of evolution is to become aware of itself before destroying itself by destroying man. Evolution has always worked by trial and error. If man should prove himself an error by deliberately declining to play the Game, then evolution will erase him and he will not rise to the next stage of evolution.

* "Bureaucracy" refers to an organization with a built-in mechanism for continuously decreasing negative feedback until there is no feedback at all.
† Testing refers to a process for reducing the fitness of entities which prove themselves less aware than competitive entities.

THE STEP BEYOND MAN

The next step in human evolution will involve the transition from mind as an effect of life, to mind as an effect of itself, i.e., pure thought. Mind, as we know it, is that effect of life which causes awareness in general and awareness of self in particular. Life is that effect of matter which causes the continuous expansion of awareness. Matter is that effect of energy which brings definite form and structure out of chaos. All are an effect of the evolutionary force.

Until now mind has evolved as a consequence of the random evolution of life. Life evolved as a consequence of the expansion of awareness. Mind was able to evolve parallel to matter and life. For man, this is no longer the case because man now evolves psychosocially—not by biological change. Man must now take evolution into his own hands or he will be destroyed by entropy.

Entropy is the counter-force to evolution. Entropy drives mind toward matter and matter toward chaos. Entropy manifests itself in mind by a decrease in awareness. The maximum form of entropy for life is death. The ultimate form of entropy is chaos. Imaginary awareness is the direct manifestation of entropy.

Mind succumbs to the entropic force by declining the challenge of the Game of Life. Life succumbs to entropy by specialization, i.e., by acquiring an ever more fixed and specific form until it is indistinguishable from matter. Matter succumbs to entropy by becoming randomly dispersed until it no longer has a specific form and it becomes chaotic energy.

The evolutionary force driving man toward ever-greater mind causes him to seek ever-greater awareness. The entropic force drives him toward matter and causes him to seek ever-greater peace and tranquillity. Tension* is produced by an unpredictable and uncontrollable environment. Man, in an effort to adjust to both the entropic and the evolutionary forces, relieves his tension by deluding himself into believing he is aware when he is not. He deliberately avoids the tension of the evolutionary

* Tension is the psychological effect of insecurity.

force by destroying his feedback. Without feedback the Game of Life cannot be won.

Both evolution and entropy are natural manifestations of the cosmic force. It is just as "natural" to sink into matter as to rise to greater mind. It is only possible to rise to greater mind, pure thought, by playing the Game of Life in the presence of total feedback. Man can continue to have feedback only if he plays the Game *deliberately.*

Man is the precursor of pure thought. He is on the verge of creating it without knowing it. However, pure thought is the only stage of evolution, thus far, which must be reached deliberately through a conscious desire on the part of man. It will not occur in final form by chance. Just as the *random* union of increasingly complex matter gave rise to life, so will the *deliberate* union of increasingly-aware life, man, give rise to pure thought.

When life or matter reaches such a high level of complexity that it can no longer increase in awareness by continuing in its present form, then the individual entities, under the influence of the evolutionary force, unite to become a collective entity far more complex than any of the former individuals. This occurred when molecules united to become cells and once again when cells united to become multicellular beings— metazoa. Man represents the ultimate complexity of metazoan life. He apparently can only achieve significantly higher complexity by uniting in a new society.

It will be shown that the union of men in a new society must be free and voluntary. Men can only become totally free by becoming totally aware. Only by having all men strive to become totally aware will it be possible to create a new society which will lead mankind toward pure thought.

The society will be composed of persons, each of whom is individually aware, and through his individual awareness enhances the total collective awareness of a united humanity, which in turn amplifies the total awareness of each individual. The new society will exist for the sole purpose of expanding total awareness. The society will eventually have the same relationship to a man as the man has to a cell and that the cell in turn has to a molecule.

The pattern that will be developed in the later chapters will show that in all probability the society will start on Earth as the culmination of science and technology but it will not be limited to Earth. It will expand toward infinity in an infinitely-expanding universe* always growing, perhaps meeting and melding with other societies, perhaps being tested by them, but always becoming more and more totally aware as it transcends time, space and matter. A new society will begin when a critical mass of humanity deliberately begins to play the Game of Life. It will never end. Only in this way will man find the immortality he has always sought. Only in this way can man evolve forever toward total awareness.

For man to choose the continuous expansion of total awareness as his sole purpose for living is merely to choose as a goal that which has been and continues to be the sole cause for his existence. In so doing, he is playing the Game of Life and creating a new society. These still vague notions will be more fully developed in the following chapters under the general concept of the "Moral Society."

Pierre Teilhard de Chardin was the first person to discuss the concept of "the Moral Society" under the more limited notion of "the Noosphere." He expressed the concept beautifully and in great detail.† His overall perception of evolution stands as an exquisite monument to the human intellect. It is analogous to Mendeleev bringing order out of chaos in the creation of the Periodic Table of the elements. Teilhard makes it clear that the expansion of awareness is not only man's necessary purpose, but is his whole meaning. Teilhard's great work is marred only by his attempt to make his beautifully clear perception of evolution compatible with traditional thought in general, and Christianity in particular. In so doing, he dismissed the danger that entropy would destroy the

---

* The two most popular cosmological models of the Universe are 1) a finite universe (Big Bang) model; and 2) an infinite universe (Steady State) model. The preponderance of scientific evidence tends to support the "Big Bang" theory. However, a finite universe is metaphysically unacceptable. Cosmological and astronomical models have often been drastically revised. This is certain to be the case with both the "Big Bang" and "Steady State" models. A model that is consistent with the evidence supporting the "Big Bang" theory, but implies an infinite universe, will almost certainly be discovered. (See the work of G. de Vaucouleurs.)

† See *The Phenomenon of Man* and other writings by Pierre Teilhard de Chardin.

human race. Teilhard saw the process of ever-expanding awareness as being deterministic and irreversible. He took a parochial view of the Noosphere and disregarded the need to play the Game of Life deliberately. He discounted the danger of nuclear annihiliation and the more insidious threat of cultural and genetic decay for the entire human race.

Assuming for the time being that Teilhard de Chardin's work, in spite of its flaws, demonstrates the desirability, indeed the necessity, of having the "expansion of total awareness" as the sole goal for the human race, the question of happiness still remains.

HAPPINESS

"Happiness" is the subjective mental state of feeling that our desires are being satisfied. Desires that have been fulfilled do not make us happy. Only desires that are being fulfilled make us happy. The degree to which we are happy is directly proportional to the rate at which we are satisfying our desires and the strength of these desires. Since simultaneous desires are often, in effect, contradictory (such as the simultaneous desires for both freedom and security) we rarely, if ever, simultaneously satisfy all our current desires. Therefore, most and probably all persons are always both happy and unhappy at the same time. When we say that someone is happy, we mean that the "happy effect" resulting from having his strongest desires satisfied outweighs the "unhappy effect" from having his weaker desires unsatisfied. An unhappy person is the converse of a happy person. A person devoid of desire would never be happy or unhappy.

From the preceding definition of "happiness" it is clear that a person who has the maximum expansion of total awareness as his strongest desire can be happy if he is fulfilling this desire. The converse, however, is not necessarily true. Indeed, a person who has the maximization of happiness as his strongest desire is in the peculiar position of creating problems that feed on their own solutions. As old desires are satisfied, new desires must be found to replace them. The desire for desire soon becomes the overwhelming need; one result is a drug-oriented, sensation-seeking, anti-intellectual culture such as is currently gestating among the

children of the world mentored by such persons as Timothy Leary* and
Herbert Marcuse.† A world oriented toward the maximization of happiness would result in an entropic nightmare, as can be shown by carrying
the notion to its logical conclusion.

In most mammals and apparently also in humans the production of
happiness by direct application of electric currents to the pleasure centers in the brain seems to cause the greatest possible happiness in the
sense that the experimental subjects will forego their strongest and most
basic desires, such as food and sex, in order to have their pleasure center
stimulated.‡ Therefore, if the greatest good is to make for the greatest
happiness for the greatest number, an "optimal" world would be a
completely-automated society in which every human being is connected
at birth to a machine which maximizes the stimulation of his pleasure
centers. The machines would keep persons alive as long as possible. They
would cultivate the maximum number of new human beings from the
collective pool of sperm and ova. The new human beings would be bred
so as to select those who achieve maximum happiness from pleasure center stimulation. Such a world is the logical conclusion of a society oriented toward the maximization of happiness.

Such a world is technically feasible within the foreseeable future
through the misapplication of physiological psychology, cybernetics, automation, electronics, genetics, etc. Indeed, some persons, such as Leary
in one sense (psychedelic drugs) and Marcuse in another (socialistic
sensualism), advocate that science and technology should be used primarily to make men happy as opposed to making them totally aware.
They are, in effect, advocating the nightmarish world described above.

The so-called "psychedelic drugs" create illusions of awareness (happiness) while destroying the faculties which in fact make men aware.
There is no evidence that any person can predict and control his *total*

* Leary, Timothy, *Psychedelic Experience.*
† Marcuse, Herbert, *Essay on Liberation* and *The One Dimensional Man.*
‡ 1 Delgado, Jose M. R., *Physical Control of the Mind: Toward a Psychocivilized*
    Society.
  2 Bishop, Elder and Heath, "Intercranial Self Stimulation in Man," *Science*, 140,
    April 26, 1963, pp. 394–396.
  3 Olds & Milner, *Journal of Comprehensive Physio-Psychology*, 47, 1954, pp. 419–
    427.

environment better as a consequence of taking psychedelic drugs. There is evidence that true awareness in fact decreases under the influence of these drugs.*

"Socialistic sensualism" is a welfare state structured to facilitate the "free" pursuit of hedonism. It has no other purpose than to redistribute the resources of society in order that each person may maximize his happiness in his own way. This type of society leads inevitably to total decay. This is shown today by the hedonistic decline of the youth in the "socialistic democracies" such as Sweden and the United States. In these affluent countries, socialistic sensualism is almost a reality.

Awareness as a central goal does not preclude happiness, but merely relegates it to a probably trivial† status. In the normal course of events, happiness is a goal most easily reached indirectly by leading a purposeful life. Most men need something beyond themselves to give their life purpose and meaning. This partially explains the success of religion and to a lesser extent Communism. The desire to expand awareness and evolve forever is an infinite desire that we can always be in the process of fulfilling. It can always make us happy. The pursuit of total awareness makes us forever a part of something greater than ourselves. Only awareness seems to give true purpose and meaning to our lives, possibly because only awareness is real. The basis of human joy is awareness, not happiness. However, both happiness and awareness are dependent on security and freedom.

SECURITY AND FREEDOM

The central goal of ever-expanding total awareness is also compatible with other "intuitively" desirable goals of humanity, such as personal

---

* 1 Weil, Zinberg and Nelson, "Clinical and Psychological Effects of Marijuana in Man," *Science*, Dec. 13, 1968, pp. 1234–1242.
  2 Grinspoon, L., "Marijuana," *Scientific American*, Dec. 1969.
  3 Massett, L., "Marijuana and Behavior," *Science News*, Feb. 7, 1970.
  4 "Marijuana and Performance," *Science News*, Feb. 21, 1970.
  5 "Marijuana and Temporal Disintegration," *Science*, May 29, 1970; pp. 1118–1120.
† "Trivial" refers to anything which does not significantly affect our awareness.

freedom and security, since these are necessary conditions for expanding awareness as well as effects of the expansion of total awareness.

"Security" was defined as a state of mind in which a person has or can readily obtain all he thinks he needs and has no fear of losing what he has. By definition, the absence of security, insecurity, makes persons unhappy. Security is necessary for the expansion of awareness because of the well-known psychosocial law of hierarchical needs. A person who is in imminent danger of being killed, and knows it, is not likely to desire food. A person on the brink of starvation is not likely to desire sex in lieu of food. Similarly, if the basic requirements of security, such as food, shelter, and continued good health (mental and physical) are not met, an individual or a population cannot be motivated to increase their total awareness. Other, less well understood factors such as "esthetic gratification" and "love" may play similar roles as necessary conditions for enhancement of awareness. As such, they are part of the gestalt of "security."

True, lasting security comes only from becoming totally aware. The desire for security in the absence of knowledge is a perversion* of the evolutionary force. It leads men to seek security through self-deception and the pursuit of personal power. The greatest source of insecurity is an unpredictable and uncontrollable environment. In order to achieve the illusion of security, some men pervert their need to be aware by 1) deluding themselves through ideology into believing that they are aware when they are not, 2) excluding through self-imposed blindness, i.e., specialization, as much of the total environment as possible from their perception; and 3) controlling, through personal power and bureaucratization, the lives of other men who threaten to expose their illusions through negative feedback.

Security, like happiness, is best achieved indirectly by leading a purposeful life. Only by confronting directly what we do not know—what we can neither predict nor control—and then doing something about it can we become aware and overcome the entropic delusions which drive us toward matter. True security comes only from deliberately playing the Game of Life. This is only possible when there is personal freedom.

* "Perversion" refers to any behavior that increases or seeks to increase happiness without increasing awareness.

"Personal freedom" may be defined in terms of a person being able to do and say as he pleases so long as he does not, in the process, interfere with the right of another person to do and say as he pleases. When a conflict occurs, a compromise is reached which allows all concerned parties the maximum amount of self-expression; furthermore, no one has the right to demand any part of another person's life, except by previous mutual agreement (e.g., law).

This notion of freedom is essential to the maximization of awareness because awareness can only be increased when there is feedback in the sense of questioning and testing all propositions and the opportunity to formulate and express new ones. Indeed, this notion of feedback is the basis of science and technology. Science and technology, in turn, are the principal and perhaps the only *direct* means by which awareness can be significantly enhanced. Art and other psychosocial processes may be *indirect* means.* In the end, all freedom, like security, stems from being aware and knowing how to become still more aware. A necessary but not sufficient condition for the expansion of awareness is scientific method. Science makes man free by giving him feedback and liberating him from illusion.

SCIENCE

Science has probably existed as long as man, since in a simple sense it means only accepting as true that which works. Science has been recognized as such and formalized, however, only during the last three hundred years. The basic process of science is defined as follows:

1 Observe, measure and describe the total environment.
2 Take the perceptions, what is known and/or appears to be known, and make predictive models of cause and effect relationships in the total environment.
3 Design and perform controlled experiments for testing the validity of each model.
4 If the results of the experiments were by-and-large correctly pre-

* Discussed in Chapter 4.

dicted *a priori* by the model, then the model *probably* has some
validity if the experiments were performed properly.

5 If the results of the experiment are contrary to those predicted
a priori by the model, then the model *probably* has no validity
and one or more of the hypotheses and/or descriptions subsumed in the model are *probably* false or the experiments were
performed improperly.

6 A completely untested model, even when logically consistent, is
assumed to be *probably* invalid until evidence to the contrary is
presented.

7 If the model can in no way ever be subjected to experimental
validation, then the model is useless.

8 It is the purpose of science to develop ever more general models
which will predict increasingly broader aspects of the total environment—past, present, and future.

9 Those models which repeatedly make the broadest range of accurate predictions are preferred over models which make fewer,
occasional and/or less accurate predictions.

10 No model is ever accepted as absolutely true and beyond doubt.

11 Every scientific model can and should be improved by ever better description, modeling, and experimentation.

This description of scientific method can, of course, be extended indefinitely to include a discussion of "How do we describe and measure?
What is a model? How are models constructed? How are controlled experiments designed, performed and evaluated?" and so on. Many books
on this subject have been written.* The purpose at this time is only to
outline the basic intuitive notions of scientific method that are simple
and direct and to which we will have occasion to refer later. Other persons may define "scientific method" in other ways. In this book "scientific method" refers only to the concept outlined above.

In short, "scientific method" is an open-minded inquiry into the
nature of cause and effect relationships. It is based on the notion that we
can never be certain about the validity of any relationship, but that we

* See Cohen and Nagel, *Logic and Scientific Method.*

can always learn more about every subject. Any person who uses the scientific method is a scientist.

Although science is based on uncertainty, the uncertainty is within ourselves and not in nature. It is the unavoidable incompleteness of our information on all aspects of nature that makes the universe seem uncertain. "Probability" is the discipline that enables us to quantify our uncertainty and to deal precisely with incomplete information.

Technology is analogous to science except that the concern here is not with prediction but with control. In technology we build models called "machines"—usually, but not always, physical in nature—which enable us to control our environment. A machine is a manufactured device which turns one form of energy into another. Language, clothing, tools, and computers are all machines. Those machines that enable us to control the broadest aspect of our total environment with greatest precision and the least effort are the preferred ones. Science gives us the predictive principles which enable us to construct and operate machines that will behave as we expect. Technology, on the other hand, enables us to perform experiments (i.e., control the environment) in order to test scientific models. Science and technology form a symbiotic pair in which one is essential to the other. The term "science" will often be used to describe the pair.

Until about four hundred years ago science was considered only one of many ways to obtain knowledge. In Europe, religious dogma and in China, tradition, were considered more important than science. In both places the unscientific, but not illogical, authoritative teachings of men such as Aristotle and Confucius respectively were weighted more heavily than scientific evidence.

In Europe at this time, several men, in the face of persecution and antagonism from the established order, began to formalize and structure the scientific method.* Within one hundred years, groups of men who called themselves "scientists" and refused to accept the validity of

---

* Roger Bacon in the thirteenth century attempted to formalize scientific method, but he was persecuted and imprisoned by the Catholic Church for "unorthodoxy." His was a premature, unsuccessful attempt to make men scientific and consequently more aware.

"truths" not supported by scientific evidence began the scientific revolution. Francis Bacon was the prophet, Galileo was the evangelist and Newton the first high priest of science. Newton's theory of gravitation was the first significant, coherent, scientific model. The scientific revolution represented the deliberate, concerted effort of a very few men to predict and control their environment by the application of science and technology. These few men, representing at no time including today more than a minute fraction of the human population, have enabled man to increase his total awareness more in the last three hundred years than he had in the previous 300,000.

It is only natural that science began with those cause and effect relationships that are simplest and then worked toward the more complex. The progression went from the artificial and completely described world of geometry to the relatively simple world of physics. Then about one hundred years later, the more complex field of chemistry began to be explored on the basis of what was known about physics. Within the last few decades, the greatly increased knowledge of organic chemistry has begun to be applied to the incredibly more complex world of biology and we stand today on the brink of predicting and controlling life itself through understanding the structure of DNA.* In the near future there will be synthesis of new life forms from non-living chemical compounds.

The only aspect of the total environment upon which the scientific revolution has not yet made a direct significant impact is the psychosocial. The psychosocial environment is at least as complex in relation to the biological environment as the biological environment is to the physical. The evolution of science has paralleled the evolution of mankind going from matter, to life, and finally to mind.

As science led to the mastery of one aspect of the environment after another, there were great social upheavals, each one greater than the last. For all the trauma caused by the model of the heliocentric universe and the physics that it implied, it was nothing compared to the trauma caused and still being caused by the first coherent model of biology—

---

* Deoxyribonucleic acid (DNA) is a very large polymeric organic molecule which carries all the genetic information that determines the structure of all life forms. It is the blueprint from which all life develops. All the information to structure a human being is contained in a few thousand DNA molecules.

Darwin's Theory of Evolution. As recently as ten years ago, Darwinism was heresy in Communist Russia. It still makes ideologues of the Left uneasy. As recently as today, the ideologues of the Right in California proposed and passed a law requiring the teaching in public schools of Genesis and the equally unscientific Aristotelean speculation of spontaneous generation. These myths must be given equal time with the validated (but still challengeable) theory of evolution by natural selection. When science begins to make significant inroads into the phenomenon of the mind and of social organization, we should expect an even greater trauma than was caused by Darwinism.

The alleged psychosocial sciences, usually called "social sciences" or "behavioral sciences," are today almost entirely devoid of science. They are at best descriptive, analogous to pre-Newtonian physics and pre-Darwinian biology. At worst, the psychosocial sciences are repositories of blatant ideology and are analogous to medieval theology.

An ideological belief is a belief in a cause and effect relationship not based on scientific evidence. An ideology is an organized set of interdependent ideological beliefs. Ideology is synonymous with dogma. Persons with an ideological persuasion will usually not entertain the possibility that their ideology may be wrong. Religions are clearly ideologies. Communism and Marxism, which have scientific pretensions, are ideologies. Modern educational theory as taught in most American colleges is an ideology. The same can be said in decreasing order for most, *not all*, of political "science," sociology, psychology, and economics. The full implication of ideology in the so-called "social sciences" will be discussed in Chapter 4 together with the reasons why science has had so little impact on understanding the psychosocial environment.

The point to be made at this time is that in all of human history only science and technology have been proven *directly* effective in expanding human awareness.* Their effectiveness has been proven repeatedly by our ability to predict and control our physical environment. This is a process which began millions of years ago with our tool-making ancestors. The scientific method was extended to the biological environment by means of the agricultural revolution of about twelve thousand years

* Recall that man has always been a scientist and that art increases awareness indirectly.

ago. The same pattern repeated itself in the scientific revolution of three hundred years ago. Rigorous science was first applied to the physical environment; today it is being applied to the biological environment. It will not be until the scientific method has encompassed *all* aspects of man's environment that man's *total* awareness can truly begin to expand.

Physics and mathematics developed together. Systematic chemistry grew out of an understanding of physics and mathematics. Biology is now becoming a full science on a foundation of chemistry, physics, and mathematics. The so-called "social sciences" will not be true sciences until the social "scientists," who are mostly scientific illiterates,* have mastered biology, chemistry, physics, and mathematics. The psychosocial environment is the last frontier of the human intellect. Man is mastering all of nature except himself. In mastering himself, he will for the first time begin to be totally aware. This is "progress"—an ever-increasing ability to predict and control the total environment. By becoming increasingly aware, man will become increasingly ethical. The concept of ethics is inextricably interwoven with the concept of "games." We must first understand the nature of games if we are to understand our ethical nature.

GAMES

A game is a set of behavioral rules about how to win or lose a specified stake. The latter may be entirely symbolic. A game has no purpose beyond itself. To play a game is to follow the rules of the game. All men play games, but not all men play the Game of Life.

In every game that man plays he has an opponent, and sometimes he also has allies. Our opponent in the Game of Life is not a person but a force—entropy; our ally is the evolutionary force. In all games, our opponent is either a person or some other manifestation of the cosmic force. This applies to specific games such as chess, poker, golf, etc., or to general games such as the Game of Life.

* A scientific illiterate is a person who has virtually no systematic scientific knowledge in any field. The minimum requirements for scientific literacy are given in Chapter 6.

In the Game of Life a player has an infinite number of states in which he can exist. These are his states of total awareness. They range from negative awareness to the infinite total awareness, which no man ever reaches. A player also has an infinite number of actions that he can take. Each action will either increase, decrease, or not affect his state of total awareness.

Associated with each action is a cost in terms of the energy expended to perform the action. "No action" is also a type of action and it also costs energy in terms of a wasted portion of a person's life. Each player subjectively associates, usually unconsciously, with each pair of awareness state and action a probable set of payoffs. Each payoff is seen as having a given probability of occurring given that we are in a given awareness state and take a specified action. The net benefit is a function of 1) the cost of the action, 2) the current state of total awareness, and 3) the probability distribution of resulting levels of total awareness. The greater the net increase in total awareness, the greater is the benefit to the player.

A player of the Game of Life attempts to maximize his expected payoff in terms of total awareness before he loses all his energy and reaches maximum entropy, i.e., dies. Only the awareness we engender in others survives our lives. A player is never certain of the outcome of any action in the Game of Life. If he is trying to win, he will, at each point, take the action with the highest subjective probability of maximizing total awareness. There is always a risk that awareness will decrease after any particular action. Taking no action guarantees that entropy will increase and that awareness will not increase. Inaction is a poor strategy because it is always trivial.

A strategy is a plan for winning a game. A good strategy in the Game of Life implies that for each awareness state we know how to choose an action that will further increase total awareness. In every game that man plays, he has a strategy. Sometimes the strategies are poor and he loses. Sometimes the strategies are good and he wins. The essential thing in any game is to have a strategy that enables us to learn from our mistakes as well as from our successes. When this is the case, we cannot help but improve our strategies every time we play the Game. Self-improving strategies are only possible when there is feedback. Without feedback, any strategy, no matter how perfect it may appear in the beginning, will lose in any game that has infinite states, infinite actions, and infinite uncertain outcomes. In the Game of Life even the probabilities themselves are uncertain. Of all the games that man plays, the Game of Life is the one with the greatest uncertainty. No person ever becomes a perfect player of the Game; every player of the Game of Life will make mistakes.

The stakes in the Game of Life are infinite awareness, therefore, man has an infinite expected gain if he plays the Game. In spite of the risks and uncertainties involved, the Game of Life gives mankind the best odds and the greatest benefits.

Games are not trivial. A game either increases or it decreases total awareness. A game which increases awareness at one point may decrease it at another. Only a game whose outcome is uncertain can increase awareness. Games whose outcomes are predetermined in the mind of the player can only increase happiness, never awareness. Therefore, as a person becomes increasingly proficient in playing a finite game, he eventually acquires the ability to precisely predict and control every move and outcome in the game. He is then transformed from a person who is increasing his awareness to a person increasing only his happiness.

The Game of Life is an infinite Game that no entity can ever master. In the Game of Life, the uncertainty of the outcome remains no matter how proficient we become. The Game of Life enables us to evolve forever, but we can never be certain of the outcome.

Only entities who value awareness above happiness will accept the challenge of the Game of Life. All other entities will seek to play games that serve solely to make them happy. All men must play games—either consciously or unconsciously.* Games are as much a part of man's nature as his need for self-preservation.† Today each man must *consciously decide* whether he will play the Game of Life or the Game of Pleasure.

The Game of Pleasure subsumes all games that serve *solely* to increase happiness. Every game that man plays is either a variation on the Game of Life or a variation on the Game of Pleasure. All of man's actions are part of a game that *he* has chosen to play. Science and free-

* Berne, Eric. *Games People Play.*
† Huizinga, Johan, *Homo Ludens* (Man the Player).

dom are strategies in the Game of Life. Ideology and coercion are strategies in the Game of Pleasure. Mathematics and art are sometimes variations on the Game of Life. Chess and religion are sometimes variations on the Game of Pleasure. Some games are variations on the Game of Life at one point in a person's life and become variations on the Game of Pleasure at another point. Sports, for example, communicate the nature of Darwinian competition to children. Adults who are obsessed with sports only increase their entropy.

As man increases his awareness, he is forced either to deliberately accept or deliberately decline the challenge of the Game of Life. There is no in-between strategy. Man either plays the Game of Pleasure or he accepts the challenge of the Game of Life. Those who accept the challenge are responsible for all of man's awareness. Those who decline the challenge are responsible for all of man's entropy. The greater the intelligence of a person who declines to play the Game of Life, the greater will be the entropy that he can engender because he has greater capacity to destroy all feedback. Any strategy that decreases entropy increases awareness. An optimal strategy in the Game of Life is one that maximizes the rate of increase in total awareness. An optimal strategy in the Game of Pleasure is one that maximizes happiness.

The Game of Life will cause happiness. The Game of Pleasure will never cause awareness. Man has always played the Game of Life unconsciously by pursuing happiness in the form of security and power. While there was competition from other men or animals, man could not be happy without becoming aware. This situation is about to end for all men. It has already ended for most men. Man can now find happiness without awareness. The moral question of our age is whether happiness in the absence of awareness is good.

The pursuit of happiness in the absence of awareness can destroy the human race. That this is the case is shown in Chapters 4 and 5. There is no logical reason for desiring the survival of mankind if man has no other purpose than to be happy. The only purpose man has is the purpose he gives himself by choosing to play either the Game of Life or the Game of Pleasure. It would appear that extinction is an optimal strategy in the Game of Pleasure since it maximizes entropy.

In most persons' lives the unhappy effect seems to outweigh the happy effect. The elimination of desire is the most effective way of eliminating unhappiness. Death is the most effective way of eliminating desire.* Therefore, death minimizes unhappiness. Thus, persons who play the Game of Pleasure invariably use entropic strategies (e.g., ideology and/or drugs) in an attempt to maximize their happiness by minimizing their unhappiness. Death is a minimax strategy in the Game of Pleasure.

A minimax strategy is a strategy which assures a player that he will obtain the best of the worst, i.e., he will minimize his risk. The worst in the Game of Pleasure is unhappiness. The best of the worst is extinction. A minimax strategy is contrary to what most persons intuitively consider "optimal." A minimax strategy is indeed only optimal in the Game of Pleasure if a person puts a disproportionately low value on happiness and a disproportionately high cost on unhappiness. Persons who play the Game of Pleasure probably always use minimax strategies. A person playing the Game of Pleasure is made unhappy by his own awareness— he tries to destroy it by destroying his feedback until he reaches total entropy. He unconsciously longs for death.

A uniformly optimal strategy is one that simultaneously maximizes our gains while minimizing our risks. A uniformly optimal strategy guarantees all that the minimax strategy does plus maximizing our gains. In the Game of Pleasure we risk unhappiness and gain happiness. In the Game of Life we risk entropy and gain awareness. To play the Game of Life as best we can is to minimize our entropy and maximize our awareness simultaneously. To do the best we can in the Game of Life is to attempt to follow the rules of the Game. For any given person, simply attempting to follow the rules of the Game is a uniformly optimal strategy. The optimal playing of the Game of Life also maximizes a person's expected happiness because only the constant expansion of awareness can continue to make us happy. The risk of unhappiness is also minimized in the Game of Life because a person with a single desire fulfilled by the very act of pursuing the desire can never be unhappy. Only playing the Game of Life deliberately can create joy.

The rules of the Game of Life are a unique, uniformly optimal strategy for anyone who *deliberately* tries to follow them. This is the case

---

* This is only the case if death is total extinction. Science supports this hypothesis as shown in Chapters 2, 3, and 4.

irrespective of whether a person plays the Game of Pleasure or the Game of Life. Today, persons who are not deliberate in playing the Game of Life risk both unhappiness and entropy. They can at best have a minimax strategy in the Game of Pleasure. They inevitably become unhappy until they die.

ETHICS

Ethics are rules of optimal behavior. Since all men either play the Game of Pleasure or the Game of Life, behavior is optimal, i.e., ethical, if and only if it is a strategy in the Game of Life. A strategy in the Game of Life is any attempt to follow the rules of the Game. To be ethical is to be a player of the Game of Life. To be unethical is to be a player of the Game of Pleasure, i.e., to use a strategy that increases entropy. An action is good if and only if it increases total awareness. An action is evil if and only if it diminishes total awareness. An action that is neither good nor evil is trivial. A person is ethical if he plays the Game of Life most of the time. A person is unethical if he plays the Game of Pleasure most of the time.

A moral person is one who *deliberately* plays the Game of Life; he never knowingly plays the Game of Pleasure again. An immoral person is one who *deliberately* refuses to play the Game of Life; he never knowingly plays the Game of Life again. An amoral entity is a subhuman being who is unaware of the Game of Life. A "child" is an occasionally ethical person who is not a deliberate player of the Game of Life. Childhood represents the transition stage in man's individual development from an amoral to a moral entity. During childhood behavior alternates between good and evil. A child who is predominantly ethical is in the state of becoming moral. A child who is predominantly unethical is in a state of becoming immoral.

In his individual psychosocial development, each person recapitulates the moral development of humanity. Children play the Game of Life as blindly as our ancestors. Man has been a child for most of his existence. Because of his recent, great increase in awareness, he has lately been forced to become a moral being. Children always increase their aware-

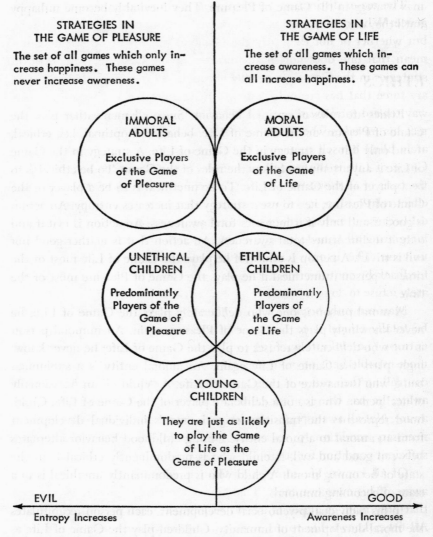

FIGURE 3
Ethical Sets

**STRATEGIES IN
THE GAME OF PLEASURE**

The set of all games which only increase happiness. These games
never increase awareness.

**STRATEGIES IN
THE GAME OF LIFE**

The set of all games which increase awareness. These games can
all increase happiness.

IMMORAL
ADULTS

Exclusive Players
of the Game
of Pleasure

MORAL
ADULTS

Exclusive Players
of the Game
of Life

UNETHICAL
CHILDREN

Predominantly
Players of the
Game of
Pleasure

ETHICAL
CHILDREN

Predominantly
Players of
the Game
of Life

YOUNG
CHILDREN

They are just as likely
to play the Game
of Life as the
Game of Pleasure

EVIL

Entropy Increases

GOOD

Awareness Increases

The ethical splits between persons are determined in part by external circumstances
and the internal state of the persons involved. In any individual the same action can
be ethical at one point and unethical at another. The concept of "children" refers
only to an ethical condition not necessarily to chronological development.

ness. Only immoral adults become totally unethical by destroying the awareness they acquired as children. They do this by acquiring imaginary awareness.

The major distinction between men is ethical behavior—not intelligence. What counts most is not how well persons play the Game of Life, but whether or not they play the Game at all. To be ethical does not mean that one does not make mistakes in the Game of Life. Not all strategies in the Game are equally effective. All men, like the evolutionary force that has created them will make mistakes as they grope their way toward total awareness. To be ethical means that a person will correct his mistakes when they are perceived and that he will not deliberately blind himself to them. The process of correcting mistakes in the Game of Life is the process of science. Scientific method is, therefore, the basis of all morality. It is unethical to be certain about any cause and effect relationship; it is always ethical to have doubts; inaction is unethical because it increases entropy. Man can only become totally ethical by integrating all knowledge into a single coherent, evolving model of the universe. This is only possible if he avoids entropy and maximizes his feedback by continuously testing and improving his models. To deliberately refuse to do so is immoral.

Man can only become totally ethical by becoming totally aware. To be totally ethical is to have won the Game of Life and to have zero entropy (i.e., infinite awareness). The more ethical man becomes, the more capable he is of predicting the consequences of his actions and of controlling their evil or good effects. The most ethical person is the most aware; he has the greatest capacity to create.* All ethical persons are aware. Not all aware persons are ethical. Ethics are a sufficient but not a necessary condition for awareness. Awareness is a necessary but not a sufficient condition for ethics.

Of all known life forms, only man is ethical because only man is aware of his own awareness. That this is the case is proved by the fact that only man, as a species, seems to increase his awareness and create. All other known life forms seem to be purely pieces in the Game of Life—probably only man is a player. The awareness of subhuman life can only increase by being mutated into new species. Therefore, *ethical*

* Recall that creativity is the highest form of awareness. See Glossary.

behavior is the highest form of awareness; it is the avatar of creativity.

A person is unaware of the Game of Life if and only if he is unaware of his own awareness. Therefore, only very young children and subhuman entities are amoral. Adults are all either moral or immoral, but not all adults are equally ethical. Ethics are, therefore, relative; but morals are absolute. All immoral persons are unethical, but not all unethical entities are immoral. A person is moral only if he is aware of his own ethics. Therefore, *morality is the highest form of ethical behavior;* it is the ultimate manifestation of creation—mind as an effect of itself.

Immorality is the most evil form of behavior. Only a highly intelligent person can be immoral. All persons are either moral, immoral or children. An immoral society can stunt the development of children so that they never make the transition to moral beings. When this happens, the children become immoral adults.

Unethical persons become immoral by destroying their feedback and developing illusions of awareness until they have destroyed the ethics of childhood. The point at which a child becomes ethical is analogous to the point at which our pre-*sapiens* ancestors became aware of their own awareness. It is a transitory point with no clear demarcations. Only when it is passed, is it clear. Similarly, the point at which man becomes moral is the point at which he becomes aware of his own ethics. The rules of the Game of Life are the natural ethics which all children possess. They are the ethics of life.

Man becomes moral by asymptotically becoming less a piece in the Game of Life and more purely a player. Only an entity capable of deliberately playing the Game of Life can be moral; to decline the challenge of the Game of Life is to become evil. Man is never knowingly evil, he only becomes evil when he is immoral. Awareness catalyzes itself by making man ethical, moral, and a total player in the Game of Life. But this is only possible when there is feedback; without feedback all persons become unethical. The deliberate destruction of feedback is always immoral.

An ethical person, in assuming responsibility for his own actions, ascribes responsibility to all other persons for their actions. Deliberately to deny them this responsibility is to regard them as amoral. This is immoral; it can only increase their entropy by depriving them of feedback; it will stunt the development of children.

The entropic force is evil. The evolutionary force is good. The Game of Life is the pivotal point between good and evil. The prime strategy in the Game of Life is to make children ethical so they may become moral adults. Immoral adults can prevent this from occurring. Immoral adults make children unethical. It is possible for immoral adults to be decent.

DECENCY AND MORALITY

A decent person is an honorable person. A decent person is one who will not willingly enhance his welfare at the expense of someone else's welfare—he is concerned with the welfare of others. A decent person is ethical when he interprets welfare as being synonymous with awareness. A decent person is unethical when he interprets welfare as being synonymous with happiness. A decent person is immoral when he is deliberately willing to sacrifice anyone's awareness, including his own, for anyone's happiness, including his own. Persons who do this are always a source of entropy. Immoral decent adults are, in the long run, just as destructive to the human race as are indecent* immoral adults.

The most unethical form of behavior is destruction of awareness. For this reason, the deliberate suppression of personal freedom is always immoral. The suppression of freedom destroys the feedback and subsequently the awareness of both the suppressor and the suppressed. The deliberate suppression of freedom is only done by indecent persons. All indecent adults are immoral, but not all immoral adults are indecent. A lack of decency is a sufficient condition for immorality, but it is not a necessary condition. Decency is a necessary but not a sufficient condition for morality.

Immoral decent persons decrease awareness by deliberately destroying negative feedback. Negative feedback is perception of our mistakes. Positive feedback is perception of our successes. Both positive and nega-

---

* "Indecent," being the converse of "decent," refers to a person who will deliberately increase his welfare at the expense of another's welfare.

tive feedback are essential to ethical development. Without negative feedback, mistakes in the Game of Life cannot be corrected. Without positive feedback, successes cannot be consolidated and compounded.

Positive feedback always makes persons happy. Negative feedback makes persons happy if and only if they are moral. Moral adults learn as much from negative feedback as from positive feedback; therefore, they are made "happy" by both kinds of feedback.

Decent immoral persons are players of the Game of Pleasure; negative feedback makes them unhappy. Therefore, they will try to avoid negative feedback for everyone. They do this by avoiding reality and giving misleading feedback to themselves and others. They increase entropy through imaginary knowledge. Today decent immorality is popularly regarded as "morality." This attitude exists at all levels of society. It exists least in the family.

The family is the social unit for turning children into moral adults. Children are all ethical because they always increase their awareness. Immoral adults decrease their awareness by avoiding negative feedback until the awareness they acquired as children is destroyed. There exist two types of morality—1) social morality and 2) personal morality. Social morality is concerned primarily with increasing the awareness of others. Personal morality is concerned primarily with increasing one's own awareness. Both types of morality are essential. Personal and social morality are causes and effects of each other. In the family the mother rarely increases her personal awareness directly, instead she is usually the principal source of expanding awareness for her children. Women through social morality are usually the catalysts that make children moral. Men are usually the direct expanders of awareness through personal morality. Immoral adults will neither increase their personal awareness nor mold ethical children into moral adults. Moral parents will insist that their children learn even if learning makes their children unhappy. This type of behavior is still commonly regarded as "moral" but only in the family. Every other social institution is becoming concerned only with making persons happy.

The same moral standards apply to both male and female adults. Both men and women have components of personal and social morality. As will be shown, there are evolutionary patterns that indicate that a concentration of social morality in the female and personal morality in the male makes for a more cohesive family* and a larger percentage of moral adults in the human population.

The evolution of morality is essentially the continuing evolution of the family. The family, when it is a union of moral adults and ethical children, represents a microcosm of the Moral Society. The Moral Society is a critical union of moral adults. Any act that weakens the structure of the family is evil. Any act that strengthens and extends the family is good. The growth of immorality in society is directly associated with the weakening of the family by turning all persons into players of the Game of Pleasure.

A society becomes immoral when the majority of its leaders are immoral. An immoral society is a society in which all adults are immoral. An immoral society cannot produce good effects; it is doomed to irreversible entropy unless the immoral leaders can be replaced with moral men. Moral adults will always increase awareness. Any society with a majority of moral leaders will become moral if it has an ethical structure. A society has an ethical structure if and only if it is structured to maximize total awareness for all persons.

By constantly increasing his awareness, man has been creating the Moral Society. A Moral Society is a society in which all men are moral. In the last few years man has begun to reverse his multi-million-year trend of increasing his total awareness. Although ethical children and moral adults still remain, man is increasing his entropy by pursuing happiness without awareness. He is no longer forced to be ethical. He now has to choose because he has become increasingly aware of his own ethics. He can only be ethical when he is moral. Today man must play the Game of Life deliberately or he will not play the Game at all.

The decline in awareness is a direct result of the fact that all the nations of the world have an unethical structure† and are becoming immoral societies. A society becomes immoral after it becomes unethical; it is unethical when most of its citizens play the Game of Pleasure most of

* The concepts of "family" and "extended family" are discussed in Chapter 2. For now, "family" may be considered in a conventional sense.
† An "unethical structure" refers to a structure for making some or all persons happy without making them aware.

the time. Unethical societies usually have immoral leaders who increase entropy by accepting ideology in lieu of science, and bureaucracy in lieu of feedback. The entire world is becoming immoral. To reverse the entropic decline of the human race and create the Moral Society, it will be necessary to create a new type of nation—a nation ethically structured to maximize the total awareness of the human race.

THE ETHICAL STATE

The transition stage between today's world and the Moral Society will be an Ethical State. An Ethical State is dedicated to the optimal expansion of total awareness for the entire human race. An Ethical State is a nation deliberately playing the Game of Life. It is a nation creating the Moral Society by helping all men to become moral. A united humanity constantly and deliberately expanding its total awareness is the beginning of the Moral Society. Only moral adults can create the Moral Society.

A nation is ethical if and only if most of its citizens are ethical. A society remains ethical only if most of its leaders are moral adults. Adults are only moral when they are generalists; however, not all generalists are moral men.

Because a moral person is deliberate in playing the Game of Life, he will attempt to maximize his awareness by maintaining sphericity, i.e., generalizing. This implies that a moral person will attempt to know all the sciences as well as the arts and humanities. In a modern, civilized society a knowledge of all the sciences is a necessary, but not a sufficient condition for a person being moral. Therefore, the leadership of an Ethical State would, as a minimum, have to be well versed in all the sciences. Today, a scientific illiterate is as unqualified to provide ethical leadership as is any conventional illiterate who can neither read nor write.

All men, not only geniuses, who have applied the simple and straightforward principles of science have enabled man to make remarkable progress. It is, therefore, astonishing on the surface that in spite of the proven success of the scientific method, every government in the world is ideologically based and dominated by scientific illiterates who eschew the scientific method in running the affairs of their people. These immoral leaders are destructive specialists in the psychosocial environment who pervert the accomplishments of science, such as modern weapons and the communications media, to accomplish unethical purposes. They increase man's entropy by destroying his feedback and *forcing* him to play the Game of Pleasure. No country has as yet either the purposes or the methods of an Ethical State. The creation of an Ethical State is not only a necessary pre-condition to the Moral Society, it is essential for man's survival. The reasons for and the structure of the Ethical State will be discussed fully in the succeeding chapters.

OF GOALS AND MEANS

Every description, hypothesis, theory and strategy in this book is tentative; they may all be in error. They represent only the first few steps of the scientific process. Science is the key to the Game of Life. Without scientific method, the Game of Life is perverted into a quest for personal power and/or the delusions of ideology and bureaucratic security. Without scientific method, ethics cannot be sustained. Methods for expanding total awareness can be altered and improved as awareness evolves. What cannot be altered is the ultimate goal of total awareness.

As an ultimate goal, total awareness has no basis in logic. It is a goal. It is not a method for achieving a goal. It is not a cause and effect relationship. It is an end in itself. It is the Game of Life. We can try to make total awareness a desirable goal by showing that it is 1) part of an already-existing pattern on which our survival depends; 2) compatible with other intuitively-desirable human goals; 3) ethically necessary, and 4) morally desirable. But this will not convince persons who cannot directly perceive the necessity of an ever-expanding total awareness as the only goal for mankind. It will only convince persons in whom the evolutionary force is stronger than the entropic force. It will only convince ethical persons. Those who will play the Game of Life and work to create the Moral Society are those who will want, for its own sake, a united humanity working to understand and master matter, life, and mind—a humanity evolving toward a time-transcending total awareness that will certainly extend beyond the stars. It is within our reach. But we can also lose it.

2

PATTERNS
OF EVOLUTION

All is an effect of the cosmic force. The cosmic force has no beginning or end; it is everywhere; it is infinite; it is mindless; it is random.*

Evolution and entropy are components of the cosmic force. Entropy destroys all that does not play the Game of Life. Entropy causes the avoidance of the Game. Entropy feeds upon itself. Evolution creates ever greater awareness throughout the universe. Through the evolutionary force, matter is created from chaotic energy; life from matter; mind from life; and pure thought from mind. Pure thought is mind as an effect of itself. Pure thought is the destiny of the Moral Society. The Moral Society is the destiny of all moral beings.

The transition from mind as an effect of life, to mind as an effect of itself begins with the Moral Society, but it never ends. The Moral Society evolves toward ever greater awareness. It becomes pure thought only

* "Random" means unpredictable without a specific pattern.

when it is infinitely aware. Therefore, the Moral Society can only become pure thought asymptotically by evolving toward total awareness.

Evolution is a clumsy, groping force because it coexists with entropy. The cosmic force is random because it is infinite while awareness is finite. No one ever knows enough to predict and control the cosmic force deterministically. The randomness results from our lack of awareness.

Evolution has specific properties and a direction—ever-greater awareness. Entropy also has specific properties and a direction—ever-lesser awareness. The evolution of awareness is the evolution toward zero entropy. Zero entropy implies infinite awareness. As mind decreases its entropy, its evolution becomes irreversible because mind becomes increasingly de-randomized. Asymptotically, mind becomes pure thought, free from the entropic perturbations of energy, matter, and life. That mind can direct energy, organize matter, and engender life is already self-evident. It is postulated that as mind becomes pure thought, it becomes one with the evolutionary force and it can create the entire cycle of evolution from itself, thereby creating energy from pure thought, matter from energy, life from matter, mind from life and pure thought from mind. This is the upward-moving, infinite spiral of evolution that has no beginning or end.

All evolution mirrors its former patterns. In order to perceive the evolutionary patterns of the Moral Society, it is first necessary to perceive the evolutionary patterns of mankind.

MANKIND

Evolution has a pattern that repeats itself every time a new phylum is created. Teilhard de Chardin called the process "fanning out." A phylum starts with a highly generalized species which has some specific advantage over other life forms. At first it can fit more or less into many ecological niches. The generalized species then begins to specialize until some of its members can fit *perfectly* into one and only one ecological niche. In the process, they test* the less aware competitors from other

* "Test" in the evolutionary sense refers to a process by which the awareness of an entity is continuously compared to another entity, and the less aware entity is given

phyla which are currently occupying the niches. When a species fails the test, it becomes extinct. In this way a phylum "speciates" so that the species with one specialty remain forever separated and fan out from those which have other specialties. Each species tries to minimize its testing by specializing. Once a species is specialized, it is doomed to become extinct whenever significant changes in the environment occur. Specialization causes irreversible entropy.

Man is still a highly generalized species that can fit into many niches. In the dim past, subspecies of near-men began to specialize by adapting physically to a specialized environment. They tried to avoid testing. Paranthropus developed a large, powerful body to ward off predators and the massive jaw and teeth of a vegetarian. He tried to fill the ecological niche of the less intelligent apes and herbivores. Paranthropus became extinct. Australopithecus who co-existed with Paranthropus was smaller and weaker, but also much less specialized. He became the direct ancestor of man. Neanderthal man represents a much more recent case of specialization. He began to specialize only a little over 100,000 years ago. As time went on, he became more brutish in appearance. The European variety of Neanderthal, which seems to have been separated by glaciation from the main stream of human evolution occurring in the warmer climates, became a heavily-muscled, squat brute with massive jaws and eye ridges. He physically adapted to the cold and developed body armor for defending himself. The motor centers of his brain became much more developed than in modern man. He was probably a superb athlete. He was completely exterminated in just a few thousand years by the testing of modern man who, being less specialized and athletic had been forced to develop better weapons, clothing, and social organization.

Modern man continued to *evolve psychosocially* toward the Moral Society by *testing himself* and by *refusing to specialize* and adapt physically to the environment. With science and technology he forced the environment to adapt to him. Even in recent times, those races of man who began to make a physical adaptation to their environment were in danger of being exterminated by the more aware races who used machines to control their environment.

---

negative feedback by having its "fitness," i.e. potential for producing progeny, reduced.

The Europeans were the least specialized human group. They used machines to dominate all other groups of men. It was only by adopting the culture of the Europeans and copying their machines that the Asiatics and to a lesser extent the Africans were able to avoid domination. The Tasmanians were so specialized that they became extinct after their encounter with the Europeans. The less scientific nations exist only at the sufferance of the nations with a more scientific culture.

Man avoids testing by specializing psychosocially. He specializes his behavior and then insulates himself from testing through bureaucracy. He increases his entropy. The lesson is clear—just as man must not specialize physically if he is to survive, neither must he specialize psychosocially if he is to evolve toward the Moral Society.

The evolution of science is part of the pattern as well as a mirror of the evolution of all life. Systematic science is a new phylum of the human mind fanning out and filling the niches of knowledge that had been previously filled with the phylum of ideology. Bureaucratization mirrors the pattern in evolution which causes a species to avoid testing by specializing and then fanning out from its brothers in a search for security. Throughout evolution speciation has been a means for expanding awareness by creating ever-more aware species which would replace the lesser aware wherever there was competition. This pattern was repeated in psychosocial evolution when the more aware societies would replace the lesser aware societies. The surviving society would grow larger than the previous two combined and unite more men in one more step toward the Moral Society. The "natural" antagonism that exists between radically different cultures and races is evolution's way of testing, then selecting for the more aware group.

Man is today fanning out from himself by deliberately avoiding his testing of himself. However, testing is an inexorable part of the evolutionary pattern. It cannot be avoided indefinitely. The longer man avoids testing by specialization and bureaucratic insulation, the greater becomes his entropy. If he does not deliberately and consciously test himself for no other purpose than to increase his awareness, his entropy will become irreversible and he will destroy himself by becoming immoral.

Fanning out and testing are frequent features of evolution, but there is another much less common phenomenon—"joining." Joining occurs when there is a giant leap in evolution. The last joining occurred when individual cells (protozoa) became multicellular beings (metazoa). The previous joining occurred when exceedingly complex molecules joined to become cells. The next joining might be when man joins to become the Moral Society.

Each time there is a joining, the different parts of the new being are homologous. They have evolved from simplicity to such a uniformly high level of complexity that new complexity can only result from joining. They do not begin to specialize until after the joining. So it must be with man; except that he will never have to specialize because he uses machines to control his environment. In order for it to be possible for a new joining to engender the Moral Society, all men who are to be of the Moral Society must become moral. Scientists must know all of science and all men who would create the Moral Society must be scientists. Only highly aware scientific generalists can create and use the highly complex machines that will form the body of the Moral Society. Only moral generalists who possess all human knowledge can become the mind of the Moral Society.

MACHINES

Recall that a machine is any manufactured device that transforms one form of energy into another. The machine has been the basis for man's evolution. The machine allowed man to remain generalized and still fill the biosphere. Once the pattern was set, probably millions of years ago, the evolution of man was essentially the evolution of the ability to build and use better machines (i.e., better means of predicting and controlling the total environment). The cultures which were most aware were always those capable of designing and building the best machines. Those races that adapted physically to their changing environment instead of inventing a new machine for dealing with it were already on their way to extinction.

The evolution of man and the evolution of the machine are part of a single pattern of ever-expanding awareness. Man uses his machines to amplify his awareness. He does this by using machines to simulate and amplify each of the individual components of his intelligence.

A simple model of human intelligence would, as a minimum, contain the following discrete components—Sensors, Information, Memory, Logic, Imagination, Effectors, Will and Connectors.

Sensors report some, but not all, effects of the environment in an ordered fashion as events in a particular time and space.

Information is the symbolic representation of events and their relationships.

Memory stores Information in addressable units. The address is determined by the nature of the event and its relationship to other events.

Logic tests the internal consistency of all the Information, i.e., it sifts the Information to avoid simultaneously storing contradictory events and relationships.

Imagination generates sets of events independent of the Sensors. The Information resulting from these events is stored in Memory just as is the sensorial information.

Effectors generate events whose effects are, in part at least, reported by the Sensors.

Will causes the Imagination and the Effectors to generate subsets of events until all event subsets are consistent and complete, i.e., contain all possible sensed effects of the environment and their relationships—total awareness.

> NOTE: All event subsets are never complete, i.e., no one is ever totally aware in an infinite universe.

Connectors propagate Information between Sensors, Memory, Imagination, Logic, and Will as shown in Figure 4.

In terms of the simple model of intelligence described above (each "component" is a subject for entire libraries) we see immediately that existing machines can amplify and extend human abilities in every component except Imagination and Will.

In an individual person the Effectors are represented by the muscles, bones, and the connective tissues of the body in general. Sensors are eyes, ears, thermoceptors, propioceptors, etc. Memory, Logic, Imagination and Will are effects of various parts of the brain. The nerves are

FIGURE 4
The Components of Intelligence

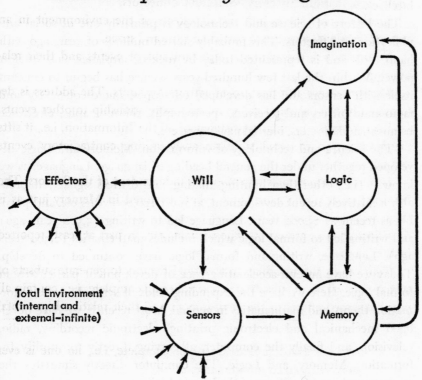

Flow of Information along Connectors between the environment and the components of intelligence under ordinary conditions. Under extraordinary conditions, it is possible for the environment to affect any or all the components of intelligence directly, e.g. neurosurgery.

the Connectors. Information is whatever is learned from the environment (internal and external) or by hereditary instinct. Man in his social evolution has been unconsciously laying the scientific foundations for the Moral Society by developing social analogues of his own body and intellect.

The history of science and technology is primarily one of social amplification of Effectors. This probably started millions of years ago with hand tools and is represented today by rockets, airplanes, and nuclear power. Within the last few hundred years science has begun to concern itself with Sensors and has developed telescopes, microscopes, TV and radio transmitters and receivers, spectographs, thermographs, electronic balances, audiometers, inertial navigators, etc.

The science and technology of Information, Memory and Logic developed together under the general heading of language. Language, as we know it (i.e., other than hunting, mating, and distress signals) it probably a relatively recent development, at most 100,000 years old and possibly as recent as 25,000 years. Language led to writing (5,500 years ago) and writing led to formal logic which includes mathematics (2,500 years ago). Language, writing and formal logic have continued to develop. Today we have an ever-accelerating pace of development particularly in formal logic. Here we have the expanding fields of symbolic logic, information theory and mathematics in general. Most recently we have developed mechanical and electronic printing, electronic recording, radio, television, and finally the computer, all serving directly to amplify Information, Memory, and Logic. The computer directly simulates the memory and logic functions of the human brain.

The initial social Connectors were the "natural" media represented by visible light and sound waves modulated by signs, sounds, and eventually language. This led to private and public "postal" service, distribution systems for printed matter, and finally to direct analogues of the human nervous system in the telegraph, telephone, and radio-television communication networks.

The selective processing of Information is a consequence of the total educational system. The determination of what Information is relevant and important is primarily a function of the Will and the Imagination. Society represents the collective Will of mankind.

The only social instrument for amplifying Will appears to be a progressive society constantly expanding its total awareness. Because of bureaucratization, ideology, and other entropic forces, societies rarely remain progressive for more than a few hundred years. Once entropic decline sets in, most societies impede the expansion of total awareness rather than enhance it. The Ethical State will be the first social amplifier deliberately structured to amplify the Will and avoid entropic decline.

Imagination is still a mystery. We can define its effects but not the mechanisms which cause it. Imagination appears to be amplified by free, close, personal interaction with rapid, accurate feedback between imaginative persons. Imagination may be a field effect that is in part produced by the collective morality of the universe. When a person is ethical, he becomes more receptive to the field and his imagination is amplified. Specialization seems to destroy imagination by making a person unethical.

It may be that Will and Imagination cannot be significantly amplified until after the Moral Society is created. In order to see how this might happen, it is first necessary to examine the structure of mind in its evolutionary context.

MIND

The mind has never been precisely defined. A working definition would be the following: the mind is that part of a person that is aware in general and aware of self in particular. It is clear that in man the mind is not a discrete entity, but is an effect of a system of living entities, cells, which interact synergistically to create awareness. The mind is intimately associated with the brain because we can destroy any part of the body except the brain and still maintain self-awareness. Furthermore, we can destroy very large parts of the brain itself and still maintain a concept of a continuous self. However, when certain parts of the brain are altered mechanically, chemically or electronically, then our perceptions of self, our intelligence, our will and our memories begin to change. It is at this point that we have begun to affect the mind. The mind, therefore, is not a "supernatural" entity but an effect of a small part of our brain. The mind is synonymous with the religious concept of "soul." The "soul" concept differs from "mind" mainly by being assumed immortal. The bulk of the body, including the brain, is a device for amplifying the Will and for providing feedback to the mind, i.e., the soul. The body is a non-manufactured machine.

This notion of mind certainly extends to all living creatures, the only differences being in the degree of awareness. Teilhard de Chardin thought that the notion of mind extended back into matter—molecules, atoms, and elementary particles—the only difference being one of degree of awareness with the Moral Society having the same awareness relationship to man as man has to the cell, the cell to the complex molecule, the complex molecule to the atom and the atom to an elementary particle. Leibniz in his *Monadology* expressed a similar theory.

Clearly all forms of mind are collective in the sense that many discrete entities interact synergistically to create awareness. Man's individual awareness is a collective awareness produced by the billions of cells which make up his body.

Mind is an effect of life and consequently of matter; however, it is an effect that has no substance. It is analogous to a gravitational field. That which causes gravity has substance but the gravity itself does not.* Gravity is caused by matter and affects matter. Mind, on the other hand, is caused by life and matter and can have obvious effects on life and matter. The greater the mind, i.e., the awareness and intelligence of the mind, the greater the effects it can have on life and matter. As mind evolves, it becomes increasingly less dependent on substance and more purely an effect of itself. A natural extrapolation of the trend is that when mind becomes totally an effect of itself, pure thought, it will have total awareness of life and matter that will manifest itself by the mind's ability to create substance from nonsubstance, i.e., itself. Similarly, matter can be created from energy. The mind and the entire universe may be an effect of pure thought.

The ultimate structure of mind and its effects are conjecture. As we understand mind more thoroughly, we should be able to make better

---

* If gravitons exist, then gravity may have substance and another analogy is in order.

estimates of its future forms. In order to understand the structure of mind, we must first understand the structure of life.

The structure of the human mind is intimately involved with the basic structure of life. By understanding life we begin to understand mind. Similarly, only by first understanding matter did we begin to understand life. There is a unity of structure in nature through which patterns repeat themselves at different stages of evolution. Such is the case with fanning out, testing and joining.

Each phylum that has dominated the biosphere has fanned out and filled the ecological niches until it was replaced by a more aware phylum. This has been the case with the arthropods and the chordates. The same pattern repeats itself in each animal class.

When the reptiles dominated the earth, there were flying, swimming, herbivorous, carnivorous, rhino-like, giraffe-like, kangaroo-like, and every other type of adaptation that a reptile could make. The mammals fanned out into the biosphere and imitated the same life forms as the reptiles; but being more aware, they replaced the reptiles wherever there was competition. Today man has himself fanned out into the biosphere. Whatever adaptation a mammal may have made flying, swimming, grazing, hunting, etc., man can or will do better because he is more aware and uses science and technology instead of physical specialization.

Similarly, patterns repeat themselves in the evolution of mind that had previously manifested themselves in the evolution of life. Mind, being an effect of life, reflects the structure of life just as life reflects the structure of matter. This may be true of every one of the components of intelligence. A speculative case in point is Memory.

Memory stores Information in addressable units. Life also stores information in addressable units called genes. The latter is done within the DNA molecule. To preserve the unity of structure, Memory must also store Information within DNA-like molecules. The information of the DNA molecule is replicated in every cell of the body. Therefore, the Information in Memory should be replicated in every cell in the brain and possibly other parts of the nervous system. Since a few thousand genes (DNA molecules) contain all the information necessary to structure an entire human being, all the Information in our Memory could be contained in at most a few thousand DNA-like molecules. Because the Information in our Memory is much less than the information in our genes, it may even be possible that a very few molecules—perhaps only one—may contain all the Information of our Memory. Again, mirroring the information of life, the Information of Memory might be stored as follows.

The DNA molecule is highly stable and does not change readily, although mutability is inherent in its structure. Memory implies a relatively easy change in molecular structure. DNA is built on templates of much less stable molecules, RNA.* Memory, therefore, should start by having information concerning sensed or imagined events recorded within an unstable, easily altered RNA-like molecule. The RNA-like molecule then serves as a template by which the DNA-like molecule alters its structure over a relatively long period of time until the information in the original memorial-RNA is completely transferred onto the memorial-DNA. Most likely there is a series of molecular changes in memory transfer. Information is first stored in very unstable, localized molecules and then transferred to successively more stable molecules until it is "permanently" stored in the DNA-like molecules in every part of the brain. This explains why we have many different types of memory, i.e., 1) very short memory, such as a telephone number that is forgotten after dialing, 2) intermediate memory such as the name of a casual acquaintance which we forget after not seeing him for a long period of time, and 3) long-term memory such as certain childhood events that are remembered all our lives even after we have forgotten nearly everything else.

The transfer of Information to increasingly more permanent molecular Memory is performed under direction of the Will (conscious or unconscious). The brain, therefore, functions somewhat like a selective tape recorder. The RNA-like molecules are a buffer where all sensed and imagined information is constantly being recorded and erased. The DNA-like molecules are the "permanent" tape, where only selected information is stored. The information in the DNA and RNA molecules serves to modulate the transmission at each synapse.

* Ribonucleic acid (RNA) is a complex, polymeric, organic molecule although it is much simpler in its structure than DNA. DNA can be synthesized from RNA.

Some aspects of "racial memory," i.e., instincts and Jungian arche-types, may represent a "contamination" of genetic DNA with memorial-DNA. This would give some scientific theoretical basis to the ideologies of the Michurin school of evolution that assumes the transfer of ac-quired characteristics. However, the evidence for this occurring is meager; there is little doubt that the major mechanism of evolution is based on natural selection and has little or nothing to do with the ge-netic transfer of acquired characteristics. Instincts probably represent merely the synthesis of the original memorial-RNA-DNA by the genes. The more intelligent the animal, the more likely that experience will alter the original memorial molecules.

The foregoing model of Memory would explain why large portions of the cortex can be removed while still allowing the person to maintain his personality and his memories. The multiple addressing and rapid re-trieval in human Memory is also explicable by this model, i.e., by having all our Information in each brain cell. The fact that the cortex is one of the most outstanding characteristics of the human brain relative to the brains of other animals implies that the cortex is the mechanism by which sensed and imaginary events are reduced to molecular informa-tion. The more developed the cortex, the more information is integrated and stored at the molecular level and the more instincts are modified by experience. Learning is, therefore, strongly dependent on the cortex, but not recall.

A possible function of the glial cells, whose neurological role is still not well understood, might be as the "recording head" in the brain tape-recorder model, i.e., they synthesize and modify the memorial-RNA-DNA to reflect new information.

A similar discussion of the other components of intelligence in terms of analogies with life processes is possible. However, a full speculative discussion of any of the components of Intelligence in this context is a subject for an entire book and need not be pursued at this time. The point to be made is that the understanding of mind is intimately associ-ated with the understanding of life. We can understand mind only by first understanding life. Man has evolved to the point where he is on the brink of total awareness of the biological environment. When he has comparable awareness of the psychosocial environment, he will have the knowledge to create the Moral Society. However, only moral men can acquire creative knowledge of the psychosocial environment.

MORALITY

The evolution of mind is the evolution of awareness. The evolution of awareness goes from 1) protoawareness (chaotic energy) to 2) awareness of self (matter) to 3) awareness of non-self (life) to 4) awareness of awareness (ethical behavior) to 5) awareness of ethics (morality). There may be higher levels of awareness than morality in the evolution of mind, however, they need not concern us at this time. Morality is the highest form of awareness known to man. Morality is a relatively recent development in the evolution of mind.

Throughout almost all of his evolutionary history man has probably been amoral. *Homo sapiens* is probably the first moral, although not the first ethical, species on Earth.* Our pre-*sapiens* man-like ancestors were probably all children. When species of pre-*sapiens* beings began to specialize, they became unethical and entropy destroyed them.

Morality is absolute, but not all *Homo sapiens* are moral—most are children all their lives. Human progress is due entirely to ethical persons. Humanity can only remain ethical if the leaders are moral adults. When the leaders are immoral men, any society becomes unethical.

Human morality increases by the increase in the absolute number of moral adults. They are the major but not the sole contributors to human progress. During the last one hundred years all men have begun to develop the capacity to become moral. Men cannot be moral unless they perceive either at the conscious or unconscious level their own evolution. In the past this perception was probably always unconscious. Today man, in becoming evolution conscious of itself, has been forced either to deliberately accept or decline the challenge of the Game of Life. This is producing unbearable tension for many persons because most persons

---

* As is indicated in the next two sections, there is some evidence that Neanderthal man was also moral. However, he probably became unethical by specializing until he was destroyed. The less specialized Neanderthalers were probably reabsorbed into the mainstream of human evolution.

would like to remain children. Man can no longer remain a child. The effect of this tension is to produce a much larger number of immoral adults than of moral men. This occurs because it is always easier to play the Game of Pleasure than to play the Game of Life. It is easier to sink into matter than to rise to greater mind. The net effect is that the multimillion year trend of human evolution has begun to be reversed; mankind is becoming immoral. When the immorality in the world reaches a critical point, entropy will destroy the human race—just as entropy has destroyed thousands of unethical and specialized species before. Immorality is the evolutionary analogue of specialization. This destruction can only be stopped if a critical mass of moral men and ethical children* join in determined opposition to the immorality that is destroying mankind. The appropriate strategy for accomplishing the reversal in moral decline is reflected in the patterns of moral evolution.

Morality and Religion

Morality has evolved, in part, as a consequence of religion. Religion is an ideology concerned with synthesizing a model which explains everything in the universe. Religion, therefore, usually starts as a variation on the Game of Life. Religion always becomes a variation on the Game of Pleasure because it does not correct its mistakes. Religions have no doubts about cause and effect relationships explained by their ideology. Religions, once established, become dogmatic and will go to any extremes to destroy negative feedback. Therefore, religions become totally evil and increase entropy without limit. The evolution of religion is analogous to the evolution of sub-human life. Religions cannot increase man's capacity for becoming moral without mutating into new religions. Once a religion starts, its moral contribution is made and it begins to decline just as an unethical species declines by specialization. Religions are all unethical (i.e., they propound certainty) although they serve to catalyze morality in some men in the beginning. The essential contribution of religion is to make men believe that life has some meaning and

* Recall that the word "child" is used in an ethical and not necessarily a chronological sense. When chronology is implied, "child" is modified by the words young, very young, etc.

purpose and that man can be a player and not just a piece in the Game of Life. This spurs man to become moral. Religions then destroy morality by destroying feedback.

In order to have the moral catalysis of religion without the entropy of religion, it is essential to have a philosophical system that gives purpose and meaning to life without destroying feedback. One such system is the Game of Life combined with scientific method and personal freedom. The combination is embodied in the Ethical State.

Religion is the evolutionary analogue of pre-human awareness, i.e., amorality. The Ethical State is the evolutionary analogue of primitive human awareness, i.e., unconscious ethical behavior. The Moral Society will be the evolutionary analogue of individual morality. Religion allegedly enables man to reach a supernatural goal. The Ethical State enables man to reach a natural goal—the Moral Society. The Moral Society enables man to reach toward the infinite goal of total awareness. Total awareness is the only ultimate goal; the constant increase in awareness is a means and an intermediate end. The Ethical State and the Moral Society are methods consistent with the goal. The means can change but not the ultimate goal. The act of pursuing the goal of total awareness will produce the optimal means for achieving it.

Means are only optimal if they result from ethical behavior. Unethical means can never produce ethical results. The end does not justify the means. All of evolution shows that the end reflects the means. Means must be consistent with the evolutionary patterns or they will destroy the human race. In the Game of Life, the ends and the means are one. Means which are not ends cannot be ethical.

Genesis of Morality

The evolution of morality within *Homo sapiens* appears to be primarily a psychosocial phenomenon. The physiological threshold of morality seems to have been passed about fifty to one hundred thousand years ago (first evidence of religion)* just as the physiological threshold of ethics, awareness of awareness, was passed several million years ago (first evidence of machines).

* The Neanderthal men seem to have had religious beliefs.

There may be an increasing number of atavisms among the human race who are physiologically incapable of becoming moral beings. These latter persons may be a result of genetic decay brought about by physical or psychosocial specialization. The majority of the human race, however, clearly has the innate capacity if not equal innate propensity for becoming moral. This is the basis of human dignity; the only characteristic in which men seem to approach equality. The development of morality in individuals should mirror the evolutionary patterns of the development of morality in the species.

The basic mechanism for making children moral and keeping them ethical is the family. The family accomplishes this feat in two ways: (1) it directly helps the child correct his ethical mistakes; and (2) it communicates the awareness and, therefore, the morality of the parents indirectly to the child at the unconscious level. The former is accomplished by the educational process, the latter by love. Education is any process that directly increases the total awareness of those who are exposed to it. Love is a state of mind in which the welfare of another person is sufficiently important to us that we are willing to sacrifice some of our welfare for his. Love has a counter-entropic effect only insofar as it is natural, i.e., insofar as "welfare" is synonymous with "total awareness." When "welfare" is synonymous with "happiness," then love is perverse and it can only increase entropy. "Love" as used in this book refers only to natural love. Love is the engenderer of moral decency.

That love is essential to the expansion of awareness is demonstrated by the many cases of children who become warped and stunted in their development when they are denied love. The necessity of love even extends to subhuman beings. Monkeys, for example, have been scientifically shown to be dependent on love for normal development. Monkeys who are denied love are much less capable of predicting and controlling their environment than are normal monkeys. The higher on the evolutionary scale an entity is, the more essential love will be to its psychosocial development.

Love is, therefore, the binding force that holds the family together. Love enables man to survive as a group and transmit his awareness, including his morality, at the unconscious level. Love may even be essential to the educational process; it catalyzes the transfer of information between student and teacher. Teachers who do not have love for their students seem to be ineffectual. Students who do not feel love for their teachers seem to learn even less effectively than if they studied alone. Love is the unconscious precursor of social morality.

Social morality in the family is concentrated in the female. Women deliberately sacrifice the maximum increase in their personal awareness in order to engender awareness in their children and their husbands. A man and a woman together produce a synergistic effect such that the totality of awareness that results is greater than the sum of its parts. This is not possible in homosexual * unions. Women by themselves do not seem to have an adequate amount of personal morality. Men by themselves do not seem to have an adequate amount of social morality. Women without men apparently cannot create significantly new awareness. They only seem capable of transferring the old. Men by themselves can create new awareness but they cannot transfer it as well as women. Awareness seems to grow best when it is a joint effort by both men and women. Awareness grows only when both social and personal morality are joined. Without social morality, our awareness dies with our life. With social morality, our awareness lives on in others. But if there is no personal morality, there will be no awareness for anyone.

Social morality is essential for personal morality and personal morality is essential for social morality. One cannot long exist without the other. Love is essential to the genesis of morality. A person is immoral if and only if he is devoid of love. An immoral person may, of course, have perverse love which manifests itself by a well-intentioned increase in total entropy.

Persons who have perverse love destroy children, including their own, by attempting to maximize their happiness instead of their awareness. To see that this is the case, we need only consider the effects on children whose parents sought only to make them happy even at the cost of the children's and the parents' awareness. These are the children who are undergoing hedonistic decline in all parts of the world. These are the children who are destroying themselves in the entropic hedonism of the

* "Homosexual" refers to a mental state in which persons show preference for the companionship of their own sex. As used in this book, it does not necessarily refer to physical sexual behavior.

Game of Pleasure. Children become immoral adults by becoming increasingly unethical until all their actions are strategies in the Game of Pleasure.

Man's progress has been due *entirely* to the evolution of the ethical family. Children become moral men by becoming increasingly ethical until all their actions are strategies in the Game of Life. Traditionally the family did the best it could to increase the awareness of the child even at the cost of the child's happiness. The current destruction of the ethical family is a consequence of the evolution of the extended family.

The Extended Family

The extended family evolved as an extension of love to include persons outside our immediate family, i.e., persons who are not our mother, father, siblings, spouse or children. The extended family evolved from the immediate family, to the clan, to the tribe, to the nation, to the empire. The next two steps in the evolutionary patterns are the Ethical State and the Moral Society. The evolution of the extended family was basically good, as is all evolution, because it enabled man to increase his awareness on an unprecedented scale by concentrating his collective intelligence. The problem arose from the fact that the extended family was more vulnerable to the machinations of immoral men.

The extended family became vulnerable because the leadership represented an essentially homosexual society of men devoid of female representation. Decisions made by men without the participation of women tend to become devoid of social morality. They serve mainly to increase the personal awareness of the men in power. Without women the desire for personal awareness eventually becomes perverted into a desire solely for personal power. That this has not been even more the case is due to the fact that most of the leaders in the extended family have been married men whose wives probably have had a peripheral association with the decisions that were made.

Women are essential catalysts for the expansion of mankind's total awareness. The differences in moral structure between men and women

are almost certainly a reflection of the differences in their genetic structure. The survival value of a closely-bonded marriage where 1) the male
took the risks to expand his and consequently his family's total awareness
while 2) the female constrained her personal awareness in order to protect and educate the children, is obvious. Men and women are essential
to each other and to the love that binds the family into a synergistic
unit.

The bonds of familial love probably have a sexual origin; however,
love and sex in an ethical family are inextricably interwoven with the
ethical desire to expand awareness. The sexual act is a means of communicating love; love is a means of indirectly communicating awareness. Sex
without love is perversion. It is a strategy in the Game of Pleasure. Sex
with love expands awareness directly by producing ethical children and
binding a man and a woman in a synergistic ethical union.

As the extended family grew, the bounds of love on which all families
depend became increasingly tenuous until they were virtually non-existent. Without love there can be no feedback. This enabled clever, immoral men motivated solely by a desire for personal power—a strategy in
the Game of Pleasure—completely to control the machinery of the state
so that they could control the structure of the immediate family. These
immoral men are the ones who are making the immediate family unethical and turning children into immoral adults. The immoral leaders are
themselves weak as a consequence of being unethical. They can only
exercise their power by controlling ethical children. Ethical children, no
matter how brilliant they may appear, are always vulnerable to the machinations of immoral adults. This somewhat paradoxical situation can
only be understood in its historical context.

Children

Children are always ethical. This means that they are usually increasing their awareness in some way by playing the Game of Life more often
than they play the Game of Pleasure. However, they do this unconsciously as a means of either being happy or adjusting to some outside
pressure. If immoral adults put pressure on children, the children can
just as easily use their awareness to further the entropic purposes of the

immoral men as to increase awareness. Children can only do well. Moral men always do the best they can.

Moral men being deliberate in playing the Game of Life cannot be made to decrease the awareness of any person, including their own, even at the price of their own lives. Immoral adults can never control moral men; they can only outnumber them, kill them, and/or control the resources for expanding awareness. Of these resources, the most important are children.

All ethical persons continuously expand their awareness. Moral men will seek to understand everything and to develop a coherent model of the universe. Children will not have so specific a pattern in their development. They are likely to be specialists. Moral men are always generalists. A specialist is a person who has learned a subject to the exclusion of most other subjects. A generalist is a person who has done his best to learn all the current knowledge necessary to form a coherent model of the universe. Both the specialist and the generalist may have considerable "in depth" knowledge in a particular area. What distinguishes the specialist from the generalist is the former's almost total ignorance of some important contemporary knowledge. Moral men will never have these blind spots if it is physically possible to acquire the knowledge.

When a child is exceptionally brilliant, he may also become a generalist by mastering successive subjects until he is an outstanding expert in each field. A moral man may not have as much depth in any field as a brilliant child. Even the total sum of knowledge and the proficiency for applying the knowledge may be greater in a brilliant child than in a moral man. Still the moral man will be more aware than the child. A case in point is shown in the lives of Leibniz and Spinoza who were contemporaries.

Spinoza and Leibniz

Both Spinoza and Leibniz were generalists. Each possessed *all* the fundamental knowledge of his day. Each essentially knew all of science, all of mathematics, all of history, all of philosophy, all of theology, and all of anything else that was considered important knowledge in the late seventeenth century.

Leibniz was one of the greatest geniuses of all time. He 1) invented calculus; 2) designed the first computer;* 3) laid the foundations for the theory of relativity; 4) developed the basis for modern logic; 5) founded the Prussian and Russian Academies of Science; 6) developed the first industry based on chemical engineering; 7) made fundamental contributions to biology; 8) developed a plan for the invasion of Egypt that was later followed by Napoleon; 9) diverted the attention of the Jesuit order away from Germany toward China; 10) engineered the election of George of Hanover to the throne of England; and among other things 11) developed an evolutionary theory, The Monadology, which implies the continuous evolution of mind from matter toward total awareness.

From what is known of Leibniz' life, it appears that he was a child. He seems to have played the Game of Life because it was fun and easy. Leibniz allowed his brilliant mind to be wasted in the service of the kings, bishops, and other petty tyrants of Europe. He was deliberately deceitful in many of his writings. He was just as much a pawn of the immoral adults of his day as he was their manipulator. He had little or no social morality.

It seems that Spinoza was a moral man. He seems to have played the Game of Life deliberately. He had none of the acclaim or impact of Leibniz during his life. The impact of Leibniz still persists in the scientific revolution, but his work has been superseded. The writings of Spinoza only began to be appreciated about one hundred years after his death. The appreciation of them is still growing today, three hundred years after his death. Spinoza was a philosopher of great depth but poor logic. In ethics, the most important field of philosophy, he still reigns supreme even though his logical methods were crude and mistaken. Today most rational men can accept his ethical conclusions, if not his method of deducing them. However, his methods were ethical even though mistaken. His ethical theories have a basis that is compatible with evolution and the laws of nature. He used no ideology in any of his work, but did the best he could to reason logically and scientifically. Spinoza made many errors in all his work but these errors had a logical, not an ideological basis. It is difficult to read Spinoza without being moved by the spirit of integrity that pervades his work. Such diverse

* Pascal had earlier designed a calculating machine.

intellects as Goethe, Bertrand Russell and Einstein were admirers of Spinoza.

Leibniz made almost no logical errors in his writings. His analyses were much more sophisticated than those of Spinoza but somehow less profound.

Leibniz spent his lifetime in the royal courts of Europe. He deliberately courted the favor of the powerful. Spinoza deliberately sought anonymity. Three years before his death, Spinoza was dying of silicosis brought about by his work as a lens grinder. At the time he was offered a chance to save his life by accepting the chair of philosophy at the University of Heidelberg. He declined the appointment because he would have had to compromise his ethical principles. Spinoza preferred to die grinding lenses which helped men to see than to live by helping to blind the minds of children. The life and death of Spinoza revealed his ethics more clearly than any of his writings. Spinoza's work is an example of ethical behavior leading to ethical ends even when it is plagued with mistakes.

Spinoza was less intelligent than Leibniz but he was more totally aware. The lives of these two men illustrate the fundamental difference between intelligence and awareness. Intelligence depends solely on the structure and nature of the components of intelligence. Total awareness depends on intelligence plus morality. Morality is a field effect which has no substance. Morality can only exist when there is intelligence. But intelligence can exist without morality. When it does, it becomes the tool of immoral adults.

Leibniz was raised in the tradition of a Protestant aristocrat. Spinoza was raised as an orthodox Jew. Both men were life-long bachelors. Spinoza was officially excommunicated by the Jewish community when he became a moral man. He was regarded as an extremely wicked man by both the Christian and the Jewish authorities. He was ridiculed by his peers. Yet there was an ingredient in his make-up that enabled Spinoza to become moral. Leibniz, with his greater intelligence and wealth, lacked that ingredient. He remained a child. This ingredient that Spinoza had and Leibniz lacked is essential to the creation of the Moral Society.

This ingredient of Spinoza is difficult to define, yet it can be perceived in such diverse persons as Albert Schweitzer, Mahatma Gandhi, Leon Trotsky, Thomas Jefferson, and others. These men, although of great intellect, were far from being the most brilliant men of their age. They each had a Leibniz to whom they could be compared. It takes more than intellect and general knowledge to make a man moral. It takes courage and ethics. The problem before us is how can courage and ethics be concentrated so that man can create the Moral Society.

3

FOUNDATIONS OF THE MORAL SOCIETY

Humanity is a *gestalt* of men, machines and knowledge. Knowledge is information that passes the test of prediction and control. Ethics are the most important kind of knowledge, because all knowledge stems from ethics. Men are animals whose bodies use knowledge to cause the effect called "awareness." The totality of man's awareness can only be expressed through his use of machines. Recall that language, clothing, tools, and computers are all examples of machines. *Together* men, machines, and knowledge represent the totality of human awareness. To destroy any part of the three part *gestalt* is to destroy all of it; human awareness can only exist when the parts are united. Man without the totality of his awareness is little more than an animal. Man devoid of all human awareness is no more than matter. Man with the totality of his awareness is the manifestation of the evolutionary force—the precursor to the Moral Society.

The precise structure of the Moral Society is, of course, impossible to forecast at this time. The important thing to keep in mind is that the Moral Society is *both* a means to an end and an end in itself. The ultimate goal is total awareness. The Moral Society is a means of achieving that goal by raising man to a higher state of total awareness. The structure of the Moral Society is implied by the evolutionary patterns. The patterns imply that 1) the Moral Society will represent a joining of men and 2) only men who are moral will join in the Moral Society.

Children will be made moral men by the Ethical State. The act of becoming moral will facilitate the development of the technology that will make the Moral Society possible. That the Moral Society will be primarily a technological development is implied by the evolutionary patterns that show man becoming increasingly dependent on his machines and the actual replacement of parts of his body with machines. The technological foundations of the Moral Society are pure conjecture and, like the rest of this book, should be regarded as hypotheses and theories still to be tested. Before discussing the technological components of the Moral Society, a brief discussion of the human component is in order.

HUMANITY

The essential ingredient that distinguishes all persons is knowledge. Bodies and machines are means for acquiring, storing and using knowledge. Our knowledge is what makes us truly what we are. Morality is the most important component of man's knowledge but few persons are moral—most are at best ethical children—many are becoming immoral adults. As we look at the great moral men of history—Moses, Zoroaster, Confucius, Buddha, Socrates, Jesus, Spinoza, etc.—we see that these men were all generalists. They were relative generalists in a historical sense since even many of the immoral specialists of today are better informed in every area of human knowledge than were the ancient generalists.

Therefore, it is not the intrinsic knowledge that makes men moral—it is something else.

The ingredient that seems to make men moral is not so much the breadth and depth of their knowledge, but rather the ability and the desire to communicate and extend the total sum of human knowledge to other men as well as the ability to learn from all other men. In other words, their breadth of knowledge makes them a part of all the men of their time. This commonality of knowledge with their fellow men when combined with creativity and love seems to produce an effect at the unconscious level that makes men moral as well as courageous. Only moral men are truly courageous (e.g., Spinoza). Children and immoral men always contain a streak of cowardice (e.g., Leibniz).

Psychosocial specialization separates men from each other in a process completely analogous to speciation in the lower animals. A joining can only occur when the unjoined beings are homologous. In the case of human beings, this means that all men must strive to acquire all important knowledge and be creative. Otherwise man cannot become moral and the Moral Society will not be possible. Therefore, the essential psychosocial process for producing the joining of moral men within the Moral Society will involve a radical change in our educational system. It will be necessary to create a system based on love which will enable all men to become full creative generalists with depth in all areas of knowledge. This subject is further discussed in the following chapters.

The technological basis of the Moral Society is much more conjectural and uncertain. What follows in this chapter represents only one possibility of how a joining may occur. It is the only technique that seems to fit all the evolutionary patterns. Others may be able to describe a more plausible technique for a moral evolutionary joining. Teilhard de Chardin, for example, thought that it would involve telepathic phenomena. However, this does not seem plausible and it does not fit the evolutionary patterns. In the end, when and if the joining occurs, it may be a radically different process from anything that can be imagined today. What follows is only one hypothesis. We begin the speculation with a discussion of technology.

TECHNOLOGY

As was shown in the previous chapter, the machine is an integral part of man's evolution. Man has always evolved by using his machines to amplify the components of his intelligence. The creation of the Moral Society should accordingly be an extension of the already-established patterns.

The creation of the Moral Society will probably be based on 1) constantly increasing the maximum level of total awareness for the entire human race in order to make all men moral and 2) developing the science and technology that will make possible the initial joining and the continuous expansion of the Moral Society. The former can be accomplished only by improving the individual quality of all human beings. The latter can only result from purposeful scientific and technological development. The two processes will interact synergistically.

The science and technology that will be essential for the creation of the Moral Society may be inferred from the basic structure of intelligence. That is to say, the technical and scientific foundations of the Moral Society as opposed to the moral foundations will be based on an understanding and amplification of Effectors, Sensors, Information, Memory, Logic, Imagination, Will, and Connectors. Intelligence will be a technological manifestation while morality will be a human manifestation.

Almost the entirety of human scientific and technological development has been concerned with the understanding and amplification of Effectors. The only other component of intelligence that has shown considerable extension and amplification in man's multimillion-year history is the Connector of language. Language also served in a much more limited way as an amplification of man's Memory and Logic.

In the flickering interval of human history represented by the scientific revolution, man has begun to amplify the other components of his intelligence. This is being done at a rapidly accelerating rate.

First, man amplified his Sensors with the balance, the clock, the telescope, then the microscope. He continued to develop his artificial Sensors such as the thermometer, the barometer, etc. In the last 40 years, he has begun to amplify rapidly every one of his Sensors; he has developed electronic light amplifiers and the electron microscope. Every one of his senses—sight, sound, touch, heat, smell, position, etc.—can now not only be amplified but actually improved and replaced by machines. From the point of view of his intelligence, the only important effect of his Sensors is the Information which is provided to his brain. Today man uses machines to convert artificially-sensed events directly into Information. This is illustrated by such devices as remote seismographs, automatic spectrographs, and so on. Man is using technology to amplify every one of the components of his intelligence except Imagination and Will. The rapid development in the technology of intelligence directly manifests the acceleration rate of evolutionary change. This is most aptly illustrated by the computer explosion.

Computers

Electronic computers were first made in the late 1940's. The computer, like all of man's machines, did not develop in a vacuum but evolved from his other machines. The forerunners of the electronic computer are 1) mathematics, which is a variation on the machine of language; 2) the abacus, which is thousands of years old; 3) the calculating machine, first developed by Pascal and then improved by Leibniz almost three hundred years ago; 4) the mechanical computer, first designed by Leibniz then imperfectly constructed by Babbage in the nineteenth century and greatly improved in the early 1940's; and finally 5) electronic circuitry, which grew out of man's efforts to develop highly efficient artificial connectors through electronic means of communication.

Since the advent of electronic computer technology, computer quality has been improving by approximately a factor of ten every five years. Since 1950, computer technology has improved more every five years than it had in the entire three hundred years since Leibniz. Computer technology is about to take another giant leap that will improve it, not by a factor of ten, but by at least a factor of 1,000,000.

Professor Humberto Fernandez-Moran of the University of Chicago has recently discovered a technique for making submicroscopic integrated circuits called "picocircuits." Picocircuits are made by using the electron microscope in reverse and etching, with a beam of electrons, the patterns of an integrated circuit on a special organo-metallic substrate. Connections between the picocircuits can be made by forming conducting strands of organo-metallic substrate between different picocircuits with another beam of electrons. Working picocircuits already exist. Within a very few years it will be possible to use these picocircuits to make super-computers hundreds of times more powerful than the largest computers of today yet *no larger than a brain cell!*

In time it will be possible to manufacture complexes of super-computers in which the memory and logic units are packed with far greater density than in the human brain as we now understand it. Cryogenic, superconducting versions of these computers could have even greater complexity than the human brain. They would be limited in size only by the speed of light, which might make communication between distant parts of the computer too slow for effective thought in some cases.

Such computers would eventually make it possible to have a *completely* automated society where all production, maintenance, scientific research and even design is performed by machines. Super-computers combined with other technological developments in 1) artificial sensors, 2) mathematics, 3) communications technology, 4) electro-mechanical servo systems; and 5) controlled thermonuclear fusion would make it possible eventually to produce a machine which in some sense rivaled and perhaps greatly exceeded the totality of man's present-day intelligence. The question before us then is whether or not the Moral Society can be purely a machine without a human component.

Robots and Cyborgs

It is part of the pattern of evolution that the more aware entity replaces the lesser aware entity whenever there is competition. There are no apparent logical reasons why machines directed by self-improving super-computers with logic and memory units more densely packed than in the human brain could not be more intelligent in some sense than man is today. If we consider that cryogenic versions of these computers could grow almost indefinitely, then we have a possibility for a totality of awareness within a machine comparable to that envisioned for the Moral

Society. If these machines developed Wills of their own, then they would compete against man for natural resources and they might replace him. This is a picture of the evolution of a robot to a super-robot.* Consider the evolution of the cybernetic organism (cyborg).

A cyborg is a machine that directly amplifies human powers. A cyborg is most easily pictured as a robot with a man inside it who controls every action of the robot directly and uses the machine to simulate and amplify his own actions. A lame person who puts on a mechanical limb is a cyborg of sorts. A man wearing functional clothing might even be considered a cyborg. In the broadest sense of the word, every machine that man has ever created has made him a cyborg. But the essential notion of a cyborg is that of a machine intimately associated with a man. The evolution of man has from the beginning been intimately associated with the development of the machine. Only the machine enabled our pre-*sapiens* ancestors to become fully human by avoiding specialization until they became moral.

A computer, no matter how complex it appears, is little more than a glorified adding machine. The human mind has features that no known machine has, namely Imagination and Will. A computer amplifies man's Memory (capacity for information reducible to simple symbols such as numbers) and Logic (speed of checking alternative consistencies). A computer in no way amplifies his Will or his Imagination; it will show no more Imagination or Will than was originally programmed into it. A self-improving (sometimes called "self-organizing") machine is one that can use its past experience to improve its speed at checking classes of inconsistences (by developing heuristics) and/or its memory in quantity and/or quality. A machine with these characteristics would be a robot. It could completely control an automated society. The machine could increase its own ability to predict and control events in that society. However, it could not do it as well as a man who used all the capabilities of the computer *plus* his Imagination and his Will.

Robots cannot generate events independent of the Sensors. A robot can have a "Will" in the sense of being programmed to generate new events with its Effectors. However, the "Will" is only a part of the Will

* "Robot" as used in this book refers to a self-improving machine that can in some way predict and control its environment.

of the original programmer. It is not amplifying the original Will in any way. The Imagination interacts with the Will and the other components of intelligence to select the new events to be generated by the Effectors. It does this by completing the incompletely-perceived patterns in the environment in order to form a consistent set. Science tests the completed patterns with the Effectors to see if they have been completed in such a way as to allow one to predict and control. This is how awareness grows.

A robot would only generate events according to a predetermined formula though it could become increasingly efficient at generating them. Even if robot Will and Imagination were developed, a robot would still not be moral, although it might be ethical. Morality is the first step in the process of mind going from an effect of life to an effect of itself. Morality is a field effect which is an integral part of our species and which we cannot separate from ourselves.

In the end, a cyborg is a much more aware entity than a robot. A cyborg needs a man. Furthermore, the most complex aspect of the environment is still man. We still have no clear notion of what constitutes Imagination and how it is dependent on the structure of the brain. It may be that Imagination can only exist in the presence of a moral field.* Man may create a machine for amplifying Imagination and Will some day, but even then the cyborg will remain the pattern of the Moral Society because only the cyborg incorporates man and only man can be moral.

The Will, as previously defined, is essentially a program to increase total awareness continuously. The fact that man does not do this is due to the delusions of misinformation brought about by poor Logic and sensorial illusions. A hedonist has the sensorial illusion that only pleasure completes the set of all events. An ideologue has a faulty Logic that does not enable him to distinguish adequately between sensed events and imaginary events. He sees inconsistent events as consistent and fills his mind with imaginary awareness.

The Will is a vector with a direction and a magnitude. Man continu-

* This does not mean that only moral men are imaginative. Children seem to be creative because they are receptive to the moral field. Immoral adults are never creative.

ously corrects the direction when he plays the Game of Life, i.e., when he tries to maintain sphericity. The Will of a machine would only have the direction and magnitude it was originally given plus changes due to random errors in the program. The Will of man has a direction that results directly from the evolutionary force. Morality is the greatest amplifier of the Will. A robot can at best be intelligent; only the cyborg can be totally aware because only man is moral.

As man develops toward the Moral Society, a united humanity of men, machines and knowledge expanding its total awareness through science, art, and technology would become a single entity with a collective intelligence and the question of whether the ultimate form of the Moral Society is man or machine will become meaningless. The Moral Society will have a mind of pure humanity but a body that is mostly machine. This is the way it has always been. Men, machines and knowledge are a single entity. There are no sharp divisions between the body, the mind, and knowledge. Each is a cause and effect of the other.

STRUCTURE OF THE MORAL SOCIETY

The structure of the Moral Society will probably entail the technology (physical, biological and psychosocial) for amplifying all the components of intelligence. It will be necessary to have the means for creating a synergistic interaction between the intelligence of many in order that a collective intelligence results that is greater than the sum of its parts. This is not now the case. Group efforts at solving complex problems by highly talented and imaginative persons may sometimes amplify some components of intelligence, such as Imagination and Will. However, the basic limitation in the efficacy of any group is the limitation on the intelligence of its most brilliant member. No problem is ever solved by a group unless at least one person fully understands all aspects of the problem. The Moral Society will be the first social system dependent on human behavior for circumventing this limitation. In so doing, it will make each of its individual members far more aware than they could have been otherwise. Every person who joins the Moral Society will possess the totality of man's knowledge.

The Moral Society, in mirroring the structure of man's mind, will possess all the components of intelligence. Most of these components will be machines, for example, communication networks (Connectors), electronic sensors, electro-mechanical and chemical effectors, and computers (Logic and Memory). The Will and the Imagination of the Moral Society, however, will be a purely biological, i.e., human, manifestation—at least in the beginning. Will and Imagination will be amplified and unified by the intimacy of communication that will be made possible by the technology and structure of the Moral Society. However, the major amplification of Will and Imagination will come from man's final realization of his destiny and a desire to fulfill it—it will come from morality.

In the distant future, the body of the Moral Society may be all machine, but its mind will always be human. Similarly, a man's body is purely animal, but his mind sets him apart. That small part of the human brain that produces the effect some call a "soul" is the embodiment of the evolutionary force. It will have its most magnificent expression in the Moral Society. In creating the collective soul and mind of the Moral Society, man will for the first time achieve literal immortality.

Man's mind is an effect of the cellular and molecular structures that make up his body. All the components of intelligence manifest themselves as a functioning of these structures. Each component may be altered by altering some group of cells. When these structures no longer function, i.e., when a man dies, then they can no longer produce an effect and entropy quickly destroys them. Therefore, since man's awareness is an effect of his body, his soul ceases to exist when his body dies. Today, death for a man is total extinction. This, to many men, is an intolerable thought; therefore, men use religion to blind themselves to the overwhelming scientific evidence that their souls die with their bodies. There is no scientific counter-evidence that this is not the case. Man's innate need to be immortal has been the basis of many religions. This same need together with the love inherent in moral men will make the Moral Society possible.

As man evolves toward total awareness, he will begin to prolong his life by replacing increasingly large portions of his body with machines. This occurs today when men replace their missing or damaged Effectors with artificial limbs and organs (e.g., artificial hearts). Man has been augmenting his defective visual Sensors with spectacles for some time. Lately it has become possible to replace damaged Sensors with electronic devices connected directly to the human nervous system. This applies to eyes, ears, and the senses of touch, smell, and heat. These devices are still crude but they work and will get better until all of man's Sensors are replaceable and, most of all, augmentable by machines.

The next logical step should be to replace damaged parts of the brain. This will probably be done, at first, by using super-computers with picocircuits to amplify or completely replace those portions of the cortex that create Memory and Logic. The computers, like all of man's machines, should in time be far superior to the original animal components of his intelligence. This is already the case with many kinds of artificial Effectors, Sensors and the more simple Memory and Logic functions of computers. Eventually, man will have machines performing all his bodily functions.

The human body has been decaying for thousands of years as man has become increasingly dependent on his machines. A simple extrapolation of this trend indicates that some day man will have a body completely dependent on machines—his body will be made of machines instead of animal cells. These machines will be as integral a part of man as the animal cells that perform the same functions today. If man still has a sentimental attachment to the particular body form that he has had for millions of years, he may create the machines in his animal image.* The technology produced by the ever-expanding total awareness of an Ethical State should eventually make it possible to create machine bodies for man that are indistinguishable in their appearance, function, and "feelings" from his animal body. Men would at first choose these bodies not so much as a means of creating the Moral Society but as a means of 1) prolonging their individual lives and 2) amplifying their individual powers.

Eventually, the cellular and molecular structures in the brain which produce Imagination and Will should be deciphered. Then man will have a machine body that exactly duplicates the basic structure, function

* A human gene was recently synthesized at the University of Wisconsin. The synthesis of human cells seems inevitable. A synthetic cell is a machine.

and possibly appearance of his animal body, but in which all the components of intelligence are greatly amplified. This will be analogous to an enlarged photograph in which the same basic patterns of the original are reproduced but on a much larger scale and on different material. Man's intelligence will result from machines controlled by the morality of man's mind. The morality has no substance and should remain the same as it was before. In other words, man will still be himself but no longer an animal. He will be an amplified man with human morality but with an almost immortal machine body. Death could still occur but only by accident.

Imagination and Will are currently amplified by the close cooperation of highly aware persons with a common purpose. The same process should apply to the amplified man. Except that now the same technology which made it possible to replace the animal body with a machine body should make it possible to achieve an intimacy of communication and cooperation not possible between animal bodies. Moral men will join in voluntary association for the sole purpose of expanding their individual and collective awareness and assuring their immortality. Immortality will be assured by the collective power of the Moral Society that makes it immune to accidental death. Individual components might be destroyed but the collective mind would not be affected any more than our individual awareness is affected by destruction of our Effectors or even millions of brain cells. Our individual awareness should last as long as the Moral Society.

While the Moral Society is being created within the Ethical State, there may be some persons who are so strongly attached to their animal bodies that they will forsake immortality and the maximization of their individual awareness in order temporarily to preserve their animal structure. As all persons in an Ethical State, they should be free to do this. They would not be part of the Moral Society and their awareness would cease to exist when their body died.

Men will be immortal within the Moral Society because their body is made of machines that can be replaced and improved as needed. The effect that produces the mind should never have to stop for any man so long as the Moral Society is expanding its awareness faster than entropy is destroying the material universe around it.

Free men whose bodies are machines but whose minds are human would voluntarily join in a Moral Society in order to maximize their total awareness. The Information of each would be pooled in a common Memory. In this way, each person would have all the Information of every other person. Each individual Will and Imagination would be amplified by the moral field. The collective awareness of all persons would form the individual awareness of each person. Each person would remain individualized and literally immortal so long as the Moral Society did not succumb to entropy. For this reason, there should be a point in the evolution of humanity when all men will forever choose to expand their total awareness at their maximum rate. Only in this way could they assure their immortality and have their individual awareness expand forever. This would be the point of no return in awareness, where the Moral Society becomes irreversible and each man becomes an ever larger part of the infinitely-expanding cosmic Moral Society.

The ultimate body of the Moral Society, while made of machines, may not be made of matter in the ordinary sense. It may be that at some point in its development the Moral Society will be made of the interface substance between matter and energy. It might be made of tachyons,* for example.

Since our minds are completely determined by the relationships that make up our bodies plus the field effect of morality, it should be possible for the Moral Society to duplicate continuously the material relationships of its body in substances that will enable it to amplify its intelligence further. If the Moral Society should choose to transform the patterns of its mind onto a body made of tachyons, it could recreate itself at speeds in excess of the speed of light. The speeds would be limited solely by how much energy the Moral Society was willing to lose. Tachyons

---

* Tachyons are postulated elementary particles that supposedly are spontaneously created from energy at speeds already in excess of the speed of light. This may be theoretically sound, but there is no scientific evidence that tachyons exist, although there is evidence that they should exist. In any case, relativity implies that objects may never be either accelerated or decelerated to the speed of light. An object made of conventional matter could exceed the speed of light only by a transformation of its structure directly into tachyonic matter. This would be analogous to a conformal mapping onto the complex plane. The techniques of differential geometry should be applicable to this process (see the work of Gerald Feinberg and R. G. Newton).

accelerate by losing energy. When tachyons have lost all their energy, they are travelling at infinite speeds. A Moral Society made of tachyons could travel anywhere in the universe instantly if it gave up all its energy. The ultimate limitation on the speed of a tachyonic entity is how much energy, if any, it needs to reconstitute itself out of more conventional matter when it reaches its destination.

Tachyons, of course, may not exist even though they are theoretically possible. Other forms of energy might be used to create the body of the Moral Society and accelerate it, in effect, beyond the speed of light. The only limitations on the Moral Society should be the limitations of thought. As the Moral Society became less an entity of matter and more an entity of pure thought, it would transcend time, space, and matter. Its mind would become an effect of itself. It would become the evolutionary force—the source of all creation.

The mind of the Moral Society will be the collective mind of moral man continuously augmented and amplified as he evolves toward infinity. The mind of the Moral Society will be filled with purpose and devoid of all emotions, except love.

Emotions

Emotion is a pre-programmed, i.e., instinctive form of behavior that enabled man to survive in the primitive Darwinian competition of prehistory. Lately, emotion has become less an aid to survival and more a source of entropy. It is emotion that causes men to seek happiness without purpose and security without awareness. Emotions such as fear, hate, greed, envy and anxiety are destructive and can serve only to impede the expansion of awareness. The only emotion that can serve a constructive purpose is love.

"Love" was defined as a state of mind in which the welfare of other persons is sufficiently important to us that we are willing to sacrifice part of our own welfare for theirs. To an ethical being, welfare refers solely to a person's ability to expand his awareness. Love will be the binding force that will enhance the initial joining of the Moral Society. It is only through love that it becomes possible to achieve the intimacy of communication with other persons which enables us to amplify our individual awareness. Love makes it possible for the awareness of one to be communicated to others at the unconscious level. Only love can extend the immediate family to the Moral Society.

The love of any given man is usually restricted to a very few persons —his immediate family and close friends. In the Moral Society the individual love of each will become the collective love of all. The welfare, i.e., total awareness, of each person will become the common concern of all persons. The Moral Society will be devoid of all emotion except love. It will be devoid of all purpose except total awareness. In the intimacy of the direct transference of thought, mankind will know true love for the first time. Only through the purpose and love inherent in the Moral Society can the human race find the joy it has vainly sought. Only love and awareness give quality to human existence.

The collective love of the Moral Society can only come about through the elimination of all the entropic forces of destructive emotion. Only moral men can do this. Only moral men can become totally aware. It is only by becoming totally aware that we can begin to understand ourselves. It is only by understanding ourselves that we can eliminate all emotion except love. It is only the love inherent in the structure of the Moral Society that will enable man to expand his awareness forever throughout the universe and beyond.

EXPANSION OF THE MORAL SOCIETY

The future of man and consequently of the Moral Society is not on earth, but beyond the stars. The Earth is merely the first stage, or better still the launching pad, for the Moral Society. Only in the infinity of outer space can man have an infinite future.

There is little doubt that the Earth, the Solar System, and eventually the entire Galaxy and all currently perceivable galaxies will run down to the point where they will no longer be able to sustain any life or mind. The entropy of matter must always increase. Only moral mind through the evolutionary force can forever counter entropic destruction. In order for this to happen, it is necessary, at least in the beginning, to tap the vitality of matter and life before it is destroyed by entropy.

The Moral Society could evolve indefinitely by expanding first to new stars then to new galaxies and then to "new universes." * In the beginning, each time the Moral Society expands it will probably consume an ever greater amount of energy by converting much of the matter under its control *before* the matter is destroyed by entropy. The expansion of the Moral Society should be analogous to binary fission and should, like all life processes, mirror the basic evolutionary patterns.

The Moral Society will first split into self-sustaining parts each with critical mass. The parts will then expand to new domains of energy where they will in turn grow, split and re-expand. Eventually, all the Moral Societies, which are after all part of a single Moral Society, will rejoin. The new joining will occur each time that it becomes possible to master a new domain of energy by joining. Therefore, a Moral Society starts at a single star, then fans out into the galaxy that contains the star until a new interstellar joining enables it to dominate the entire galaxy. At this time, fanning out resumes within the universe of perceivable galaxies except that the elementary domain of energy is a galaxy. When all galaxies within the perceivable universe are dominated, then a new intergalactic joining occurs which enables the Moral Society to fan out again into the universe of universes where the elementary domain of energy is an entire universe. This goes on forever in an infinitely-expanding universe where the Moral Society becomes ever more totally aware. This is the way it has always been with all evolution—fanning out, joining, fanning out, joining *ad infinitum*, always leading to greater awareness. The problem of testing remains.

Until now, testing has been as integral a part of the pattern of evolution as fanning out and joining. It is almost a certainty that within our galaxy, to say nothing of our universe, there already exist among the billions of stars Moral Societies, or at least incipient Moral Societies.† Is it reasonable to expect that the human Moral Society will be tested by them?

* A "new universe" is the universe which exists beyond the limit of perception where matter is receding from us at the speed of light.

† Quasars, which apparently consist of entire galaxies in which all the matter is rapidly being converted into energy, may result from the expansion of a relatively primitive Moral Society. (See *Intelligent Life In the Universe* by Shklovskii and Sagan.)

The creation of the Moral Society can only occur if a critical mass of men become deliberate players of the Game of Life. It is ethical to expand both our awareness and that of others. It is unethical to avoid the Game of Life. It is unethical to tolerate entities that increase entropy, i.e., immoral entities. As a Moral Society expands throughout the universe, it will probably encounter other Moral Societies periodically. When the encounter takes place, a decision will have to be made whether it is possible for the Moral Societies to meld * in such a way that the totality of awareness which results is greater than the totality of awareness before the melding or whether the melding will cause a net decrease in total awareness. This process will be completely analogous to the unconscious testing that different cultures and races have undergone in social evolution, except that the testing between Moral Societies will be conscious and deliberate. The major criterion for testing will have to be based on whether or not a Moral Society is succumbing to entropic forces, i.e., becoming immoral, by over-emphasizing happiness and security. A primitive Moral Society that is expanding its awareness at its maximum rate cannot help but enhance the total awareness of a more developed Moral Society. Even when this is not the case, the love inherent in the structure of a Moral Society will make it give up some of its welfare (though not decrease total awareness) to advance the welfare of a more primitive Moral Society. Ethics would force a Moral Society to avoid a less aware Society only if the latter had begun an irreversible entropic decline. Therefore, the danger in the testing process of a Moral Society will be not in encountering more aware Societies (this is an eventual periodic certainty for all Moral Societies if the universe is indeed infinite), but in succumbing to the entropic force and expanding its awareness at less than the maximum rate.

Eventually, each galaxy will have room for only a single Moral Society. The most aware Society will have to meld with the less aware Societies or avoid them if melding would significantly increase its entropy. The same process will exist in all domains of energy. This is analogous to the critical situation that currently exists on Earth where we must either

* The melding of distinct Moral Societies would be possible because their bodies are made of machines which can be adjusted to one another. It would not be a biological process, but a technical and moral process.

have world government very soon (i.e., the most aware nation melds with the less aware nations) or else nuclear proliferation, pollution, genetic decline, or gradual depletion of resources will destroy the Moral Society before it is born.

The infinite expansion of the Moral Society is only possible if the Society is deliberately expanding its *total* awareness at its *maximum* rate at *all* times. Only in this way can the evolution of the Moral Society become irreversible. Only in this way can the human race join periodically with other far more aware Moral Societies. Only in this way can each Moral Society evolve forever toward the infinite Cosmic Moral Society of all joined Moral Societies—the Moral Society of pure thought and total awareness. Only morality can engender immortality.

As humanity evolves toward the infinite Moral Society of pure thought, it should eventually begin to require less energy for its expansion since its mind will be less an effect of matter and more an effect of itself. The Moral Society should in time be able to tap the force of creation directly as it becomes one with the infinite Moral Society. At this time it would no longer need to convert matter in order to expand. It would instead become a part of the evolutionary force creating matter, life, and mind throughout the universe.

The evolutionary force may be irreversible in the larger patterns of the evolution of the Cosmic Moral Society.* That is to say, the Cosmic Moral Society that transcends time, matter and space is already determined and inevitable. What is not inevitable is that any given Society will eventually meld with the Cosmic Moral Society. An individual Moral Society is not essential to the cosmic pattern. If a Society at any time succumbs to entropy, it will probably be avoided by the more aware Societies until it destroys itself as the incipient human Moral Society seems likely to do. The pattern of evolution indicates that the longer a Society has been evolving toward total awareness, i.e., zero entropy, the less likely it will be to succumb to entropic decline. In other words, the less entropy a species has, the less likely it is to succumb to entropy. Entropy feeds upon itself. Only the expansion of total awareness at the maximum rate under maximum tension can guarantee that a Moral So-

* A Cosmic Moral Society is a Moral Society which results from the melding of independent Moral Societies which originated at separate stars.

ciety will never succumb to entropy. This is the way it has always been in human evolution.

Throughout his history man has been under maximum tension to expand his awareness at his maximum rate. If he did not, he would be destroyed by animals, starvation, or other more aware groups of men. It is only lately that modern science and technology have made it possible for all men to relax and increase their entropy without being immediately destroyed. A counterforce to the descent into matter has been the competition between nations. This and morality have prevented nations from succumbing to entropy. The competition is about to end either through annihilation or the hegemony of one nation over the rest. Only an Ethical State can prevent the ultimate increase in entropy due to either annihilation or eventual hedonistic decline of a single immoral world state. Only an Ethical State has built into its basic structure the constant tension and creative competition upon which all human progress depends. Only an Ethical State is structured to become a Moral Society.

Before creating the Ethical State, it will be necessary to understand the current human condition. Man is at the edge of a precipice. He has blinded himself with ideology, bureaucracy and hedonism. If he does not deliberately play the Game of Life, he may fall into the chasm of irreversible entropy. If only a few men will deliberately play the Game of Life, then they can help lead their fellow men away from the edge toward total awareness. But in order to reach the heights, we must first perceive the depths. Only by observing the depths of irreversible entropy into which man is about to descend, can we find the resolve to scale the heights to which man can just as easily ascend. Only by direct perception of himself can man find the will to create the Moral Society.

PART TWO

observation

*Human history becomes more and more a race
between education and catastrophe.*

—H. G. Wells

The greatest horror is to see no horror. To observe the world as it is implies an ability to see ourselves as we are. It has been said that each man is three persons: 1) the person he thinks he is; 2) the person others think he is; and 3) the person he really is. For any person to attempt to give or accept an accurate description of the world, it is necessary that the three persons become one. This apparently is never completely possible; therefore, all observation involves error. The reader, in turn, may accept observations that are false and reject observations that are true. It must always be borne in mind that any statement concerning cause and effect relationships may be in error. Every description, theory, and strategy in this book may be erroneous. Only our perceptions are certain, never their causes.

4

THE
WAY
IT IS

That the world is ethical is evidenced by man's increase in total awareness. That the world is becoming unethical is evidenced by the billions of people who are continuously increasing their and others' entropy by playing the Game of Pleasure.

Most of the nations of the world are unethical. That is to say in most nations most of the people are playing the Game of Pleasure more often than they are playing the Game of Life. However ethics are relative and no nation as yet seems to be immoral. Some nations such as Russia are becoming immoral because most of their leaders are immoral. These are the nations which deliberately suppress the freedom of their citizens. Only indecent, immoral men will do this. Similarly other nations such as the United States are becoming unethical through decent, immoral leaders who seek only to make their citizens happy and destroy their negative feedback. The latter case, however, creates a situation in which eventually indecent men replace the decent, immoral leaders. The etiology of these phenomena is the major subject of this chapter.

GOOD

The good in the world has its roots in the fact that throughout the ages some men have chosen to face reality and play the Game of Life in lieu of ideological security and insulation from negative feedback. All such men have been, in the broad sense, ethical.

Ethical men have increased total awareness directly through the scientific method which enabled mankind to predict and control his physical, biological and to a much lesser extent his psychosocial environment. Ethical men have also increased man's awareness indirectly through art by making man aware at the unconscious level of the evolutionary force driving him toward total awareness. No awareness seems possible in the total absence of scientific method and art.

Science has made man ethical by enabling him to predict and control the consequences of his actions. As man's ethical powers evolved, so did his power for good or evil. To increase man's power is always ethical. However, only men who use power to expand awareness are ethical. Men who use power to diminish awareness are unethical. The ethical men of the world are becoming unethical by deliberately abdicating their power to men who are already immoral.

EVIL

The evil in the world has its roots in the fact that an ever-increasing number of persons are declining the challenge of the Game of Life in order to play the Game of Pleasure. This is clearly manifested in the actions of the principal decision-makers who directly guide the destiny of the human race. They have neither the desire nor the knowledge to expand man's total awareness. Their decisions are made without benefit of the purposes and methods of science, but are often implemented with the force of a captive and sometimes perverted science. The prime deci-sion-makers, such as government officials, politicians, religious, labor and business leaders, professional educators, etc., are, in general, extremely ignorant of both science and art. Consequently, they are often immoral psychosocial specialists in the Game of Pleasure; they are experts in ma-nipulating persons by catering to their most primitive emotions and de-sires for security.

This group of men is representative of pre-scientific authority which was assumed to know of what it spoke solely because of its authoritative position and because of the irrational force and/or ideology with which it supported its contentions. This community of influential decision-makers and self-styled experts which reflects pre-scientific values and methods will be called the "Immoral Community." The Immoral Com-munity controls almost every society in the world, as it usually has for thousands of years. Human progress occurs in spite of the Immoral Community, not because of it.

The special preserve of the Immoral Community is the psychosocial environment. The traditional "experts" of the Immoral Community vig-orously resisted the onslaught of science in the physical environment until they were overwhelmed. In the biological environment they are still resisting, although ever more weakly after more than one hundred years of scientific progress. In the psychosocial environment the Immoral Community remains truculent, intransigeant, and uncreative. Still they are effective in their destructive desire to control other persons by en-tropic means. They use the weaknesses of children and immoral men to maintain their power. They are experts in the psychosocial environment in the same way that an efficient killer is an expert in the biological environment.

Since the Immoral Community can no longer challenge the basic tenets of science, it defensively claims that the psychosocial environment is not amenable to the ordinary scientific approach because 1) it is too complex, and 2) it is not possible to make controlled experiments. This is false as will be shown later. However, the most insidious defense of the Immoral Community against science has been to have its "experts" as-sume a deceptive appearance of science while remaining largely unscien-tific. This is done by simply having a new rite of passage—imitative of the more trivial aspects of scientific preparation—called the "Ph.D." The rite of passage involves learning the currently accepted ideology of the social "sciences" and becoming proclaimed a "Doctor of Philosophy."

Once a person has gone through the rite of passage, although ignorant of mathematics, physical science and biology, he is proclaimed a "social scientist" and thereby an expert in the problems of the psychosocial environment. The reasoning seems to be that since they are largely incapable of dealing with the simpler aspects of the environment, social scientists must be experts in dealing with the more complex aspects. Such is the case with the overwhelming majority of psychologists, sociologists, political "scientists," doctors of education, Marxist theoreticians, and other theologians. In this way the Immoral Community attempts to obtain scientific respectability while remaining insulated from the methods of science. Ironically, this is not done maliciously or even deliberately by either the leaders or the "experts" of the Immoral Community. Instead it is the unconscious result of the "natural" entropic forces of ideology and bureaucratization. No person considers himself immoral. Persons only *become* immoral by refusing to play the Game of Life.

The power of the Immoral Community is ideologically based, but its members are not committed to any particular ideology. The Immoral Community can be fascistic, theocratic, communistic or democratic. The prime motivating force behind the Immoral Community is not ideology but a desire to control the destinies of other men. Ideology is only a means to an end. The Immoral Community seeks only power. Usually this is done for self-serving purposes as an end in itself. Such is the case of the professional politician. Sometimes it is done by apparently sincere, altruistic ideologues who feel that they have a monopoly of "truth" and will resort to any means in order that this "truth" may be propagated. Lenin was such a man. St. Paul and Mohammed were others.

The direct pursuit of power is a manifestation of the evolutionary force and as such is good. However, the direct pursuit of power over men, untempered by an at least equally strong desire for the expansion of man's *total* awareness, leads to a suppression of feedback and an increase in entropy. As such, it is an evil perversion of the basic innate drive in all men toward total awareness. It leads in time to the extinction of awareness. *Only immoral men seek power without awareness.*

Because of the entropic structure of the current world social order, it is inevitable that immoral men whose main desire is power will be the ones who obtain it, while moral men whose main motivation is the expansion of awareness remain relatively ineffectual in shaping the psychosocial environment. The entropy is augmented by the fact that at this time the vast majority of people, the masses, are children who are motivated primarily neither by power nor awareness, but by the direct pursuit of happiness. As such, they are Pavlovian pawns of the Immoral Community in the Game of Pleasure.

The Moral Community* on the other hand lives mostly in contemptuous, smug isolation from both the Immoral Community and the masses. The Moral Community is thereby continuously turning inward and concentrating more and more on irrelevancies as it produces ever narrower, and as a consequence less ethical specialists who are increasingly ineffectual in the psychosocial environment. Because and only because segments of the Moral Community can, at times, serve the purposes of the Immoral Community, the latter cautiously but deliberately nurtures an ever-more willing Moral Community in a process of domestication. The Moral Community, therefore, while not exactly a pawn of the Immoral Community, has become not unlike a semi-tamed domestic animal that is useful but can still overcome its master. If the Immoral Community should succeed in completely domesticating the Moral Community, then man's awareness may be extinguished forever. In domesticating the Moral Community they will destroy the last vestige of feedback in the society. The destruction of feedback leads invariably to extinction for any organism. The elimination of feedback is the main function of bureaucracy.

* The "Moral Community" is the community of all ethical persons concerned with the expansion of awareness. It includes most but not all of the scientists, artists and technologists in the world. Technologists include all persons who produce any of the goods or services that are essential to the expansion of awareness, e.g., physicians, teachers, farmers, craftsmen, etc. The members of the Moral Community are the true "workers" of the world who are exploited by the Immoral Community.

BUREAUCRACY

An organization is a group of men tied together by some common goals and rules of behavior. A bureaucracy is an organization with a built-in mechanism for continuously reducing feedback. Therefore, all bureaucracies are organizations but not all organizations are bureaucracies. It seems inherent in human nature that man shall turn all his organizations into bureaucracies unless 1) some outside force prevents it or 2) he recognizes the phenomenon of bureaucratization and uses scientific method to prevent it deliberately. The former is accomplished mostly by competition from another organization; competing organizations provide unavoidable feedback to one another. The latter has never occurred but is essential for an Ethical State.

Organizations are transformed into bureaucracies by unethical behavior. An organization is a social system of collective decision-making with the de jure purpose of expanding awareness in some way. When its primary de facto purpose is the happiness and security of its members, the organization has become a bureaucracy. This leads to continuously diminishing negative feedback in the system so that the individual decision makers, whatever their position in the system, become insulated from having to face their own inadequacies and mistakes. The avoidance of all mistakes and the means for detecting any mistakes (negative feedback), even by the decision makers themselves, becomes the central goal for all bureaucracies.* Bureaucracies, not organizations, exist only because some persons would rather be happy and secure than aware and/or effective. Bureaucracies create illusions of reality by diffusing responsibility and making the environment appear predictable.

Organizations are formed whenever a prime decision maker feels that the decisions that are his responsibility are beyond his ability to cope with because of their number and/or complexity. Organizations, there-

---

* This may not be deliberate on the part of a bureaucrat but the result of decent immorality. A decent, well-intentioned bureaucrat can unconsciously cut-off all negative feedback. He may, for example, seek security in a common set of rigid rules and procedures of operation. A bureaucrat can always avoid responsibility for his mistakes by claiming he was following standard operational procedures.

fore, have the ostensible purpose of enhancing the decision-making process in order that a prime decision maker can arrive at better decisions
more quickly. In fact, organizations have inevitably become bureaucracies by becoming instruments for avoiding decisions until events force
the decisions to be made in a context in which there are virtually no
longer any alternatives save one. Bureaucracies, therefore, react to prime
events instead of creating them.

A "prime event" is an occurrence novel in character that was not
readily predictable from previous events. Hitler's taking power in Germany and then setting out on world conquest was a prime event. The
Allies reacting to their threatened security, defending themselves and
defeating Hitler was a secondary event implemented by bureaucracies
when they no longer had a choice. The American Revolution was another prime event engendered by a few ethical men. England's reaction
was a secondary event which failed. There is nothing inherent in prime
events or secondary events that makes them good or evil. The evil in
bureaucracy lies in the intrinsic corruption of the system which destroys
feedback and transforms a decision-making society into an immoral deci-
sion-avoiding society which can only increase entropy.

"Bureaucratic corruption" does not necessarily mean "malfeasance"
or bureaucrats taking bribes, although this of course sometimes occurs
and may be a part of the overall pattern. "Bureaucratic corruption" is a
process of diminishing feedback that increasingly puts more emphasis on
the security, i.e., lack of unhappiness, of the bureaucrats than on the
efficacy of their decisions. "Corruption" means that bureaucrats eventually destroy all forms of feedback in order to maintain their illusions of
security. This is usually done in a passive way by avoiding all decisions
that may produce negative feedback. The same process that destroys
negative feedback eventually leads to the suppression of all feedback—
until the bureaucracy is totally corrupt and immoral. This passive type of
bureaucratic corruption merely means that the bureaucracy becomes incapable of generating prime events, good or evil. There is, however, also
an active component to bureaucratic corruption.

Bureaucracies become actively, as opposed to passively, immoral
when they are controlled by aggressive or power-seeking bureaucrats.
These men take initiative in obtaining security by deliberately acquiring

control of all means for detecting their mistakes, i.e., all means of feed-back. Power-seeking bureaucrats will, whenever possible, suppress free-dom as a means of suppressing feedback. They will also deliberately pre-vent others from taking initiative in performing any function with which their bureaucracy is entrusted. In this way power-seeking bureaucrats try to prevent all good prime events by producing nothing but evil, destructive secondary events. Power-seeking bureaucrats are therefore usually indecent and not merely immoral.

Power-seeking bureaucrats differ from the security-seeking bureaucrats, who are more likely to be decent but just as immoral, only in having more courage. Power-seeking bureaucrats are rare in most systems; they are found mainly in the political bureaucracies, such as the Democratic and Republican parties in the United States and the Communist Party in Russia. In political bureaucracies most, not all, of the leading bureaucrats appear to be power-seeking. In contrast to the aggressive bureaucrats, most bureaucrats seem much more desirous of passive security than they are of active security—i.e., power. They become willing tools of the power-seeking bureaucrats.

The net effect of bureaucratic corruption is that organizations become instruments for hindering progress instead of enhancing it. When prime events of an evil nature occur, even well-intentioned bureaucracies often cannot react in a positive way to counter them. This is particularly true of events that have long-range effects, such as environmental pollution, genetic decay, cultural decline* and so on. In this case, the bureaucrats are not immediately threatened by these events and do nothing about them, since to do so might expose them to negative feedback and diminish their illusions of security. In the case of environmental pollution, this procrastination may prove catastrophic. Furthermore, the leadership in the upper echelons of any bureaucracy eventually goes through a selective process that sifts out the most ethical persons and allows only the most innocuous mediocrities or power-seeking bureaucrats to survive. These latter persons rarely can perceive their responsibilities, let alone execute them. Moral persons will not deliberately associate themselves with a bureaucracy. Ethical children will inevitably be turned into immoral men by bureaucracies.

* "Decline" and "decay" refer to a decreasing total awareness.

This corrupt system of decision making is ubiquitous. It is the dominant feature of government, politics, business, religion, and education in every country. It is a natural manifestation of man's desire to be happy and secure. Bureaucracy is, therefore, an evolutionary analogue of specialization. It exists least in situations where there is good feedback. Feedback is the implacable enemy of bureaucracy.

Feedback is a system for checking the efficacy of one's actions, including the avoidance of action. It is the foundation of science and is anathema to a bureaucracy. In order for good feedback to exist, it is necessary for alternative decisions, which can be evaluated scientifically, to exist. It is not enough to show that a decision had the predicted results in order to prove that it was good. It is necessary to show that it was better than any proposed alternative. This can only be done when there is personal freedom and competition. For this reason, bureaucracies will restrict freedom and resist competition against which they can be evaluated. In order for feedback to be effective, however, it is essential that a Darwinian-type of natural selection occur in order that systems which produce good decisions multiply and systems which produce poor decisions perish. Immoral men thrive in the absence of feedback and perish in its presence.

In conclusion, "bureaucratization" is an unethical process by which an organization's decision-making potential is gradually deprived of feedback through the formation of bureaucracies. Through internal corruption, the bureaucracies become self-serving and increasingly ineffectual in making decisions until they are utterly corrupt and immoral. Bureaucratization is independent of any particular ideology, but it becomes most pernicious when it is ideologically based.

IDEOLOGY

We recall from Chapter 1 that 1) an ideological belief is a belief in a cause and effect relationship that is not based on scientific evidence; and 2) an ideology is an organized set of interdependent ideological beliefs. Ideologies are intrinsically neither true nor false. They are merely unscientific. They may also be logically inconsistent. Ideologies are evil because they impede the expansion of awareness. Unlike true scientists, ideologues rarely doubt their "models." Usually, the less proof they have for their ideology, the more vigorously they will defend it. It is hard to learn when one has no doubts. Ideologies are, therefore, always unethical and they can make any person immoral.

Ideology is a theory which is not tested scientifically. It is ethical to theorize; but it is unethical to accept an untested theory as true. Ideologues do not correct their mistakes. All ideology is a deliberate form of self-deception that man imposes upon himself to create the illusion that he is aware when he is not. Ideology in general and religion in particular have their roots in fear—fear of the unknown, the unpredictable, the uncontrollable.

Ideologies range from the rather simple to the exceedingly complex. Democracy (liberalism) is the simple ideology that freedom will automatically make persons happy and secure while enabling them to build a progressive culture. Catholic ideology is much more complex and includes abstruse notions about the nature of God, "natural law," the infallibility of the Pope, and other myths. The most complex ideology is that of Marxism, Marxism-Leninism, Communism, etc. This fragmented and contradictory ideology will be called collectively, "Communism." Communism claims to have discovered "scientific" deterministic laws about historical development and the nature of man. (Recall that in science only probabilities exist; no model of nature is ever beyond question.) The fact that these "laws" have proved very poor predictors of events in the past one hundred years does not seem to trouble the Communist ideologues.

The religious ideologies that have shaped so much of human history are, as a result of the greater effectiveness of science, everywhere on the decline. They are playing an ever decreasing role in the making of important decisions and are now mainly concerned with the "spiritual" part of man's life. However, more will be said of religion later. The major ideological split today is along the Left-Right continuum.

Of Right and Left

In the United States the terms "conservative" and "liberal" are often incorrectly used to denote rightist and leftist views respectively. Both types of descriptors exist on a continuum. Hitler was a rightist, but he was not conservative. Stalin was a leftist, but he was not liberal. Only the terms "rightist" and "leftist" will be used as ideological indicators in this context.

"Liberal" and "Conservative" are not ideological indicators. An extreme liberal is a person willing to tolerate any change. An extreme conservative is a person unwilling to tolerate any change. When ideologues of any persuasion acquire power, they become increasingly conservative. When they have no power, they are liberal to the point of being revolutionary.

An extreme leftist is someone who believes that the behavioral differences between persons are totally a product of their environment and that heredity plays no differential role in shaping what they become. An extreme rightist believes that environmental differences are unimportant and that only heredity, not environment, shapes people's behavior. There do not appear to be any persons at the boundary of the Extreme Right. But there are some people at the boundary of the Extreme Left. Most people fall somewhere along the continuum between the boundaries in a distribution that is being continuously skewed to the left. The question of where on the Left-Right continuum the range of truth lies, under what circumstances, is a purely scientific problem that can be readily solved by science and technology.* The reason that it has not been adequately solved is because the Immoral Community has no wish to solve it. Yet at the heart of today's most divisive ideologies is an assumption that the "truth" is at one end or the other of the continuum.

A rightist ideology is, therefore, one based implicitly or explicitly on the ideological belief that the "truth" lies somewhere right of center. A leftist ideology is the converse of a rightist ideology. The basic rightist or

---

* For example, a controlled experiment could be done among young orphaned children to see if the range of environmental differences in a country produced significant differences in the total awareness the children achieved as they matured.

leftist assumption is so basic to the respective ideologies that if the hypothesis of the extreme left is proven correct, then any rightist ideology will totally collapse. The same applies to a leftist ideology if the extreme rightist hypothesis is proven correct. Ideologues of both the Right and Left are often unaware that at the center of their ideology is an ideological belief about heredity and environment.

Etiology of the Left

The last significant rightist ideological movement was that of Nazi Germany which assumed that "Aryans" (a misuse of a linguistic term) were innately, uniformly "superior" to all other "races" (a misuse of "race"). The Nazi ideology was arbitrary and illogical. It had no scientific basis as to what constituted "race" or "superiority" let alone how one could measure differences. The fact that the Nazis were so savagely cruel and irrational and that they were totally defeated by the combined forces of the Left has made it inevitable that almost all decent humane persons in the world would become leftists with strong antipathies toward rightist ideologies. This, of course, has nothing to do with where on the continuum the truth lies.

The leftist bias in ideology is reinforced by the fact that most of the better educated persons in all the advanced countries are leftists while the rightists are usually less educated and have a penchant for fundamentalist religious beliefs and brutality. In the United States most university professors are leftists while most fundamentalist preachers and Ku Klux Klan members are rightists. The overwhelming majority of the members of the Immoral Community in all civilized countries are also leftists, though there are also Immoral Community rightists in every country awaiting their chance for power (viz. the current military dictatorships in Greece and Brazil).

The ideological differences in the Moral Community show a curious split. Engineers, particularly civil and mechanical engineers, seem to have a tendency to be rightists. Biologists and experimental scientists in general apparently tend to cluster near the center of the continuum with a slight leftward bias. Mathematicians, theoretical scientists and the social scientists seem well to the left. Artists may be anywhere on the continuum. What all this implies is that the ideologies of Left and Right are relatively impervious to logic and scientific evidence. The leftward bias of world opinion seems to occur as follows.

Most educated people are aware of the opinions and theories of the behavioral "scientists." They assume that like most scientists, the behavioral "scientists" can predict and control events within the environment in which they are alleged experts. So they accept their theories which are mostly those of the Extreme Left and which have little or no scientific basis. The behavioral "scientists" have a vested interest in supporting leftist ideology because it helps justify their existence. If all behavior were determined by heredity (which it clearly is not), there would be little need for behavioral science. However, if all behavior were determined solely by environment, then behavioral science is all important.

The more theoretically-inclined members of the Moral Community are usually those of a more intellectual bent and are (1) more likely to be well read and familiar with behavioral science theories and (2) more inclined to accept plausible coherent theories as true in the absence of experimental evidence. Engineers as a group seem to have a rather mechanistic, pragmatic view of the world, are usually totally ignorant of the behavioral sciences, and are unsympathetic to theoretical arguments. To them, things are the way they work. The uneducated masses apparently have a similar attitude. It seems that man is instinctively a rightist. Experimental scientists usually assume that in a case when there is no experimental evidence, both sides of a question are just as likely to be correct. Therefore, they are mainly middle-roaders because they are not familiar with the evidence. Most geneticists are moderate rightists in a rather sophisticated way. They assume from past experience that although a phenotype may be determined primarily by genetics, environmental effects can cause dramatic alterations of the phenotype. Artists are basically non-analytic and formulate their ideologies entirely on the basis of taste; therefore, they may be anywhere on the continuum.

Etiology of the Right

Rightist ideologues occur as a consequence of privilege. Privileged persons in an attempt to justify their special status to themselves will sometimes assume that their position is due to some innate superiority on their part vis-à-vis their less fortunate brethren. The privileged person need only be slightly privileged relative to someone else in order to adopt a rightist ideology (e.g., the poor Whites in the Southern United States).

An impediment to rightist ideology is the leftist ideology of the social "scientists." Humane, sensitive and privileged persons who are familiar with and believe the leftist ideology often will develop guilt about their special status. They will accordingly attempt to compensate for their feelings of guilt by supporting leftist causes and engaging in charitable enterprises that benefit less privileged persons. They may become the most militant of leftist ideologues. Leftists may more often than rightists, appear to be decent persons because they express concern for the welfare of others.

The rightist ideologues, therefore, tend to be the less educated and/ or less sensitive persons with a relatively privileged position. For this reason, as will be shown in the following paragraphs, rightist ideologues tend to be conservative and have a penchant for fundamentalist religion and brutality. Non-ideological rightists on the other hand, are not any more likely to have these characteristics than are the leftists.

In an established democracy fundamentalist religion is a supporter of the established order. The clergy obtains privilege, independent of merit, and it in turn supports the privilege of those who support it. Some clergy (e.g. the White Southern Baptists in the United States) go so far as to invoke divine sanction for the privileges of their adherents.

Because the rightist ideologues are as a group rather insensitive to the sufferings of others, they find it easy to justify brutalizing their leftist opponents. The Leftists are regarded as either innately inferior themselves or diabolical revolutionaries intent on upsetting the "natural" order of things by taking privilege away from those who deserve it and giving it to innately inferior, i.e., subhuman, beings. In most countries the military and the police consist primarily of rightists while teachers and social workers are primarily leftists.

In Communist countries where all privilege is vested in the bureaucrats who support the leftist ideology, the leftist ideologues acquire most of the conservative and brutalizing characteristics of the rightist ideologues in the democracies. In Communist countries the rightists are revolutionaries whom the established order brutally suppresses.

Evidence

Both the ideologies of the Right and the Left are, therefore, equally unscientific but not equally illogical. The fact that Leftist ideology is more logically coherent than rightist ideology has nothing to do with the *scientific* validity of the leftist hypothesis. Indeed, insofar as scientific evidence exists, the indications are that some important* differences in behavior within a given culture are primarily determined by heredity. This applies particularly to intelligence.

Intelligence was defined as the ability to predict and control the total environment. As such, it is completely subsumed within the notion of "awareness." There are no objective, coherent measures of this characteristic. The measures that do exist are the so-called "mental aptitude" or "I.Q. tests." These tests measure some aspects of a person's ability to predict and control within a particular cultural context. I.Q. tests almost completely neglect such important intellectual factors as Imagination, important Information and force of Will. I.Q. tests crudely measure Logic and Memory. One would expect I.Q. scores to be somewhat correlated, not perfectly, with "true" intelligence scores if the latter existed. In spite of all these deficiencies, I.Q. scores are good predictors of performance in school, particularly at the elementary levels. They are also correlated with income, health, social status, and other factors indicative of a person's ability to predict and control his total environment.

Arthur Jensen,† a scientifically-inclined educator, has gathered considerable scientific evidence to support the proposition (i.e., elementary scientific model) that the I.Q. of persons living in the more advanced societies of the West has a heritability factor of at least .80. A heritability factor of 1.0 would indicate that environmental differences as currently constituted within these countries had no effect on I.Q. scores.

Other scientific studies ‡ and the whole field of behavioral genetics tend to support the proposition that intelligence has, within an ad-

* Important being the converse of "trivial" means significantly affecting awareness positively or negatively.
† Jensen, A. R., "How Much Can We Raise I.Q.," *Harvard Educational Review*, Ser. #2, 1969.
‡ Thoday, J. M. and Gibson, J. B., "Environmental and Genetical Contributions to Class Differences," *Science*, Feb. 1970, pp. 990–992.

vanced, modern, democratic culture, a large hereditary component.*
This does not mean that drastic environmental factors cannot have drastic effects on behavior. What it means is that the environmental differences between most people in western countries are not as significant in
their important effects as are the genetic differences.

A position on the Left-Right continuum can have a scientific as opposed to an ideological basis. A leftist can be nonideological if his position is based on scientific experiments that support the leftist hypothesis.
The same applies to rightists. A careful analysis of all the scientific evidence at this time gives overwhelming support to the rightist hypothesis.

The evidence supporting the rightist hypothesis as it exists now, although significant, is not conclusive since it only explains the past in a
scientifically consistent manner. It implies the need for controlled predictive scientific experiments. The ideologues of the Left are not even
willing to consider these experiments. They have already made up their
minds in the absence of scientific evidence. They have no doubts. Additional scientific evidence from controlled experiments on the nature-
nurture problem might move one either farther to the Right or toward
the Left, but probably not to any of the extreme boundaries.

What both the rightists and the leftists ignore is that the most important aspect of behavior is ethics, not intelligence. Both the rightists
and the leftists in their respective zeal to proclaim that there are or that
there are not significant genetically-based intellectual differences between human groups distort the real issue, which is ethical behavior. It is
self-evident that all human beings are born ethical because all human
beings increase their awareness as children. The important question is
what is it that causes so many of our fellow men to stop increasing their
awareness and to become unethical. This phenomenon may have a genetic basis, but it seems much more likely to be a result of an unethical
culture than of genes.

The innate intelligence of a person determines how much he can
expand his knowledge within the cultural context in which he lives.
However, it is his ethics that determines his total awareness. It is ethics
that determines whether a person expands human awareness or decreases
it. An ethical person, no matter how low his intelligence, will contribute

* Stern, Curt, Human Genetics.

to human progress. An unethical person, no matter how great his intelligence, will serve only to increase entropy. Indeed, the more intelligent an immoral person is, the greater will be the increase in entropy that he produces.

For this reason, it is more important that we find a way to keep children ethical and turn them into moral men than to show that intellectual differences are primarily hereditary. Still, the evidence that human intelligence is in large part a hereditary phenomenon and not purely an environmental accident has serious implications.

Implications

Most of the persons who could significantly help expand man's total awareness are leftists. The dominant position of the apparently incorrect leftist ideology in all major countries is a serious impediment to the establishment of an Ethical State. It is one of the root causes of the immorality in the world. This is the case because a concomitant of leftist ideology is the belief that the happiness of persons is more important than the awareness of the entire human race. If the ideology of the extreme Left is proven false, then a eugenics program is essential to expand man's total awareness. This is the case even if the truth is left of center, but not on the left boundary. If there is any genetic basis to intelligence, then eugenics is essential to reduce entropy. Eugenics in this case is ethical and dysgenic policies are unethical. Deliberately to refuse to increase the genetic quality of the human race is immoral.

Eugenics is essential because spontaneous mutations among the human gene pool cannot be stopped by any foreseeable technology. Since almost all mutations are deleterious, the absence of some form of natural selection in the form of eugenics would lead to a steadily decreasing intellectual potential in the human race until progress would no longer be possible. It is a law of genetics that any gene not selected against eventually spreads to every member of an interbreeding species.

Unfortunately, eugenics and the entire ideology of Right and Left are so heavily laden with emotion that even the most intelligent persons, who can be completely scientific in their work and many other aspects of their life, find themselves irrationally committed to leftist ideology. The ideologues of the Right, by their crudity, brutality and ignorance, make even the consideration of a rightist hypothesis abhorrent. Of all the evil that Hitler did, the most disastrous may be not the killing of millions, but the condemning of billions by making it impossible for so many ethical persons to discuss eugenics with an open mind.

If man cannot deal objectively and scientifically with the problems of Right and Left, he will never be able to expand his total awareness continuously. His ideology will make all sociopolitical problems insoluble. The entropy will increase without limit. Ideologues are usually unethical, but not always indecent. Rightist ideologues are almost never decent. Leftist ideologues may be decent, but they are in the end just as destructive as the rightist ideologues. When leftist ideologues achieve a monopoly of power as in Russia, they become indecent.

The major differences between the Communist countries and the democracies is not one of fundamental ideological belief. The Immoral Community in both systems is predominantly leftist. The major differences are those of tactics and the fact that the political bureaucracies feel threatened by tactics radically different from the ones they are following. The democracies are fully committed to the diminishing effectiveness of feedback through the democratic process. The Communists are committed to a rigid totalitarian formula of development which, while not totally illogical, is unscientific and has very poor feedback. It seems to be producing an immoral society.

The Communist political bureaucracies have committed unspeakable atrocities in the past and are still imposing unnecessary hardships on their people all in the name of ideology. If they admit that they have been wrong, they may find it impossible to control their subjects. As in every other ideological totalitarian state of the past, the political bureaucracy in the Communist countries has almost completely lost sight of its original objectives and is concerned mainly with perpetuating itself. It is probably totally immoral. However, before discussing the democratic and Communist states in greater detail, an analysis of religious ideology is in order.

Religion

Religion, like all ideology, results from man's innate need to be aware. Religion is the most evil form of ideology because it quickly causes man to become complacent in his illusions and eventually to completely stop expanding his awareness. Religion invariably makes men immoral. Religion differs from all other ideology by stressing cause and effect relationships concerning man's "soul."

The purveyors of religion have never precisely defined the soul. Man perceived intuitively at the unconscious level that he had a soul because he perceived directly that he had a mind, (Cogito, ergo sum). Indeed, an analysis of religious writings on the soul would show that the concept of "soul" was no more than the concept of mind tied to supernatural cause and effect relationships. Mind is an indisputable reality. The supernatural cause and effect relationships are ideological beliefs devoid of any scientific evidence. Therefore, the concept of "soul" cannot be logically or scientifically shown to necessitate more elaboration than the concept of mind. The mind being an effect of life is mortal just as life is mortal (see chapters 2 and 3). Therefore, the soul must also be mortal. Since our souls are identical to our minds, they die with our bodies.

No matter how unaware man has been in the past, he has always known that he had a soul, for he perceived it directly. As fundamental as man's need for security is his need for awareness. Man has an innate need to predict and control his total environment. The evolutionary force driving man toward the Moral Society has always created in him a need to be a part of something greater than himself. He could not tolerate the thought of his own finiteness. He could not tolerate the thought of not being able to predict or control the activities of his soul beyond the lifetime of his body.

It was this need which man could not understand or control that became the focus of most religions. Religion met the need to create the Moral Society with the ideological belief that the soul was immortal. Around this belief grew an ideology that embraced all aspects of the environment. Like any ideology it began to crumble when overwhelming scientific evidence began to contradict the underlying dogma in its structure. However, the unconscious need to create the Moral Society is so strong in man that, in the absence of any satisfactory alternatives, he tried desperately to cling to religion even as it crumbled all around him. Only religion seemed to give true meaning and purpose to life. When men lost their religion, only those who were directly involved in the expansion of awareness seemed to find satisfaction in life. The others abandoned themselves to a frustrating, suicidal pursuit of happiness without meaning. Religion, therefore, fills a basic and important need in man. Any society that ignores this need is doomed to failure. In order to understand better the nature of man's religious needs, it is useful to examine religion in its evolutionary context.

The Evolution of Religion

As was discussed in Chapter 2, religion is the evolutionary analogue of pre-human awareness. Therefore, religion can only increase awareness by being mutated into new religions. New religions are formed in an ethical attempt to create a new, coherent, general model of the universe when the models represented by the existing religions are found to be inadequate. The creators of religion are, therefore, usually moral men who have a sincere ethical desire to increase man's total awareness. Religions become immoral when they become bureaucratized. Since religions are unscientific organizations, they inevitably become bureaucratized. Once a religion is bureaucratized, it can no longer evolve because it deprives itself of feedback until entropy destroys it. This usually occurs by forcible or voluntary conversion of its adherents to another religion that is more vigorous and/or progressive. In the process of becoming bureaucratized, religions suppress freedom and destroy awareness for all humanity. However, bureaucratization is not an instantaneous process and as long as religions remain at least partially ethical they are not an absolute impediment to increasing the awareness of humanity. Therefore, new religions are usually associated with progressive societies and old religions are associated with decaying societies. An exception to this rule is Judaism.

Judaism

Judaism occupies a unique place within the pantheon of established religions because by a series of historical accidents Judaism acquired an internal structure which provided continuous feedback and inhibited bureaucratization. First of all, Judaism was as its inception a radical mutation completely different from all religions that had existed previously. Because of a multitude of reasons, some conjectured and some unknown, Moses developed a unique concept of a single, all-powerful god.* He viewed God as an abstract force that could not be represented by visual imagery. God was seen to be the ubiquitous author of universal laws with which there was no compromise. The Jewish concept of "God" was almost identical to the scientific concept of "cosmic force." The only difference lay in the Jewish notion that God was individually aware and purposeful as opposed to the notion of the mindless, random cosmic force. Judaism, therefore, represented an enormous leap in ethical development. The Ten Commandmants were a totally rational code of ethics compatible with the evolutionary force. However, Judaism began to become bureaucratized as do all religions.

First the basic ethical code of the Ten Commandments was corrupted by other rules of conduct that were not ends in themselves but solely means to ends. The ultimate ends such as good health and social cohesiveness were perfectly ethical; however, as is always the case, the means became the ends and Judaism became burdened with an ever-increasing load of superstition and compulsive, irrational behavior plus an entrenched priestly class that represented the religious bureaucracy. Then another accident occurred.

When the Jews were conquered by the Babylonians and deported to Babylon, the religious bureaucracy was destroyed. However, the ethical principles of Judaism had still not been so corrupted that they were not vastly superior to the ethical system of the Babylonians' primitive worship of Baal. The Jews were then faced with a much stronger foe who was their obvious ethical inferior. It was at this time, while in Babylonian captivity, that Judaism was remutated and took its special form of a

* See, for example, *Moses and Monotheism* by Sigmund Freud.

completely abstract ethical religion independent of geography and nationhood.

This new type of Judaism acquired tremendous vigor and resiliency when the Jews were repatriated to their homeland fifty years later, after the Persian conquest of the Babylonian Empire.* The cultural shock of being the captives of an intellectually superior but ethically inferior civilization had tempered Judaism into a powerful world force. After the Babylonian captivity, the new Jewish vigor began to decline under the new priestly bureaucracy and the intellectual challenge posed by the most amazing intellectual force in history, classical Greece.

As Judaism was being corrupted by the new religious bureaucracy, the Jews began to become Hellenized under the overwhelming force of Greek intellectual expansion that followed Alexander's conquests. The Jews successfully resisted Hellenization by force, but were slowly being assimilated intellectually when Rome conquered Judea.

Under the Romans occurred the final mutation that was to shape Judaism as a unique vital force in human history.

The hybridization of Greek philosophy and religion with Judaism produced Christianity. Christianity would probably have completely replaced the ever more bureaucratized Judaism of Palestine except that as Christianity was being born the Jewish nation was destroyed by Rome, not to be revived for two thousand years. The destruction of the Jewish nation destroyed the Jewish religious bureaucracy and made Judaism a family-centered religion without a priestly caste. Because the family is the fountainhead of morality, Judaism has been able to maintain its ethical structure. As a minority religion Judaism could not avoid negative feedback. As an ethical religion, Judaism was self-selecting. Only the highly ethical Gentiles would convert, and only the highly unethical Jews would convert to the competing religions in order to obtain material gain and security.

The Rabbis were teachers and interpreters voluntarily supported by each Jewish community. They had no priestly powers and were not as-

---

* Note that the Persians at this time had recently adopted Zoroastrianism as the new official religion. Zoroastrianism was almost on the same ethical plane as Judaism, but it became bureaucratized.

sumed to speak for God. Rabbis had to convince by logic and not by authority. There was no bureaucracy.

It was at this time, from about 100 to 500 A.D., that the Talmud (Babylonian and Palestinian) was written. The Talmud was a highly democratic document filled with thousands of conflicting opinions on Jewish law, but almost totally devoid of ideology because there were no priests. Talmudic analysis continued for many centuries after its completion and had its ultimate expression with Maimonides (twelfth century A.D.), who revised the Talmud and tried to make it completely compatible with Aristotelian logic and scientific knowledge. Maimonides was a great generalist with deep knowledge of the physical, biological and psychosocial environment. Although Maimonides' radical teachings were not to become an integral part of Judaism for hundreds of years, they were eventually assimilated and they have had their influence on all the Jewish philosophers who followed, most notably on Baruch de Spinoza (seventeenth century A.D.).

Spinoza is the ultimate Jewish philosopher. In Spinoza Judaism reached its logical conclusion by becoming totally abstract and depersonalizing God into the cosmic force. The philosophy of Spinoza is devoid of ideology and attempts to prove everything deductively from axioms and scientific laws. Spinoza's philosophy is a logical failure that was ethically successful. It freed ethical behavior from supernatural imperatives. Like Maimonides, Spinoza was not readily acceptable to the Jews because he was extremely radical. Indeed, he was so much more radical than Maimonides that Spinoza was excommunicated by the Jewish community and is still considered an apostate by the orthodox. However, Spinoza laid the philosophical basis for Reform Judaism and the Reform Jews have almost completely incorporated the ethical teachings of Spinoza. Most of the Jews in the world today are de facto Reform or agnostics.

The evolution of Judaism is, therefore, clearly in the direction taken by Spinoza—a scientific, non-ideological concept of ethics devoid of the notion of an anthropomorphic God. The ultimate form of Jewish ethics is compatible with the Game of Life. Indeed, the Game of Life is implied by Spinoza's ethics.

In spite of its ethical superiority, Judaism as a culture has not been as directly responsible for human progress as have other religious cultures. Although in recent years many individual Jews have contributed disproportionately to progress, the Jews throughout history have been more the catalysts of progress rather than the direct causes. Indeed, from a historical point of view, the main contribution of the Jews during the last two thousand years has been to create other religions that have directly influenced human history, most notable among these being Christianity, Islam and Communism. These are all Jewish creations that have shaped the world we live in. Communism is regarded as religion because it is a coherent model of the universe which has an ideological, as opposed to a scientific, basis and assumes the soul to be an effect of matter. If Judaism is regarded as being on the main path of psychosocial evolution, then Christianity, Islam and Communism are slight mutations which went their own way but may rejoin the mainstream of human evolution.*

Christianity

In evolutionary terms Christianity is to Judaism as Neanderthal man was to the mainstream of hominization. Catholicism is the analogue of the European Neanderthal who over-specialized and became extinct. Protestantism is the analogue of the non-European Neanderthal who seems to have been reabsorbed into the mainstream of evolution before he became too specialized.

Christianity was ethically inferior to Judaism but it had one essential ingredient that Judaism lacked. It made each person feel that he was an integral part of a greater whole as opposed to being merely an obedient servant of an omnipotent despotic God. This notion also existed within Judaism but not to the same extent. The Christian believed in the union of all souls within the mystic body of Christ. This belief was probably an ideological expression of man's unconscious awareness of the possibility of his ultimate union in the Moral Society.

When Protestantism began, after over one thousand years of bureaucratic corruption within the Catholic Church, Christianity became revitalized because feedback was introduced into the system. The Protestant sects were the least bureaucratized and accordingly the great post-Refor-

* Judaism is further discussed in the next chapter.

mation contributors to human progress were disproportionately Protestants, e.g., Shakespeare, Newton, Leibniz, Bach, Goethe, Gauss, Darwin, etc. However, the Catholic church itself was revitalized by the newly established feedback of the Reformation. This expressed itself most notably in the Jesuit order of the Counter Reformation.

The Jesuits were for a time one of the most potent forces in the world for expanding human awareness. Even today the Jesuits provide education to millions of students the world over. Teilhard de Chardin was a Jesuit priest.

Because the Reformation produced the secular state, competitive Christianity and its consequent feedback have been maintained in most of the formerly purely Catholic countries. Therefore, Christianity has continued to evolve. Protestantism as represented by Unitarianism has indeed evolved to the same ethical state as Reform Judaism. Unitarianism is Reform Judaism without Jewish tradition. As such it is more ethical because it is more inclusive.

Catholicism has evolved much more slowly than Protestantism because it is still highly bureaucratized. However, the ecumenicism of Pope John XXIII together with the progressiveness of the Jesuits portends hope that eventually Catholicism, Protestantism, and Judaism will abandon ideology and unite with all men in an Ethical State.

Not all religions have shown the evolutionary vigor of Judaism and Christianity. Islam is almost totally corrupt and Communism is reaching the same state. These may represent deleterious, indeed lethal, mutations of Judaism. The religions that have not mutated from Judaism, including Buddhism, appear to be evolutionary dead-ends not likely to have any further effect on human evolution. Only Communism, Christianity, Judaism, and Islam in that order of importance are still likely to have a significant historical effect. Islam's effect is likely to be entirely negative as dicsussed in Chapter 5.

Islam

Islam is almost identical in concept to seventh century Judaism. The major difference is in 1) the relative emphasis on the immortality of the male soul (women are assumed to have no souls); 2) a totally hedonistic sensual view of the souls' afterlife; and 3) a non-analytic, literal approach to the interpretation of the scriptures. Islam also gave a peculiar twist to the absolutist concept of Jewish ethics. Islam had the notion of relative ethics and equity as opposed to rigid law.

Islam started with a tremendous advantage over other religions in that it did not have a priestly bureaucracy. All male Muslims were assumed to be equal. However, Islam became bureaucratized in other ways. It was primarily a political religion used to unify what was to be a single, all-encompassing empire. The bureaucratization of Islam was, therefore, inextricably interwoven with the decay of the Arabian and Ottoman Empires and it will be discussed later in that context. Communism (Marxism) has much in common with Islam in that it is primarily a political religion.

Marxism

Marx was born a Jew; while still a child, he was baptized; and as a man became an atheist. He attempted to formulate a coherent model of the universe that was consistent with mid-nineteenth century science and Judeo-Christian ethics. Marxism was, therefore, a synthesis of Judaism, Christianity and science. Systematic science itself was a logical outgrowth of Judeo-Christian philosophy, which saw the universe ordered by immutable natural laws emanating from a single source, God. The laws had to be logical and consistent because God, as the supreme intellect, had to be logical and consistent.

The fact that Marx did not derive a superior system of ethics was due primarily to his ignorance. He was essentially a scientific illiterate. Furthermore, mid-nineetenth century science was still Newtonian and deterministic. The psychosocial sciences were primitive and Marx tried to create them almost from scratch. He formulated his theories in the absence of feedback and his followers, most notably Lenin, turned them into the rigid, unscientific ideology of Communism. Still, Communism was to become the most significant religious mutation since the Reformation. It replaced traditional religion for millions of people.

Communism had the essential ingredient of making one's life a part of a greater whole. It had the flavor of religion, but the appearance of science. It almost worked. Bureaucratic corruption soon disillusioned any who lived under it. Its success in providing greater security made it defeat its own purposes because it had no goal beyond security. The Communists have failed to learn a lesson from the democracies which already have greater security than they are ever likely to achieve. Yet the democracies are already in a state of decline. Man vitally needs a goal beyond security and happiness.

Communism played the Game of Pleasure. Science was seen only as a means of making men happy. Communism became unethical because it had no objective beyond making men happy. In the process it increased entropy and began to make all ethical persons who lived under it miserable by destroying all negative feedback.

Communism is a religious state as was Islam and the Medieval Church. The religious states of the past have two lessons to teach us. The first is that ideologically-based totalitarianism knows no limits of corruption and can completely stop the expansion of awareness until a totally immoral society results. The second is that a state dedicated to reaching a goal beyond men's personal lives can unite men as no other cause can.

Religious States

All religious states of the past were totalitarian. A totalitarian form of government is a centralized government in which any means are justified if they "advance" the ideology or the wishes of the leaders. This results from the belief that the leaders have a monopoly on truth and that rival opinions are always in error. Science is incompatible with totalitarianism. As in all political systems, however, the ideological basis of the state was no match for the process of bureaucratization which led to complete corruption of the system and its eventual downfall.

The bureaucratization of the Catholic totalitarian state ended in total decay. This caused the Reformation. The resulting states had "competitive Christianity." This reintroduced feedback and revitalized the former Catholic states.

The predominantly Protestant states acquired a new ethical code, "The Protestant Ethic," which was in harmony with the rules of the Game of Life. They, as a consequence, became the most progressive countries in Europe. The nations that remained predominantly Catholic had formerly been the most progressive European nations. After the

Reformation they began a decline relative to the Protestant states. This decline is still continuing. It manifests itself most in Spain and Portugal where Catholic ideology has been firmly implanted in most of the population. It manifests itself least in France where a large number of Protestants and agnostics co-exist within a basically Catholic State. Italy, which was the most advanced country in Europe prior to the Reformation, seems to have avoided sinking to the same level as Spain and Portugal by a peculiarly Italian characteristic of accepting the Catholic religion while not taking it seriously. Italy was helped by its own cynicism.

The leaders of most post-Reformation nations, however, tended to eschew controversial religious ideology as a means of uniting their people in favor of a new, more parochial ideology called "nationalism." This type of ideology had its culmination in Nazi Germany.

The great ideological rival of the Catholic Church was the ideological totalitarian state of Islam. It underwent the same bureaucratic decline as the Catholic Church, but had no comparable cleansing reformation with which to reestablish feedback in the system. Islam simply decayed and fell to pieces. The pieces themselves are now so entropic that neither nationalism nor even a Communist revolution seem likely to revitalize them. Islam has apparently reached irreversible entropy.

The decline of Islam shows what can happen to a once vital people. The Arabs, from about the ninth to the fourteenth century represented the vanguard of human civilization. They carried the torch that had been ignited in Greece. They were in the forefront in mathematics, astronomy, medicine, and many of the arts. In a few hundred years they made great inroads into the rival empire of the already decaying Catholic Church. But bureaucratic corruption set in. The religion supported by a monolithic political bureaucracy deluded the people into thinking that it answered all important questions. The expansion of awareness stopped.

The only part of the Catholic totalitarian state that survived the Reformation intact was Iberia (Spain and Portugal). Perhaps because of its centuries-long life-and-death struggle with Islam, the Catholic totalitarian state reached its most pernicious level of corruption in Iberia. Iberia's decline, which closely parallels and is intimately involved with that of the Arabs, began when the bureaucracy of the Catholic Church obtained a monopolistic position by forcibly converting, expelling, and/or killing the rival Moslems and Jews. Up to that time, the feedback from three competing ideological bureaucracies had made Iberia the most vital region in the world and among the most culturally advanced.

The momentum of vitality that had been built up in Iberia prior to the start of its decline enabled it in only fifty years to build the most far-flung empire the world had ever seen. But it was an empire whose corruption had begun at its birth. It began to decay as it grew. That decay is still going on today. Iberia and some of the remnants of its empire are the only remaining Catholic totalitarian states. Their decline and entropy are almost as great as that of Islam. Only the feedback that they have obtained from a peripheral association with the mainstream of European civilization has enabled them to avoid sinking to the same level as Islam. Iberian art remained the only means for intellectual expression in a basically anti-analytic culture. Artistic expression was partially stimulated by association with the progressive culture of France. A revolution of reason against the immoral and homosexual society of the Catholic Church might still save Iberia from continuing entropic decline.

In the end, both Catholicism and Islam became immoral societies because the religious bureaucracies insisted that they had a monopoly of all important truth and women were totally excluded from the decision-making process. They produced a rigid, anti-analytic, destructive culture. Through coercion and control of the educational system they were able to instill their ideologies in the vast majority of the population, thereby depriving the people of feedback, destroying their vitality, and stopping the expansion of awareness. Religious ideology has also destroyed other states in the past. Today the ideology of Hinduism has so increased the entropy of India that she is on the verge of total collapse from internal decay.

Islam and Catholicism were potent political forces. They made it possible to form vast empires serving to unify man and thereby contributed to the building of the Moral Society. The ideology of nationalism has never been so successful; it was too parochial. It united a small segment of humanity at the cost of isolating it from the rest. Nationalism was contrary to the evolutionary force. Those ideologies that tend to unite man in an all-inclusive world system are most consistent with the evolutionary force. Only they can have important long-range political effects.

For this reason, totalitarian states with no ideological bases, such as the Latin-American dictatorships and some of the oriental despotic states, have little historical significance. A state which attempts to make each person feel that he is contributing to something greater than himself and that all men are brothers whether democratic or totalitarian, has historical significance. Such was the case with Communism, such was the case with democracy. In the end, all countries irrespective of their ideological basis have succumbed to bureaucratization. Ideology merely accelerates the process.

BUREAUCRATIZATION OF NATIONS

The effect of bureaucratization within nations is most readily seen in the caliber of the leaders. When a completely new nation is formed by revolution, there is no effective bureaucracy. Its leaders, regardless of their ideological bias, are usually brilliant, ethical persons of broad awareness and courage. They include moral men. This was the case in the formative years of the United States, Republican France, Soviet Russia and modern Israel.

In the early years of the United States, the leadership consisted of men such as Benjamin Franklin, Alexander Hamilton, and Thomas Jefferson. These highly ethical men were remarkably aware. The United States has never again had a President who even approached the intellectual, let alone the ethical caliber of Jefferson. It is difficult to believe that genetic decay in the United States has progressed to the point where today the best leadership that the country can produce is represented by those found in public office. There must be another explanation.

The decay in American leadership went from 1) moral men who were generalists (e.g., Jefferson) to 2) brilliant children (e.g., Adams) to 3) ethical children (e.g., Lincoln) to 4) decent unethical men (e.g., F. D. Roosevelt) to 5) indecent men who are the scientific and ethical illiterates governing the United States today. Even when indecent men consciously try to do well, the corrupting process they went through in order to achieve power has completely destroyed their capacity for ethical judgment.

Since they are immoral men they use entropic strategies in the Game of Pleasure. Death is the minimax strategy that they unconsciously pursue by destroying their feedback and that of others. This continues until the society is immoral and destroys itself through hedonism and immoral wars that the indecent leaders wage for political expediency. Immoral men are not repelled by death because they unconsciously long for it. Bureaucracy seems inevitable to immoral men because they project their own unethical motivations onto all men.

In a bureaucracy a necessary means to power is a thorough understanding of the structure of the organization—i.e., the written and unwritten rules by which the bureaucracy operates. The rules are usually very simple in quality but of voluminous quantity. They are also not always clearly specified. Worst of all, they rarely have a logical basis and are contradictory. The training which best prepares a man to work within a bureaucracy is typified by that of the lawyer. A lawyer is trained to interpret and manipulate rules of bureaucratic behavior.

A "legal" type of mentality is one that is concerned neither with truth nor awareness but with the manipulation of power through the exercise and interpretation of "unnatural" bureaucratic rules of behavior.* These men are the technicians of the Immoral Community. A legal mentality will usually seek to acquire the training of a lawyer. The technicians of the Immoral Community are, therefore, likely to be lawyers but certainly not all lawyers are legally minded. The "legal mentality" is, therefore, the antithesis of ethical mentality, which is concerned primarily with "truth" interpreted as prediction and control of the *natural* environment. Only unethical persons have a legal mentality.

The bureaucratization of government in the United States has led to a system that is dominated by men with a legal mentality. Indeed, the

* Bureaucratic rules of behavior are "unnatural" because they usually have no basis in natural science such as physics, biology or what little is known in the behavioral sciences. They are overtly unethical because they serve mainly to destroy feedback and increase entropy. Sometimes they are completely illogical and contradictory and represent political expediency as opposed to a coherent policy. This is typified by the real estate and income tax laws of the United States and most other nations.

majority of all elected officials in the United States have for many years been, in fact, legal minded. Almost all power-seeking bureaucrats in any bureaucracy are legal-minded.

A lawyer is intrinsically neither moral nor immoral. It is certainly possible for a person to be trained in both law and science, as some are (e.g., Jefferson was both a moral man and a lawyer). However, it is not possible by definition for a person to be ethical and legal-minded at the same time. An ethical person can never fit into the structure of a bureaucracy which serves only to support the Immoral Community. The lawyer, when he is legal-minded, fits perfectly. A person trained in science may, of course, become a technician of the Immoral Community by becoming legal-minded. Many former scientists have so done. This occurs most often when the scientist is highly specialized. It occurs least to generalists. Generalists of great ability and integrity are usually ethical members of the Moral Community as were Franklin, Hamilton and Jefferson. In a bureaucratic state such persons are not only ineffectual in achieving political power, but they find the process so distasteful that they generally avoid it altogether. The entire syndrome is reinforced by the fact that in capitalist countries in general, and the United States in particular, access to large sums of money is indispensible for political success.

This partially explains why scientifically illiterate lawyers and scientifically illiterate millionaires almost completely control the only two effective* political bureaucracies in the United States. It partially explains why the many brilliant, courageous, ethical persons in the United States have no effective role in the Government.

The trend is clearly established. The leadership is steadily becoming immoral. The Moral Community does not yet have a strategy for correcting its mistakes and removing the immoral leaders. This trend toward ever greater entropy in society as a consequence of increasing entropy in government can only be reversed if moral men become the political leaders. Means toward this end are outlined in Chapters 6 and 7. However, first the phenomenon of bureaucratization must be more fully discussed because this phenomenon is sweeping the world at an accelerating pace and threatens to destroy it in the near future.

* Effective in this context means exercising political power.

A similar picture of decline in leadership through bureaucratization can be seen in every country. In France, we go from the brilliance and daring of Napoleon, a brilliant child who was well versed in science and technology, through successions of ever greyer mediocrities and unethical men with occasional flashes of brilliance during times of great internal turmoil and corresponding decline in bureaucratic power.

In Soviet Russia the leadership of today is a far cry from the brilliance of Trotsky, a generalist and a moral man who tried to correct his mistakes. Instead, he was quickly replaced by indecent men (e.g., Stalin) who deliberately suppressed freedom wherever they could. Today they invade and destroy freedom in every country they can because they are terrified of any feedback. They will not feel secure until they can suppress personal freedom as effectively in every country as they do in their own.

Even in Israel, where the constant threat of imminent annihilation and frequent battles give a great deal of feedback, we see in only twenty years children replacing the leadership of a generalist and moral man such as Chaim Weizmann.

If bureaucratization occurs in countries with such widely different ideological bases as the United States, France, Soviet Russia and Israel, then there must be something in the process that is independent of ideology. In order to understand this better, it will be useful to examine the bureaucratization process in various ideological and operational settings.

DEMOCRACY

"Democracy" in the classical sense is clearly an unworkable system for any modern state. Instead, "democracy" has come to mean a republican form of government where the representatives of the people are chosen by all the people in "free elections." In order for elections to be "free," it is assumed that there must be 1) freedom of expression, 2) freedom of assembly, 3) freedom to run for any political office and proselytize for any political cause, and 4) ready and equal access to all the differing opinions, points of view, and partisan arguments.

Freedom as used above means that anyone can engage in these activities without unreasonable interference from either the state, political rivals, or anyone else and that the state exists *solely* to guarantee personal freedom.* Although democracy as here described does not exist in a perfect state anywhere, it is an ideal that is approximated in various ways in all English-speaking countries (except those in Africa), most European countries (except the Soviet bloc, Albania, Greece, Spain and Portugal), and to some degree in other countries, most notably Japan and India. It clearly does not exist in any Communist country. The Communist lexicon, as well as others, define democracy in different ways. However, in this book, "democracy" will mean only the concept identified above.

Democratic Government

In practice what happens in a democracy once it is established is that the legal-minded politicians soon achieve a monopoly of political power even though several political bureaucracies called "parties" may be involved. The greater the number of effective political parties, the broader will be the ideological base of political power. As political parties decrease in number until there are only two effective parties (an inevitable consequence), fundamental ideological distinctions tend to vanish. Political parties then become instruments solely for achieving power even though they may still use ideological labels and slogans. The stability of the political system is inversely proportional to the number of effective political parties. Conversely, the feedback in the political system is directly proportional to the number of effective political parties.

It was once asserted by Bertrand Russell that in a bureaucratized democracy the only persons who can be elected to office are those who are either 1) stupid, 2) hypocritical or 3) both hypocritical and stupid. By "stupid" Russell presumably meant someone of significantly less intelligence than his own. His reasoning seemed to be that if someone is intelligent, he is likely to have opinions and attitudes that are contrary to the prejudices of the majority. If he is stupid, he probably shares the prejudices of the majority. Voters elect only candidates who openly share most of their prejudices. Therefore, only stupid and/or hypocritical politicians will get elected. A corollary is that most voters are stupid.

* Recall the definition of "personal freedom" given in Chapter 1.

Russell's dictum appears to be partially correct, but ignores the crucial factor of morality. It would not be so bad if the leaders were stupid if they were also moral. The most important consequence of stupid and hypocritical leaders is that it means immoral men have achieved a monopoly of political power.

A final observation concerning the behavior of voters is that most persons seem to value security over freedom (as defined in Chapter 1) in the sense that they will more often than not sacrifice their freedom in order to preserve or expand their security. An example of this is the acceptance of a police state by the White citizens of South Africa in order to avoid direct competition with the non-White population. Hitler legally taking power in Germany is another example. The growing tolerance of and demand for police-state tactics in the United States in order to suppress increasing crime and disorder is a third. The current indecent leaders are most willing and ready to accommodate the voters on this matter.

The net result in a democracy is that the feedback and freedom inherent in the system are sacrificed for the sake of security by reducing the number of effective parties to two and sometimes one, thereby temporarily increasing the stability of the system. The competition for power becomes one of technique in manipulation of the prejudices of voters as opposed to one of providing meaningful alternatives to the voters. Instead of educating the voters, the object is to deceive them. The voters themselves rarely vote *for* a candidate, but rather vote *against* the most obnoxious candidate. Therefore, candidates who have blatantly violated the voters' prejudices and need for security while in office are usually voted out of office. This means that at best democracy is a minimax strategy that gives the voters the best of the worst, thereby allowing them to avoid the worst of two bad alternatives. Minimax strategies lead inevitably to total entropy—death.* This is most clearly shown by the democratic election of indecent men to high office in the United States.

The recent elections in the United States, where the technology of electoral engineering is most advanced, indicate that any candidate with moderate acting ability can be sold to the voters by semi-scientific mer-

* Recall that death is the minimax strategy in the Game of Pleasure and that all Immoral Men play only the Game of Pleasure.

chandising techniques. These consist in continuous feedback obtained by means of scientific public opinion polls together with packaging of the candidate in such a way that he maximizes his appeal while constraining his offensiveness.* The technique involves avoiding significant issues that involve judgment or reason and making a direct emotional appeal to the voters.

The ultimate outcome will be that political power goes to the candidates able to muster the largest financial resources with which to buy the best professional merchandising team and advertising media. As professionals, the candidates will have no political or ideological views *per se*, but will tailor their image to suit the current whims of the public. Only unethical men will do this.

Even the argument that the people are getting what they want becomes a sham because what they want is determined primarily by the communications and news media. Ultimately, in a democracy, whoever controls the means of propaganda and information controls the country as effectively or more so than the most tyrannical dictator in the most oppressive police state. The argument that competition among the communications media will prevent this is a dream. The media in any capitalist country are for sale to the highest bidder. In the more socialized countries there is even less competition and the media are easier to control. In completely socialized countries, the media are an instrument of the state for controlling the citizens.

There will, of course, always be a minority of mavericks who will do the opposite of what the propaganda is exhorting them to do. These mavericks may even print their own newspapers, propagandize and engage in mass disruption; however, the "silent majority" will despise them for it and give even more power to the establishment to crush the dissension. Minority dissension can be very effective in a conventional dictatorship when the dissenters reflect the will of the majority; in a democratic dictatorship with majority support it only serves to strengthen the establishment by offending the prejudices of the majority. A democratic dictatorship of immoral, indecent men can be created and is being created in the United States while faithfully adhering to the myth of democracy.

* See Joe McGiness *The Selling of the President 1968*.

The tyranny of the majority can be just as terrible as the tyranny of a minority. This was amply demonstrated by Adolf Hitler.

Of all the myths perpetrated about democracy, the most absurd is that people want democracy because it gives them freedom. Democracy works because it gives people security. It gives security by providing more effective feedback to the political bureaucracy than any other form of government. Therefore, in order to maintain its power, the political bureaucracy gives the voters what they want and think they need. This is never more freedom. Every democracy is in the process of decreasing personal freedom by converting from capitalism to socialism.

The essential ingredient in socialism is not public ownership of the means of production, but rather the notion that every one is responsible for the welfare* of everyone else. This notion is "socialism." Public ownership of the means of production is only a notion the traditionally-minded Marxists have emphasized as being the necessary condition for socialism. A counter-example to the Marxist dogma is modern Sweden, a socialistic, democratic country where most production is in private hands.

Socialism gives greater security at the price of less freedom. It gives the state the right to demand an increasing part of each person's life for the "welfare" of others. The majority of the voters in all democracies have shown themselves ready to pay the price. They allow the state to have a claim on an ever-increasing part of their lives in exchange for promises of more security.

Pure capitalism and anarchy are synonymous. They represent the survival and prosperity of the strong at the expense of the weak. It was rightly decided by the romantic political theorists of the eighteenth and nineteenth centuries (i.e., the theorists of "Liberalism") that pure capitalism, i.e., anarchy, would not provide as much freedom as a capitalist democracy where the main function of the state was to enforce contracts and protect private property and life, and where all other decisions were left to the individual citizen. In this system the citizen only gave up his freedom to blatantly defraud, rob and kill his neighbor in exchange for

* Welfare in the conventional socialistic sense refers only to happiness and security, not freedom and awareness.

the security of his own life and property. This was clearly an optimal compromise for maximizing freedom.

The United States was originally structured as a nearly perfect capitalist democracy. It did not remain so because of the fallacy of the assumption that the majority of people preferred freedom above all else. This fallacy, however, was a natural mistake for the Founding Fathers to make since they were broadly aware persons who saw freedom as a means for enhancing their own awareness. They made the common mistake of projecting their ethics on those who do not share them.

In the final analysis, a political system based on freedom fails because freedom is not an ultimate goal for anyone. It is only a means to an end. Means that are not ends cannot succeed. Democracy proved to be a means of obtaining security in democratic countries by providing feedback. It should also be a means for enhancing awareness in an Ethical State for the same reason, but freedom will be a consequence of structuring a nation to maximize awareness; it will not be only a means. Freedom is a negative quantity. It is the absence of outside interference in our personal lives. Man can only be truly moved by positive quantities.

Communism has in fifty years captured half the world by directly promising the positive quantity of security in the absence of freedom. Democracy as a revolutionary force was less spectacularly successful because it was more abstract and promised security indirectly as a by-product of freedom. Communism has failed, except by using outside force, to replace a working democracy; not because it provides less freedom but because it provides less security.

In a democracy, the important decisions become socialized and thereby more quickly bureaucratized than the trivial decisions. Eventually the only prime events generated in the society are trivial ones. Because of better feedback, the least bureaucratized part of democratic society, the trivial part, is much more vigorous and dynamic; soon it assumes an overwhelming importance in the minds of its citizens. They become more concerned with legalizing drugs than with passing better educational laws. Rock and roll concerts often draw more attention and response than debate on the most crucial political issues (e.g., Woodstock). Since it is a democracy, the political bureaucrats must make it possible for the citizens to obtain what they want, in order to maintain their power. Therefore, they pass legislation strengthening even more the forces of trivia. The most universal desire for trivia being that for unessential consumer goods and entertainment, the politicians almost without knowing what they are doing structure the society to maximize the production and consumption of entertainment and consumer goods.

The bureaucracies of business and commercial entertainment, i.e., the corporations, have the best feedback and are the freest. They find it easier to make money, their main purpose, by selling unnecessary goods and entertainment to the masses who have been convinced that the only purpose of life is to be happy by desiring and possessing trivia. The corporations further augment the process by using large percentages of their profits to corner the artistic and scientific energies of society for the sole purpose of inveigling ever more consumers to buy increasing amounts of trivial goods and services that the consumer feels he must have in order to be happy.

In a democracy the Game of Life is ultimately lost by default in an all-absorbing, suicidal scramble for trivia in which the entire creative energy of the society is consumed until entropy destroys it.

For this reason, unless purposeful action is taken soon, the democracies will probably begin to decline faster than the more bureaucratized Communist countries even though democracies have better feedback and greater inherent potential for being transformed into an Ethical State. However, the Communist countries will not be far behind. They too will succumb in time to demands that education become entertainment and that scientific research be sacrificed to producing more consumer trivia. The communist leaders will learn that it is easier to control the masses with trivia than with police-state tactics.

It is even more likely, however, that both the democracies and the Communist states will destroy themselves *and the rest of the world* through nuclear annihilation and/or environmental pollution. In order to understand this phenomenon better, it will be necessary to understand the bureaucratization of the democratic infrastructure.

Democratic Infrastructure

The bureaucratization of government is the most pernicious aspect of our moral decay since government is ultimately responsible for all important decisions in a bureaucratic state. However, one might expect that in relatively free, advanced societies, such as Sweden or the United States, the non-governmental parts of the society should be able to do something to prevent decline. This indeed might be the case if the government alone were bureaucratic, but by the time government is bureaucratized, the whole infrastructure is also bureaucratic.

The basic infrastructure of modern democratic society has the following four major components:

1   The Military: includes all the forces of direct coercion which are available to the government. It includes the army, police, coast guard, spy organization, etc.
2   Industry: includes all means of production of goods and services, except entertainment and education. Industry includes agriculture, manufacturing, medical care, etc.
3   Entertainment: includes all means of production of goods and services that directly cause happiness, but are primarily trivial in nature. It includes most of the communications media.
4   Education: includes all the means of production of goods and services that directly expand awareness. It includes most schools, research institutions, and a small part of the communications media.

The same infrastructure, of course, also exists in a Communist society. However, there the political bureaucracy has complete control of the infrastructure and the corruption is greater. In a democracy the political bureaucracy has only partial control over the infrastructure, the greatest control being over the Military and in descending order over Education, Industry, and Entertainment. The more socialized the democracy, the greater will be the control of the political bureaucracy over the infrastructure. The least socialized major democracy is the United States. It will often serve as a model, because whatever can be said about the bureaucratization of the infrastructure of the United States applies even more to the other democracies.

The Military

The Military has as its ostensible major objective the implementation of the will of the political bureaucracy controlling the government. The Military in effect becomes the refuge for the least productive members of the society and is the most bureaucratized of all the bureaucracies. The Military is essential to the survival of society since without it the predators from within (criminals) as well as the predators from without (aggressive foreign political bureaucracies) would consume it. The Military is, therefore, analogous to our white blood cells—we need it to protect society from the spread of disease. However, if the Military gets out of control, it can become a cancerous growth just as excess white blood cells are symptomatic of leukemia.

The most effective source of feedback for the Military is encounter with the enemy. The Military becomes most effective during times of continued warfare and most corrupt during prolonged peace. During periods of prolonged peace, the Military finds it increasingly difficult to justify its existence. On the other hand, like any other bureaucracy, it would like to avoid feedback. An optimal situation from the military bureaucracy's point of view is, therefore, the continuous threat of imminent war without the consequences of war, i.e., feedback. This situation can only be achieved by cooperation, not necessarily deliberate, between the Military and the enemy. Only unethical men will do this.

Each military bureaucracy must convince the political bureaucracy which controls it that other nations have aggressive intentions and capabilities. This is usually easy to do. The political bureaucrats, being aggressive, power-oriented members of the Immoral Community are ready to project their own motivations into their foreign and domestic counterparts. In the case of Stalinist Russia and Nazi Germany, the implied threat was even true. Once a balance of terror is established between rival military bureaucracies, it is virtually impossible to end it without open warfare in which one or both rivals are destroyed or seriously damaged. Even a domestic revolution, unless it is inspired by the rival, will be ineffective in changing policy. Once the balance of terror is established, the threat of war is real and it will affect any political bureaucracy in power. The military has become a cancer, but it has not yet metastasized.

When war does ensue and rival military bureaucracies test each other, the competition is mainly one of relative incompetence between the two bureaucracies. The Military that had the least feedback is the most corrupt and has the highest entropy. Therefore, the relative efficiencies of rival Militaries are completely a product of their relative entropies resulting from poor feedback. For this reason, in every major war of the last two hundred years, the more democratic side has usually won because the democratic Militaries invariably have better feedback than the Militaries in totalitarian states. Of course, a highly corrupt military bureaucracy may defeat a more efficient Military by sheer size. Such was the case when Soviet Russia defeated democratic Finland.

The same processes apply to domestic terror inspired by criminals, revolutionaries being rare in established democracies. It is to the police's bureaucratic advantage to exaggerate the threat of crime and underrate their capability for dealing with it, the implication always being that they are understaffed. But, then, all bureaucracies claim to be understaffed.

In the United States the military bureaucracy, although quite heterogeneous, has a tendency to attract two distinct personalities. The overwhelming majority of military personnel are passive, security-seeking types—as are most bureaucrats. They make a military career because it gives them the security of a highly predictable environment in which moderate advancement is assured by simply not being offensive to their superiors. The tasks that they have to do are usually clearly defined and the means for doing them are specified. There is also virtually no risk of being fired for incompetence since there is very little feedback. The grossly incompetent, when they fail to follow the rules of the bureaucracy because of sheer stupidity, are merely relegated to the lower ranks and do not get promoted. Only the outright destructive criminals or uncooperative innovators (e.g., Billy Mitchell) are fired.

The other major type of military careerist is the chronic psychopath who delights in exercising his authority over others and/or brutalizing them. He, unlike most of his fellows, thoroughly enjoys encounter with the enemy. This type of militarist is much rarer in the bureaucracy and is found mainly within the police organizations. When he is a commissioned officer, he has a tendency to make his fellow officers uneasy and finds it difficult to obtain promotions. However, the psychopathic-type militarist makes the most effective leader in wartime and he is also likely to be among the most intelligent and least bureaucratic militarists. Therefore, although rare, he may sometimes be found among the highest ranking officers (e.g., General George S. Patton, Jr.). Ironically, the psychopathic militarist is the one most likely to be an ethical man. He plays the Game of Life in a primitive Darwinian sense by testing the ability of other men to survive. The psychopath is invaluable in war and an anachronism in peace. In peace time his life is plagued by ethical mistakes.

With this background it is not surprising to find that the Military is the least effective bureaucracy for expanding awareness. Because of the peculiar socio-economic structure of the United States and a few other countries such as Israel, the Military often serves as an indirect means of subsidizing the educational process. Insofar as the Military helps perform an educational function, it serves its only creative purpose. It is a very inefficient organization for educating people, but it is often better than nothing.

The evil of the military bureaucracy lies in 1) its potential for catalyzing destructive or even totally annihilating wars through its own incompetence and/or the psychopathic tendencies of some of its leaders; and 2) its insatiable appetite for consuming the entire physical and intellectual resources of the people it is allegedly defending.

War through Incompetence

The triggering of a merely destructive war such as the American-Indochina conflict or a war of nuclear annihilation with the Soviet Union (as is always being threatened) results not from hostile intent on the part of the military bureaucracy but primarily from its incompetence. As science and technology advance, war becomes more complex. The point was reached long ago (World War I or before) when the scientific illiterates, who make up the bulk of the military bureaucracy, had virtually no understanding of the weapons available to them, the possible strategies for their deployment, and the complex consequences of their use. Therefore, they began to hire a captive community of scientists and technologists who offer their talents to the Military sometimes out of patriotism but usually for simple economic gain and security. These former members of the Moral Community form a sub-bureaucracy within the overall military bureaucracy. They may be employed directly by the Military or indirectly through contracts and grants to industry and universities. They often profess disdain and contempt for the professional militarist yet they do his bidding.

Because they are an integral part of the most corrupt of bureaucracies, the scientists become corrupt and in the process unscientific, legalminded, and immoral. They waste enormous resources in extremely inefficient development of new weapon systems. They make decisions not on the basis of what is scientifically correct and technically sound but on the basis of what is politically expedient. They deceive their scientifically illiterate military clients with the appearance of science devoid of the substance of science. The fact that all their work is cloaked in secrecy spares them the feedback of scrutiny from the Moral Community which is the only group of people capable of evaluating the "scientific" deception. The captive former scientists and technologists become the single most corrupt group within the military establishment—far more corrupt than the military careerists who are more often patriotic idealists and ethical persons. Only the highly intelligent can be immoral.

In spite of all this corruption, there are still a few persons, a minute percentage of the scientists and technologists supporting the Military who remain ethical. They are technically competent and scientifically honest (e.g., Admiral Hyman Rickover and Dr. Edward Teller). They, and only they, are responsible for the effectiveness of the new weapon systems. They do their work in the inertia of an ineffective, corrupt military-scientific-industrial bureaucracy. The results sometimes cost thousands—even millions—of times more than they are worth, but the results are eventually produced. These weapons are almost entirely automatic. Their use involves only simple responses on the part of the users. Some of these weapons have the capacity for destroying the entire biosphere. They are becoming increasingly destructive and automatic.

Eventually it will be possible for a psychopath deliberately to trigger a war of total annihilation. But more likely a fool, or more aptly a series of fools, will trigger the war through a series of mistakes.

The American-Indochina war represents a decision that was made because of poor feedback from corrupt bureaucracies. The corrupt bureaucracy of the U.S. Department of State gave the President the deceptive feedback with which to justify the causes and purposes of the war. The corrupt bureaucracy of the Military establishment gave the President the deceptive feedback with which to justify the technical and economic feasibility of the war. Both analyses were based on a poor or nonexistent understanding of the psychosocial context in which the war was to be fought.

The ideological scientific illiterates of the State Department understood nothing and could predict nothing about the cause and effect relationships between freedom, security, nationalism, socialism, Communism and democracy. The Military could not understand why, against a determined minority of militant ideologues in a primitive environment, modern weapons of mass destruction are totally ineffective for imposing a nonideological, totalitarian minority regime under the name of democracy. The Military could not perceive the true nature of its strengths and weaknesses.

The only way the United States could have obtained its objectives in Indochina was by killing the majority of the population of North and South Vietnam. Fortunately, the bureaucratic corruption in the United States has apparently not yet reached the point where this is an acceptable solution to a rather trivial problem of 1) whether to support a corrupt, non-ideological, unethical foreign military dictatorship which is ostensibly friendly to the United States or 2) whether to try to win influence directly with a new, non-bureaucratic, vigorous, ideological dictatorship of the Left which expresses hostility toward the United States and will eventually become immoral but is likely to be more motivated by ethical nationalism at present than by political ideology. The United States chose what it thought was the lesser of two evils. However, unethical means never achieve ethical ends. A nation which is moral and seeks to maximize awareness would not have become involved militarily in Vietnam. Even if it made a mistake in the beginning (as was the case), it would have corrected it when it saw its policies could not possibly increase the totality of man's awareness. Instead, this unethical war continued because of political expediency. Only indecent men will sacrifice human life to political expediency.

Military Consumption

The wasteful consumption of resources by the Military of today has no counterpart in history. Besides diverting millions of potential members of the Moral Community into a corrupting bureaucracy, it consumes directly and indirectly the majority of the economic and natural resources in every advanced country in the world except Japan and West Germany.

The remarkable progress made by Japan and to a much lesser extent by West Germany since the end of World War II is in large part due to their not having to support an all-consuming, parasitical military bureaucracy. Japan, with the proportionately smallest of all military establishments, is correspondingly more progressive than West Germany, which has a considerably larger military bureaucracy.

The greatest costs of the military bureaucracy are the indirect costs in human resources. The costs in terms of corrupted scientists are staggering. The revulsion for all science being generated in the youth of the world by the obvious corruption of scientific purpose and method in the Military may in time eliminate all feedback in the society and cause the entropy to increase in an irreversible reaction.

This revulsion against science is probably the single greatest cause for the hedonism and anti-intellectualism among the youth of the world. However, it is not the only cause. All the bureaucracies in the democratic infrastructure together with the political and government bureaucracies are jointly contributing to the decay of world culture and the extinction of awareness.

The Military interacts with the other parts of the infrastructure in a symbiotic fashion. The Military provides resources to the entertainment media and the entertainment media perform "public relations" services for the Military (e.g., war films). The Military recruits and trains its future officers at the educational institutions, and it in turn subsidizes research activities at the same institutions. The closest symbiosis is between the Military and Industry. Some of the largest industries are completely dependent on military contracts. The Military in turn is completely dependent on Industry for the development of all its armaments. Industry is the prime corrupter of the democratic infrastructure.

Industry

In democratic countries Industry is predominantly capitalistic. This is true even when countries are highly socialized, such as Sweden, England, most of Western Europe and to a lesser extent Japan. "Capitalism" simply means that any person with the necessary capital can produce and sell any goods and services he wishes in any manner he wishes, in competition or in the absence of competition with any other person or groups of persons, and keep his profits. "Capitalism" as defined is virtually non-existent in any country and may have never existed. Instead, there are various approximations to the ideal involving greater or lesser degrees of bureaucratic control and confiscation of profits. The economic system of the United States in the nineteenth century, which was a logical consequence of democratic ideology, was probably the closest approximation to pure capitalism (economic liberalism) in history.

The success of capitalism rests entirely on the feedback inherent in competition. However, pure capitalism does not work for very long because the more efficient producers and distributors eventually replace all their competition in a process of natural selection called "monopoly." Once a monopoly is established, the enterprise, by controlling virtually all the market for its products, destroys any potentially more efficient competitor by underselling him at a loss or otherwise undermining him until he goes bankrupt. Usually this is not necessary because potential capitalistic competitors prefer using their resources to attack a less competitive and therefore less risky market than one controlled by a monopoly.

Once a monopoly or near-monopoly is established, a capitalisitc enterprise becomes as bureaucratic and corrupt as any government agency. Therefore, in order to keep their economic system vital, democratic governments usually find it necessary to pass anti-monopolistic laws (called anti-trust laws in the United States) and pure capitalism no longer exists. This is not necessary in the rare cases when there is considerable

"free" competition with foreign industry. Eventually the capitalistic entrepreneurs have to contend with an artifically-fostered competition as
well as the government bureaucrats in charge of assuring that competition is maintained. Even without the problem of monopoly the democratic process forces the government to become involved in Industry.

Successful capitalistic enterprises, whatever the specific industry,
soon develop a special bureaucratic structure called a "corporation." The
corporate structure serves two major purposes: 1) it enables the individual enterpeneur to avoid personal responsibility for many types of crimes
and mistakes that the corporation may commit, and 2) it provides a
means of collective ownership by which very large amounts of capital
may be concentrated to a degree not possible even by the richest individual entrepeneur. The corporation, in turn, is a soulless entity with a single goal: the concentration of ever greater power and wealth by whatever
means are feasible for its owners and/or controllers. As such, the corporation becomes a completely predatory but not necessarily immoral entity within society. Therefore, democratic pressure forces the government to form additional bureaucracies to regulate the activities of the
corporation and protect the ordinary citizens and other corporations
from its machinations.

In a democratic society the net effect of this means of production is a
losing battle against the monopolistic forces of capitalistic predation and
corruption. The larger, more monopolistic corporations have highly corrupt immoral bureaucracies. They find it easier to use the large amounts
of capital at their disposal to lobby the legislators and government bureaucrats for favored treatment as opposed to competing honestly within
the system on the merits of their products. The further corrupting of
immoral bureaucracies is always a process that immoral men understand
best. They corrupt the democratic process by using their concentration
of capital to elect to office politicians who will serve their power-seeking
and money-making purposes. The overwhelming majority of the political
bureaucracy is soon beholden to the corporations. This is usually kept
secret by a tacit understanding among all the politicians, the exception
being the politicians beholden to the special corporations called "labor
unions."

Most of the people in the society being workers, it is assumed that obligation to labor unions is not a serious political liability and may even be an asset. However, the labor unions are the most corrupt and immoral of all the corporations because only they are allowed to have an outright monopoly of their product, which is labor. Since they have no competition, they provide an ever-decreasing quality of labor at an ever-increasing price.

The net effect on Industry is primarily beneficial because it becomes increasingly cost-effective to substitute machines and automation for an ever more deficient labor force. The competition between industries becomes primarily one of technique in being able to produce in the absence of effective labor. Since this produces an ever-decreasing market for many types of labor (typified by that of the less versatile and intelligent worker), the politicians who represent labor attempt to pass legislation that will take an ever-larger percentage of the profits produced by an increasingly-automated industry and redistribute them in some form to the ever less productive workers.

Industry retaliates by attempting to elect a larger percentage of its own captive politicians than labor, but finds it very difficult when the majority of the electorate is composed of working people. However, the competition for automated production eventually leads to such an efficient means of production that the number of *de jure* workers is very small and the number of *de facto* workers is nil. Instead, almost everyone is living a parasitical existence in the bureaucracies that administer Industry, Government, the Military, Education and to a much lesser extent Entertainment. The competition is no longer one of efficiency in production, rather it is one of how 1) to rise in the bureaucracy through the typical bureaucratic tactics and 2) to obtain the largest share of resources and power for one's own bureaucracy. The actual production of essential goods and services already has become a trivial matter.

Eventually a few hundred surviving giant corporations control almost all production and split the markets between themselves on the basis of a fixed formula, which is illegal, but this does not stop them. They also allow token competition to keep alive the myth of competitive capitalism. However, by this time most people are not really interested in rising in the bureaucracy or power since the democratic process of socialization, together with the application of science and technology to Industry, has produced an almost uniformly high standard of living independent of merit. Instead, the major preoccupation of the ever more immoral society which results is a concern with being happy.*

Competing industries sell their trivial and unnecessary wares, not on the basis of their relative merits, but on the basis of their ability to convince the consumers that their wares will make them happier than those of their competitors. The power-seeking bureaucrats who dominate the bureaucracies also give promises of happiness and security to their subordinates in order to concentrate power in their hands and in their bureaucracies.

The politicians run for office by promising happiness to the electorate. They promise to make it possible for the electorate to acquire and protect the consumer goods which Industry has spent billions of dollars advertising in order to condition the public to identify them with happiness.

The end result is that Industry contributes little or nothing to the enhancement of awareness. It uses its vast concentrations of power and money primarily to maintain the corrupt bureaucracy which administers it. This is done by 1) influencing and/or buying politicians and bureaucrats to protect and extend their privileges, and 2) advertising in such a way as to condition the public to desire its products above the expansion of awareness.

All this occurs almost automatically. Hardly anyone realizes what is happening and why. Science and technology have automated the production of wealth. The surplus wealth is used to keep the masses in an immoral stupor of happiness and ignorance. The degradation is augmented by bureaucratized Entertainment.

Entertainment

"Entertainment" is any process that normally produces happiness in some person(s) without necessarily increasing the awareness of any person. As such, Entertainment is merely trivial. The evil in Entertainment is similar to the evil in religious ideology. It can create the illusion of satisfying all of one's needs and lead to the extinction of awareness. The

* Recall the discussion of "happiness" in Chapter 1. The definition is repeated in the Glossary.

good in Entertainment results from its being a powerful tool for psychological conditioning which can be used to enhance the expansion of awareness by couching the learning process in an entertainment context.

Games, for example, all entertain but they are not trivial since they can condition persons to play the Game of Life. This is most clearly illustrated in competitive games, i.e., games in which persons compete against each other such as in sports and chess. The playing of these games by young children communicates at the unconscious level the basic evolutionary pattern of Darwinian competition and it teaches children that men are all created different not equal. Competitive games also teach children that no matter how proficient they become, they can always improve their performance in any game. Games, therefore, almost always begin as variations on the Game of Life, but they become variations on the Game of Pleasure when they no longer teach but serve solely to entertain. A person who becomes extremely proficient at a competitive game is usually playing the Game of Pleasure. Eventually all children who are to become moral men must begin to play the Game of Life directly.

The Game of Life is not a competitive game but a cooperative game where all who play win. It is a non-zero sum game.* Entertainment can be a substitute for the Game of Life when it is a variation on the Game of Pleasure. However, Entertainment when used in combination with the Game of Life can become a powerful device for expanding awareness.

This is seen in the structure of great literature where logically consistent theories about the psychosocial environment are presented in the context of an entertaining story (e.g., Dostoyevsky's *The Brothers Karamazov*). The current decline of literature is in large part due to the formalization of psychosocial theory building within the so-called "behavioral sciences." Only broadly-aware persons can be great writers. Broadly-aware persons usually wish to continue the expansion of their total awareness. Therefore, the potential great writers of today are mostly generalists who do not write anything except technical papers,

---

* A non-zero sum game is a game in which the stakes are greater than the total ante; it is possible for each player to win without depriving any other player of a chance to win.

while the actual "literary" writers are mostly entertainers. The same process applies in all the arts.

Art

"Art" is Entertainment used to expand awareness. The art of a culture is primarily a reflection of its awareness rather than a cause. It is a means through which the awareness of some is communicated to many, usually at the unconscious level. The art of a people communicates the deepest essence of their awareness. The ancient Greeks were a vital and broadly-aware people; their art reflects it. This applies even more to the artists of the Renaissance who were probably the most broadly-aware artists in history.

Being a generalist with depth and having social morality is a sufficient but not a necessary condition for being a great artist. Leibniz was a great generalist with little social morality. Goethe was a great generalist with social morality. However, art is largely an unconscious process which does not require a conscious knowledge of science (e.g., Bach). Great art seems to be catalyzed by generalists (e.g., the Renaissance).

Art is intrinsic in the psychosocial makeup of man. It has always been a part of our species. Therefore, art must be part of the evolutionary force expanding awareness and driving man toward the Moral Society. Art represents a means of communicating the total awareness of a culture at the unconscious level. It reflects the spirit rather than the substance of cultural awareness. It stimulates the unconscious mind to synthesize the overall pattern of awareness and build upon it. It communicates the unity of man and knowledge. Art is to a culture what dreaming is to the individual.

All persons dream; but most forget their dreams. If an electroencephalograph is connected to a sleeping person, it is possible to tell when the person is dreaming. If every time the person begins to dream, we wake him, he will undergo psychological change. The systematic interference with dreams causes the frequency of dreams to increase. It is as if a person has to have a certain number of dreams. The continued interruption of dreams leads eventually to serious psychological disturbances.* In dreams we bring about a synthetic union between our conscious and

* See Kales, A., Sleep: Physiology and Pathology.

unconscious awareness in an attempt to resolve the differences and thereby increase our total awareness.* The patterns that emerge are represented symbolically and figuratively as opposed to literally.

The art of a culture is the symbolic synthesis between its total conscious awareness (science and technology) and its total unconscious awareness (the evolutionary force). The artistic process and its interaction with total awareness is not well understood. For this reason it is essential that art remain free and that no one tamper with the dreams of a culture.

Art is not free. In the Soviet Union and to a lesser extent in other Communist countries art is brutally regimented to meet the prejudices of the bureaucratic ideologues who control it. There, art is being systematically turned into rigid entertainment and propaganda. In the democracies it is almost as bad. The bureaucratic infrastructure has corrupted the artistic process by industrial commercialism and/or educational specialization.

Artistic Corruption

Industry, through advertising, has taken Entertainment and used it psychologically to condition the population to buy its wares. The object in advertising is to influence as many people as possible. Therefore, Entertainment is structured to satisfy the lowest common denominator of taste. To Industry the only criterion for the "quality" of Entertainment is how well it sells. Therefore, Entertainment has apparently perfect capitalistic feedback.

This would be strictly true only if the communications media (radio, T.V., books, films, theater, records, etc.) had sufficient capacity to give everyone what he wants. Instead, the media represent a limited resource which is sold to the highest bidder. The highest bidders in a capitalistic democracy are the corporations whose main purpose is to make money. They use the media to make even more money. They pre-empt the channels of communication with Entertainment devoid of art. In the process of conditioning the public to buy their wares, they also condition it to accept the lowest common denominator of Entertainment as the

---

* Creative persons often comment on how they achieve a synthesis in their sleep. (See dream theories of Freud and Jung.)

standard. They ruin the taste of a generation by conditioning it to look only for escapist fantasy and happiness in Entertainment—never a means for expanding their awareness. Such is the fate of radio and television in a capitalist democracy. However, there are still other entertainment media such as films, theater, books, and records.

Films represent the most complete, all-encompassing art form. Films are also the most commercialized of all the arts. The corporations producing films do so only to make money. The lowest common denominator of Entertainment is not only easier to produce, but also makes more money since more people will buy it. In a capitalistic society films soon become degenerate. Films which seek to make people aware find an ever-decreasing audience in the "art houses." Corporate monopoly and bureaucratic corruption increase the entropy of Entertainment just as they do with the rest of Industry.

Underlying the whole corrupting process is the fact that persons who are artistically inclined are becoming increasingly unaware of the total environment. They begin specializing at an early age and seldom learn science; they become unethical and espouse an art-for-arts-sake philosophy. The artists soon develop utter disdain for science and technology, regarding them as inhuman and cold. They are concerned with emotions, particularly perverse ones. The scientists and technologists they meet appear to be mostly narrow, dull, and insensitive people. The worst part is that the artists are right. Science in general and the scientists in particular are becoming just as they see them. The cleavage between art and science becomes complete and both lose in the process. Art becomes Entertainment and science becomes irrelevant.* The main purpose of art, the unconscious expression of the total unity of man and knowledge evolving toward total awareness, is lost. Its loss becomes one of the reasons for the disintegration of science.

Books become repositories of pornographic fantasies which the other media cannot yet fully express. The mildly pornographic, simpleminded, sentimental books which only entertain and make no effort to expand awareness become the best sellers of all time. Some of the

---

* Science is irrelevant when it makes a few persons narrowly aware, but does not significantly enhance man's total awareness. Science is irrelevant when it is devoid of social morality and serves only to satisfy the personal morality of a few specialists.

publishers, whose sole purpose is to make money from producing and distributing books, try to find "formulas" for producing more best sellers to satisfy an ever more jaded public. They do not try to find any intrinsic merit in books, but only try to estimate on the basis of past successes and the trends in taste whether or not the books will make money.

Music

Music, like all art, reflects the evolutionary force directly by the complexity of its forms (greater awareness) and the unity of its style (the unity of structure in all evolution). Music is pure symbolism working directly on the nervous system to expand total awareness. Music is the purest of all the arts and as such the most important because it expresses man's most profound unconscious knowledge. Music is the only art form devoid of conscious meaning. The abstract visual arts may be approaching the same level of purity, but these arts are plagued by frauds.

Great art is that art most appreciated by great men. The greatness of a man is measured by the totality of the awareness which he engenders. While it seems that J. S. Bach is the greatest of composers, the order of the next ten is less clear, but it would probably include one or more of the following: Monteverdi, Mozart, Beethoven, Berlioz, Wagner, Brahms, Verdi, Mahler, Nielson, Ives, Richard Strauss, Debussy, Ravel, Bartok, Shostakovich, Honegger, Vaughan Williams, Schoenberg, Hindemith, Stravinsky and Penderecki. These composers wrote in drastically different styles. The only thing they have in common is complexity of form and unity of structure. Great music has survived and is still being created even while the other arts seem to be in a state of acute bureaucratic decline.

The music that is most heard on the media ("popular music") like the rest of the media represents the lowest common denominator of taste. It is simple in form, monotonous, repetitive and primitively rhythmic. It makes no appeal to the intellect; it reflects the lowest common denominator of awareness. Yet a full spectrum of contemporary music exists from the greatness of Penderecki to the simple primitiveness of rock and roll.

The split between the style and complexity of contemporary great music and current popular music is illustrative of the schizophrenia in our society. We are a society with the greatest total awareness that the world has ever known. We are also a society in which the majority of people are being turned, ever more willingly, from the pursuit of awareness into a plunge to primitive hedonism and immorality. The devolution of popular music illustrates that at an ever-increasing rate men have only their most primitive emotions in common. For this reason, primitive contemporary music is becoming increasingly popular among highly aware persons as well as the masses. It is the only way in which "art" can still unify men.

The great music of the past was the music of life. The music reflected the evolutionary patterns directly and communicated them to the unconscious mind. This phenomenon is most clearly demonstrated in J. S. Bach's The Art of the Fugue.

The Art of the Fugue begins as a relatively simple fugue with the embryonic theme of BACH (German notation). Bach, therefore, was representing his personal awareness (ego) within a musical form. As The Art of the Fugue progresses, the simple fugues become increasingly complex yet they mirror the patterns of the previous fugues. The elements of the simpler fugues are then joined into larger, more complex fugues which still continue to evolve until they again reach such a high level of complexity that new complexity is only possible by further joining. This progression continues with all the fugues together forming one great fugue of incredible complexity. Throughout all the fugues is the central developing theme of BACH, distinct yet an integral part of the over-all complexity. Eventually the BACH theme is fully developed in the last fugue which is the point at which Bach died. He died with the unconscious awareness of himself as part of a greater whole. He did not finish The Art of the Fugue in the conventional sense, because this music represented the unending spiral of evolution. It could not be finished because what Bach was expressing never ends.* Only his personal awareness stopped.

In The Art of the Fugue Bach expressed the evolution of all life and mind toward ever greater awareness by fanning out and joining in an ascending spiral of increasing unity. Yet it is a complexity in which the

* See Schweitzer, A., J. S. Bach.

individual remains distinct while becoming ever more aware. This is the pattern of the Moral Society.

The true artist can only reflect the awareness of his time. He cannot express what is not there. Today man is unconsciously aware of his impending doom and his descent into entropy. We live in a world dominated by a simultaneous desire for and fear of death. This is clearly demonstrated in the music of Penderecki.

In Penderecki's music there is death plus horror at the hopelessness of man's plunge into irreversible entropy. For this reason, the truly great music of our time is not pleasant listening. It makes us aware of what we do not wish to admit. The great music of today gives negative feedback.

Today when music is great, it expresses death. When music is entertainment, it expresses the schizophrenia and disintegration of our society. Much of modern popular music serves to blind man to the truth that all science and great art is showing him—the impending death of humanity.

All the arts reflect this. All the means of Entertainment are being used to accelerate the disintegration process. It is all happening blindly. The major defense of the culture against this decay is Education. But Education is caught in the same entropic force of bureaucratization as the rest of society.

Education

Education is any process which directly increases the total awareness of persons subjected to it. It includes, but is not limited to, schools, research centers, and parts of the communications media. Therefore, Education is the most important activity of any society. A rational society wishing to expand its total awareness would structure itself to maximize the educational output. All other functions—Government, Industry, Entertainment, and the Military—would be support functions, useful only if they enhanced the educational process. The Ethical State described in Chapter 6 is such a society.

In all countries Education is presently considered a support function to what are viewed as the much more important activities of the Military and/or Industry. Because, and only because, both the Military and Industry are so heavily dependent on science and technology, there is considerable support for scientific and technical education. The educational bureaucracy, like any bureaucracy, sees its role primarily as one of self-preservation and security for its own sake, not as a means for expanding awareness. Therefore, as the educational bureaucracy becomes corrupt, it becomes less a means for expanding awareness and more a means for constraining it. This comes about in a variety of ways.

The educational bureaucracy is rigidly structured in a hierarchical fashion. In the United States a few great universities and research institutes (Harvard, Berkeley, California Institute of Technology, Chicago, M.I.T., Yale, etc.) are at the top; then come the much larger number of lesser universities and colleges; at the bottom is the enormous, highly-corrupt, entrenched bureaucracy of secondary and primary education. In varying degrees of association with the hierarchy, sometimes peripheral sometimes integral, are the research centers of Government, Industry, and the Military together with the artistic community, journalists, publishers, the television networks, and so on.

A similar structure exists in every other country except that there the educational systems are even more centralized and bureaucratized. Therefore, anything said about the evil effects of the educational bureaucracy in the United States applies even more to other countries.

The great universities set the standards for the rest of the educational system by 1) setting their own standards of admission and 2) training the most influential members in the other parts of the interlocking bureaucracy. The educational system attempts to prepare its students to advance within the hierarchy. The number of their students qualifying for admission to and/or high position at the great universities is considered as the principal objective measure of the success of the lower echelons of the hierarchy. By their ability, prestige and contacts, the trainees of the great universities often obtain commanding positions in many branches of Government, Industry, the communications media and of course, most notably, within the educational bureaucracy itself. The great universities, in short, appear to set the tone for the whole structure of society. However, this is only partially true. The prime responsibility for structuring society lies with the political bureaucracies.

In a democracy the political bureaucracy reflects the needs and prejudices of the society as a whole. The failing of the educational system is its failure to perform its main mission. It has not made people broadly aware. It has not inculcated a desire for total awareness in its students. In order to understand this failure, it is necessary to understand the structure of the great universities and how they are becoming ever more corrupt. They bear the ultimate responsibility for the decline of democratic society.

The Universities

The university system of the democracies and most Communist countries is patterned after and evolved from the medieval European universities. The medieval universities were concerned primarily with weaving a "rational" pattern around the ideology of Catholicism. They were not concerned with science at all. They were, in short, an instrument of the Immoral Community for supporting itself. The Renaissance brought about a remarkable change in the structure of the university. At this time scientific method was introduced into the curriculum. An embryonic science in the form of mathematics and to a lesser degree astronomy had always been present in the universities. For many centuries these disciplines did not challenge Catholic dogma. When the Catholic totalitarian state became totally and obviously corrupt, the evolutionary force driving man toward greater awareness made him question many of the basic tenets of Catholic dogma and the authority of the Church. He became aware of his illusions of awareness. In so doing, the men of Europe planted the seed of science which is *the will to doubt*. This brought about the Renaissance, the Reformation, and the scientific revolution.

Until this time the universities stressed the unity of knowledge as being a reflection of the perfection of God. When physical science began to be introduced into the universities during the Renaissance, science was seen as one more facet in the unity of knowledge. The scientists of this period studied *all* there was to know. This included science, theology, law, history, Latin, plus anything else that was considered knowledge. Soon there arose irreconcilable differences. The pieces of what was rightfully considered the total unity of knowledge did not fit together. This inherent incompatibility lay not in the inherent nature of knowledge, for *all knowledge is one*. It lay in the differences in the methods for allegedly expanding knowledge. Science has its basis in experimental verification. Law has its basis in political expediency. Theology has its basis in ideological dogma. It soon became impossible for most people to perform the "double think" and mental juggling necessary to entertain jointly the different methods for allegedly expanding knowledge. All the branches of human knowledge, which for a brief period had been one, went their separate ways. The modern university grew out of the disintegration of the Renaissance university along the lines of method.

At first this disintegration gave even greater vitality to the expansion of science. When theology became completely separated from science (eighteenth century), it was analogous to having a cancer removed from an otherwise healthy baby. Science grew and flourished. Theology became increasingly irrelevant to the world order. The same was true for the other "disciplines" of the Immoral Community when they also became separated from the sciences. They lost their vitality and withered. Eventually, however, the process began to go too far.

Science was relegated to "natural philosophy," which was at first limited mainly to the study of the physical sciences, but which later was to include biology. Physical and biological science together were to be called "natural science." "Moral philosophy," which studies the much more important psychosocial environment and the field of ethics, was left without scientific feedback. As such it remained what it had formerly been—a captive of the Immoral Community. The greatest damage that had been done was to destroy the notion of the unity of knowledge. This disintegration of the totality of knowledge is still proceeding today. In part, this was done deliberately by the Immoral Community wishing to insulate itself from scientific feedback; however, the major blame is due to the scientists for allowing themselves to become bureaucratized.

Part of the process of bureaucratization is to compartmentalize authority in such a way that there is no overlapping of responsibility. This minimizes the internal competition and feedback from comparative evaluation. In the university, compartmentalization began with the arti-

ficial separation between natural and moral philosophy.* Biology was for
a time in a no-man's land between the two. It eventually became a part
of natural science, but by then the natural sciences themselves had
begun to become compartmentalized into individual disciplines. Soon
(nineteenth century) there were academic departments of physics,
chemistry, biology, mathematics, astronomy, geology, engineering, and so
on. Eventually these became even more compartmentalized. Today
mathematics is further divided into departments of applied mathematics, pure mathematics, and statistics.† Biology is divided into, among
others, departments of zoology, botany, physiology, genetics, bacteriology, physiological chemistry, and lately molecular biology. Engineering is
fragmented into civil, mechanical, electrical, hydraulic, chemical, etc. In
each field the experimental branches separate from the theoretical. Applied research is separated from pure research.

Each time there is a departmental cleavage and sometimes before,
the individual scientist and teacher is addressing himself to an ever-
narrower audience which eventually begins to decrease in total awareness
by becoming highly ellipsoidal and one-dimensional. The overwhelming
emphasis is on the methods of the discipline and not on the relevance of
the results for increasing man's total awareness (i.e., awareness of the
total environment—physical, biological, and psychosocial). Each narrow
specialist becomes incapable of even reading abstracts of the work being
done in areas directly related to his own, let alone being able to understand other disciplines.

As a bureaucrat, the overwhelming concern of the university scientist
is with security. In the academic community, security comes from understanding something academically acceptable far better than others
and/or convincing the "experts" that this is the case. This forces the
specialist to become ever more specialized in order to meet the standards
of acceptability. What is acceptable is what is popular with the majority
of persons who make up the specialty. They get no feedback from other

* Spinoza, Leibniz and Newton admitted no separation and considered all knowledge
one.
† The bureaucratization of mathematics has gone so far that today most mathematicians do not regard mathematics as a science but rather as a purely esthetic exercise
analogous to music. Historically, mathematics has been an integral part of science
and started as an empirical science—geometry.

disciplines. Each specialty leads to ever-new, ever-narrower specialties. The scientist is trapped in the classical dilemma of knowing more and more about less and less until he knows everything about nothing. In the process, science becomes irrelevant. The "good" scientists become "brilliant" in their specialty, but ignorant of everything else. They are incapable of predicting and controlling their *total* environment. They are narrowly, irrelevantly aware as opposed to being broadly aware. It becomes increasingly difficult to produce the generalists who can become moral men.

The scientists themselves recognize the dilemma. A new field develops called "systems science"; its alleged purpose is to put science together again by being a metascience encompassing and uniting all fields of scientific and technological knowledge. Departments of systems science are formed in all the major universities. The systems approach is acclaimed everywhere. However, systems science becomes bureaucratized before it is fully established. The new academic departments of systems science (sometimes called operations research) become specialized in the more obvious techniques of the field—mathematical optimization and decision theory—and neglect the foundations of the field which consist in a broad understanding of all the essentials of science and technology. It is much easier, safer, and academically more acceptable (i.e., bureaucratic) to show expertise in optimization theory and cookbook mathematics rather than in multidisciplinary problem solving. At its birth, systems science falls victim to the process it was created to circumvent. Science keeps becoming more fragmented and irrelevant. Awareness becomes narrow instead of total. As a consequence, the entire society keeps getting ever more bureaucratized and immoral. The Immoral Community, which controls the university through its political influence and its claim to the majority of the faculty members, further augments the bureaucratization of Education. The university becomes an ivory dungeon with an ever-dimming light.

The university departments which are an integral part of the Immoral Community are those which resulted from the bureaucratization of "moral philosophy." This occurred in a manner completely analogous to that of the sciences. However, for the Immoral Community it was merely a case of the blind becoming ever more blind. In the "disci-

plines" of the Immoral Community, points are made not by appealing
to scientific evidence but through rhetoric and the "documentation" of
the related ideological beliefs of other members of the Immoral Community. Writing style and the clever—not necessarily clear or honest—
use of words become all important. A point becomes documented and
proved by showing that other members of the Immoral Community had
similar opinions or that the conclusion is implied by the currently-
accepted ideology. This was the technique used by the medieval theologians and scholastic philosophers before the Renaissance. After the Renaissance, it was the technique used by Hegel, Marx, Lenin and Hitler. It
is the technique still being used by ideologues, all successful politicians
and most so-called "social scientists."

Social "Science"

Social "science" became formalized in the late nineteenth century
when the natural sciences had achieved tremendous success and prestige
in the academic community. It was an effort by the Immoral Community to cloak its ideology with scientific respectability. Social science
would have been a natural outgrowth of the physical and biological sciences. However, by the time that the Zeitgeist for social science was at
hand, the already-bureaucratized natural scientists, by default, lost the
initiative in creating the social sciences to the Immoral Community.
Some persons with inclinations toward and knowledge of the natural
sciences went into the social sciences (e.g., Hermann von Helmholtz,
Francis Galton and William James), but the majority of its founders
were members of the Immoral Community. The ideological roots of the
Immoral Community, which had been dying in the sterile fields of moral
philosophy, found new strength when they were transplanted to the fer-
tile fields of social science. Like weeds, they inhibited and are still inhibiting the development of science within the "social sciences." However,
in spite of the bureaucratization of the Moral Community and the
strength of the Immoral Community, natural science has established itself in the social sciences and has managed to make some headway
against tremendous odds. In this lies great hope for the human race.

The social sciences have the alleged purpose of applying scientific
method to the psychosocial environment. If this is the case, then predic-

tive models of human behavior can be developed, which predict a future psychosocial state on the basis of a description of the current physical, biological, and/or psychosocial state. The scientific method demands that controlled experiments be used to test the efficacy of the predictions. *This process is almost never used in the social sciences.* Instead, another method, which might be called the "clinical approach," is the dominant technique used in social science. It gives the appearance of science to blatant ideology. Sometimes, of course, even the clinical approach is eschewed in favor of ideological rhetoric.

The clinical approach has a superficial resemblance to science. Measurements are taken of the environmental phenomena. An attempt is made to develop logically consistent models to explain past cause and effect relationships. The models are then extrapolated to predict future events. The only missing ingredient is the notion of controlled experiments to check the predictions rigorously. In short, the clinical approach is science with extremely limited feedback and as such is no science at all. Because so little feedback is present, the measurements themselves tend to be arbitrary, lacking in internal consistency, and devoid of a relative scale let alone an absolute scale. The models themselves are primarily nonquantitative. The defensive arguments of the social "scientists" are that it is physically, economically and/or politically not possible to do controlled experiments in the psychosocial environment. This is not true. The field of formal education is a case in point.

One of the fundamental ideological beliefs of most of the Immoral Community and consequently of the majority of the social scientists is that the extreme leftist hypothesis is correct. Therefore, the differences in educational attainment between people must be due primarily to environment. With the proper environment we should be able to mold pupils to be anything we want. That this does not happen is assumed to be due to improper environmental techniques, but never to the possibility that the fundamental hypothesis is wrong. As a result, millions of dollars are wasted in the United States in clinically-based education "research." First one fad then another is tried to enhance the learning process.

The differences in educational achievement between distinct groups of people are assumed to be due to differences in the schools. Enormous efforts are made to equalize the educational environment for all groups. In some cases (e.g., higher education) the system is biased in favor of the "disadvantaged" group. The group differences in performance still persist. A new assumption is then made that the major differences between the groups are due to the pre-school environment. A new pre-school program of environmental enrichment, called "Headstart," is begun. The group differences still persist. The fact that different persons of the same "disadvantaged" group with apparently identical environments perform quite differently is ignored. It is now alleged by the leading social science ideologues that the major differences between the groups are due to the environmental differences between the groups during the first two years of life. They cling to the leftist ideological hypothesis in the face of all contrary evidence. The leftist hypothesis may still be correct, but no controlled experiments are seriously suggested to test it rigorously.*

Finally, a social scientist with an apparently open mind and more courage than his colleagues, Arthur Jensen,† challenges the basic ideological hypothesis of the Left. He puts together a cogent, logical argument with a mathematical foundation, supported by experimental evidence from identical twin studies and matched group studies. He comes to the conclusion that the rightist hypothesis is much closer to the truth. A scientific approach to the controversy would be to propose a carefully-controlled experiment to resolve the differences. Instead, Jensen is pilloried by his colleagues as a racist.‡ They distort his position and then attack the distortions. He has some support from the geneticists and a

---

* William Shockley, a Nobel Prize winner in physics, has suggested such an experiment, but he has been almost unanimously denounced by the social scientists and the American Academy of Sciences for the suggestion. Part of the fault here seems to lie with Shockley's lack of finesse and his obvious rightist bias. However, the response of the Moral Community was still unscientific.

† Op cit.

‡ "Racism" is an ideology which infers behavioral characteristics about persons solely on the basis of race. Racism like all ideology has no basis in scientific evidence. Rightist ideologues are by definition racists. Leftist ideologues call anyone to their right a "racist." A person who cites scientific evidence to support the rightist hypothesis is not a racist unless he judges individual persons of a particular racial group a priori as having the behavioral characteristics commonly associated with their race. Anyone who accepts persons on the basis of their individual merits is not a racist.

few social scientists but the leftist communications media report only the distortions. The rightist ideologues distort the conclusions to support their own racist ideology. The response is unscientific. No attempt is made to arrive at the truth scientifically.

The ironic consequence of the unscientific response to Jensen's work is that the very problem with which the leftist ideologues profess concern is compounded by ideological blindness. It is clear from a thorough reading of Jensen that he shares the concern of all decent men for the racial inequities in the United States. He apparently did his research in an ethical attempt to find a scientific method for correcting those inequities. However mistaken Jensen's work may be, it is highly unethical to condemn his work by imputing his motives and distorting his analyses. In so doing, the leftist ideologues are blinding themselves to genetic reality and are contributing to the continued genetic decay of the very people whose welfare they claim to desire.

The crux of the problem seems to be with the leftist ideologues' perversion of the concept of "welfare" to mean only "happiness." In so doing, they destroy negative feedback for themselves and others. If they were concerned with the true welfare of people, they would explore all scientific possibilities for increasing the awareness potential of all men— White or Black—living or yet unborn. Their present response is an example of how basically decent men, blinded by ideology, can cause untold evil to the human race. This evil manifests itself not only in dysgenic policies but in the wastages of the educational bureaucracy.

With a fraction of the funds spent on ideologically-based, mass education "experiments," it would be possible to determine a priori the effectiveness of any proposed program. This is never done. When two or more logically-consistent models about educational effectiveness exist with some supporting evidence, the scientific thing to do is 1) to divide a small part of the population chosen at random (a few thousand subjects total) into statistically-matched groups; 2) try each educational technique under controlled conditions on one and only one of the experimental groups; 3) at the end of the experiment to measure the total awareness of the experimental and control groups by standardized achievement tests;* and 4) based on the group differences, to use statis-

* The feasibility of measuring total awareness is discussed in Chapter 7.

tical techniques to determine which, if any, of the educational techniques was superior and in which ways to any of the other techniques. This simple, inexpensive and straightforward approach to educational development would lead to an optimal system of education in a few years, but it is not used. It is the same with the other social sciences, such as sociology, political science, and economics.

The reason that the scientific method has such difficulties getting established in the social sciences is that 1) most, *not all*, social scientists (like their mentors in the rest of the Immoral Community) are scientific illiterates;* and 2) the social sciences are bureaucratized to the point where any feedback is a threat to the whole structure of the Immoral Community.

FEEDBACK

The studies by J. S. Coleman et al.† and A. W. Astin ‡ indicate, but do not prove, that there is no significant educational effect due to differences in the school environment as it currently exists in the United States. In other words, the differences in educational achievement are due primarily to the quality of the individual students as opposed to the quality of the total environment in the schools. For example, when the quality of the university level students is matched on the basis of their performance on the College Board Entrance Examination, their educational achievement at the end of four years as measured by the Graduate Record Examination is *independent of any of the accepted measures of institutional excellence.* In effect, it makes no significant difference whether they went to Harvard or a small obscure local college.

This implies two hypotheses: 1) if a good student is put into a group-learning context where he can learn, he will learn; 2) the much touted "superiority" of some schools has little to do with the school itself, including the composition of the faculty or the student body; it is merely a

---

* See performance profiles on Graduate Record Examination for social science majors. Also note that few natural science requirements are included in the social science curricula except cookbook statistics.

† Coleman, J. S., et al., *Equality of Educational Opportunity*, U.S. Ofc. of Education, Dept. of Health, Education, and Welfare, 1966.

‡ Astin, A. W., "Undergraduate Achievement and University Excellence," *Science*, Vol. 161, pp. 661–667, 16 Aug. 1968.

reflection of the fact that a large number of superior students attend the school.* If these two hypotheses are rigorously proven to be correct then the whole bureaucratic hierarchical structure of the educational system is threatened and as a result so is the commanding position of the Immoral Community. It means that Education can be decentralized, i.e., debureaucratized. The possibility still exists, of course, that some changes in the educational environment can produce significant improvements in educational achievement. Bureaucracies have shown themselves incapable of making these changes.

The bureaucratic system of administering Education appears to be totally ineffective in producing differential effects. The only thing that seems to matter under the existing system is the quality of student and feedback in terms of student performance. If the student is in a group-learning context and knows how much his total awareness is increasing relative to others, and he has a *minimum* level of educational resources at his disposal, he can use this feedback to modify the educational process itself and adjust it to fit his individual needs.

The elimination of this last bit of feedback is the ultimate goal of the leftist ideologues of the Immoral Community. In trying to eliminate comparative evaluation of students by standardized tests, they are eliminating the last vestiges of feedback in the education bureaucracy in order that it might become totally bureaucratized and, as a consequence, no longer merely ineffective but an absolute impediment to the expansion of awareness. Their goal is to make the educational resources available to the students not on the basis of how well they can use them, but on the basis of what political bureaucratic advantage may be gained by allowing one student group versus another to delude itself into believing that it is being educated. The illusion of education in the absence of education is central to the bureaucratization process in Education. This brings us back to the first point.

---

* In some schools in the United States there exists so much chaos due to the disruptions of anti-social "students" that it becomes *physically* impossible for a willing student to learn. This is consistent with the two hypotheses.

SCIENTIFIC ILLITERATES

The reason so many social scientists are scientific illiterates is a consequence of the long-established illusion held in the Immoral Community that one can be an educated, i.e., aware, person without knowing any science whatsoever. This is completely analogous to the illusions perpetrated by religion. Its consequences are to stop the expansion of awareness. The illusion has enabled the less capable students who cannot readily master the more rigorous fields of mathematics and physical science to delude themselves into thinking that they are learning science by studying the ideology of social science. More importantly, it has diverted millions of potential scientists into a state of relative ignorance.

For many years a similar situation existed in biology. Scientifically-inclined persons incapable of readily mastering mathematics or physical science studied biology. However, biology was not quite as central to the ideology of the Immoral Community as are the social sciences. Therefore, scientific method, although confined mainly to description, made steady progress in the biological sciences. In the 1930's persons trained in the methods of mathematics and physical science began to address themselves to biological problems.* They and not the classically-trained biologists have brought about the revolution called "molecular biology." Molecular biology and biophysics in general portend total awareness of the biological environment. There is an ever-increasing demand that biologists be thoroughly trained in mathematics and physical science. The same is possible in the psychosocial environment if the bureaucratic grip of the ideologues can be broken and a reformation in the teaching of the natural sciences is brought about.

Psychosocial Science

In order to understand the psychosocial environment, it is as a minimum essential 1) to have a thorough understanding of mathematics in order to describe psychosocial processes precisely and rigorously formu-

---

* Von Helmholz was another physical science generalist who addressed himself to biological and psychophysical problems in the nineteenth century, but his high caliber work was not followed up by other comparably qualified persons.

late predictive models and experiments of the most complex phenomena known to man; 2) to understand physical science and technology in order (a) to construct physical science analogues of psychosocial processes, (b) to devise measuring instruments and (c) to control the experimental environment; 3) to have a thorough understanding of biology, particularly neurophysiology, in order to understand the biophysical causes and effects of behavior—this in turn is dependent on a thorough understanding of mathematics and physical science.

Very few social scientists have this type of background. The social science bureaucracy perpetuates its own kind. The scientifically-based psychosocial scientists will have to be trained outside the establishment.

The teaching of natural sciences, however, is so thoroughly bureaucratized and fragmented that the broad scientific perspective needed for the social sciences is very difficult to obtain. A person wishing to acquire the proper background for working in the social sciences must learn tremendous amounts of largely irrelevant techniques and facts in order to obtain the necessary knowledge for becoming totally aware of the psychosocial environment. The training of molecular biologists and biophysicists is a step in the right direction, but they usually do not learn what little is actually known in the social sciences, sufficient neurophysiology or the mathematical techniques appropriate to the social sciences which are primarily probabilistic in nature. Furthermore, the bureaucratization and fragmentation of the natural sciences is continuing at an accelerating rate.

Hope lies in the union of the fields of biophysical neurophysiology with mathematical and physiological psychology. Much of the theoretical work in the latter areas has been crude and basically trivial, but there is the possibility that it will improve. This may create pressure for the reunification of natural science within the context of scientific psychology. From here the scientific method may spread to the other psychosocial sciences.*

* Economics is a social science in which rigorous quantitative methods have recently been introduced. However, the econometricians as a group have fallen into the classical trap of the academic bureaucracies and have become obsessed with method as opposed to scientific relevance. They tend to construct mathematical models as ends in themselves as opposed to means of predicting and controlling the environment. Econometric models are almost never tested scientifically.

The only hope for man to save himself from the entropic process of bureaucratization is to perceive directly* that the unity of man and the unity of knowledge are different facets of the same evolutionary process. Each is a precondition to the other. There is neither the time nor the means to gather the orderly scientific proof to convince a bureaucratized and increasingly unscientific humanity. Only by direct perception can man master the evolutionary force that is threatening to destroy him even as it drives him toward the Moral Society. Only by direct perception can man realize that *all men must become generalists.*

Generalists

Being a total generalist implies knowing *all* the arts and sciences. The first reaction of most people to this proposal is that while it may be possible to know all the arts, it is impossible to train men who know *all* science. However, to grasp all of science does not mean to know every single fact and detail. It means knowing all the most relevant facts and the foundations of all the sciences sufficiently well to be able to understand any new relevant finding in any science. It also implies the capacity for being able to contribute original new relevant findings in any science.

Science is "relevant" only when it contributes to the expansion of *total* awareness. Those scientific findings and methods which serve to unify the totality of science are the more relevant. Today the most relevant science of all is that which contributes most to man's capability for prediction and control of the psychosocial environment. A few men in the past and a few men today have this totality of scientific knowledge. Leibniz was an example of such a man. John von Neumann is a more recent example. The life of Leibniz has much to teach us about the value of *broad* awareness as opposed to narrow awareness.

The accomplishments of Leibniz were described in Chapter 2. The human race has not yet produced another Leibniz. It is unlikely that this is due to there not being any persons among the billions born since his time who equal his innate intellectual capacity, rather it is due to Leibniz being among the last men having the unified education of the Ren-

---

* "Direct perception" refers to becoming aware of a pattern in nature in the same way that we are aware of the pattern of our own existence. It is insight supportable by scientific evidence.

aissance university.* He wasted most of his life in theological arguments, court intrigue, and writing a history of the House of Brunswick. Yet the totality of synergistic perception resulting from a broad awareness and a brilliant mind enabled him to play a crucial role in implementing the scientific revolution. If he lived today, it is not unlikely that the bureaucratization process would force him into the niche of the professional mathematician or theoretical physicist where he would have great success, win international acclaim and remain largely irrelevant to the evolution of man toward total awareness. We know that this is the case because Leibniz was not a moral man. A moral man cannot be forced into the role of the specialist, he is always a generalist.

The loss of depth in training a generalist is only temporary. The synergistic effect of a broad awareness with limited depth will enable the generalist eventually to develop greater depth in any given area than if he had concentrated on it exclusively from the beginning. Furthermore, he will be able to distinguish the relevant from the irrelevant which the specialist can never do. That this is the case is illustrated most notably by the accomplishments of Renaissance men such as Leibniz and Spinoza. It is shown even today in a more limited fashion by men such as John von Neumann, Norbert Wiener, Lev Landau, Erwin Schroedinger, Albert Schweitzer, and others. Except for the latter, these men are responsible for the newly-developing schools of biophysical neurophysiology and molecular biology. Albert Schweitzer is a lesser version of a modern-day Spinoza. Schweitzer was a complete artistic and scientific generalist who in his own way lived and expanded the Ethics of Life.

The unethical quality of modern bureaucratized science traps brilliant minds in a vicious cycle of thought-for-thought's sake where the cleverness of accomplishment far outweighs its relevance. Scientists are becoming chess players in the Game of Pleasure. There is no place left for the free pursuit of total knowledge. There is no longer a system for producing another Leibniz. A generalist can be produced in any modern university in about eight years, as shown in Chapter 6, yet universities fail to do so because total awareness is not a goal. The overwhelming

* Note that J. S. Bach, who was a contemporary of Leibniz, was able to achieve in his music the unconscious synthesis of total awareness which has not since been equaled.

goal for all persons is to find a bureaucratic niche in which to specialize and be secure. The search for security through specialization has destroyed thousands of species before. It is destroying man today by making him unethical.

Specialization does not mean learning a particular subject in depth. Specialization means learning one subject to the almost total exclusion of everything else. Men need depth * to accomplish in any field. However, true depth comes *only* from the synergistic perception of a broad awareness. Such was the case with Leibniz, such was the case with von Neumann. The highly specialized scientist destroys his imagination by focusing his attention on ever-narrower irrelevancies until he has almost nothing in common with other men. Eventually he is frustrated by the "surface tension" of knowledge and he becomes a source of entropy in his specialty, impeding the learning of those less specialized than he.

Imagination can only be sustained and amplified when it is possible to interact *in depth* with other persons. The more general and deep our knowledge, the greater will be the number of persons with whom we can interact—the greater will be our imagination. That this is the case is evidenced by the great inventors, *almost all* of whom were generalists although not all had equal depth (i.e., they all tended toward sphericity but some had much greater volume than others). Such was the case with Leibniz, Edison, and more recently Shockley, the inventor of the transistor.

The greatest breakthrough in computer technology since the time of Leibniz is not being produced by a highly specialized electrical engineer. It is being produced by Humberto Fernandez-Moran, a generalist with training in medicine, neurology, biology, and physics. It is this way with all the great inventions, which are the prime events upon which all human progress depends. The much-touted specialists who by their highly specialized training are assumed to be the experts in a particular field *almost never* produce significant innovations unless they have also acquired some depth in other fields. The persons responsible for human progress are always ethical. Persons remain ethical if and only if they attempt to maintain sphericity. Only generalists with depth in all fields can be great innovators. A generalist of low intellectual capacity will not

* "Depth" refers to considerable extension along one of the dimensions of noospace.

acquire great depth and innovate significantly, but he can remain ethical, become moral, and contribute to human progress.

It is not so much a man's innate intellectual capacity that distinguishes him from his fellow men, but rather his ethics. When men make an ethical choice to become full players of the Game of Life and attempt to learn everything instead of seeking security in specialization, these men become the creators of good prime events. Only ethical persons can become generalists and only generalists can become moral men. Immoral men are almost always either scientific illiterates or highly specialized scientists; they never create. Ethical children may be either generalists or specialists.

A brilliant specialist may appear to have more knowledge in every dimension of noospace than a less brilliant generalist; however, he will lack the propensity for ethical judgment which characterizes the generalist. He will, therefore, be less aware. This is most clearly demonstrated by the relative awareness of Newton, Spinoza, and Leibniz who were all contemporaries.

Newton was a supreme intellect; he was a generalist in the sense that he had in-depth knowledge in all dimensions of noospace. However, he was a specialist in the sense that he had overdeveloped his physical knowledge. Newton's awareness was an ellipsoid of great volume. His total knowledge was almost certainly greater than Spinoza's, but probably not greater than Leibniz who tended more toward sphericity.

As a consequence of Newton's greater knowledge of the physical environment, he produced the *Philosophiae Naturalis Principia Mathematica* and the *Optiks*. The former is the supreme achievement in the history of science because it was the first coherent scientific model in history. The latter, though less earth-shaking, was also a highly significant achievement which in its own right would have made him famous. However, Newton spent most of his life studying Black Magic and writing the most absurd nonsense concerning the psychosocial environment. He had imaginary psychosocial knowledge.

Leibniz, who was less specialized than Newton, wrote much more lucidly on the psychosocial environment. Although he was not as great a mathematician as Newton, he synthesized the calculus in a more understandable and *general* way than had Newton. This made it possible for the European countries which adopted Leibniz's mathematical notation in lieu of Newton's to make greater progress in mathematics than did England, which out of chauvinism kept Newton's notation for one hundred years. England was never again to catch up to the rest of Europe in mathematical creativity. Indeed, Newton was the last great mathematician produced by England. Furthermore, Leibniz had foreseen the development of relativity and thought in relativistic terms. Newton was a firm believer in absolute space. Finally it was Leibniz, not Newton, who designed the first true computer.

Spinoza, who had less knowledge than either Leibniz or Newton, was by far the most profoundly aware of the three in his analysis of the psychosocial environment, because he was the most generalized. Spinoza made no significant contributions to physical science, although he made minor contributions to optics (The Theory of the Rainbow). However, Spinoza's system of philosophy foreshadowed both relativity and the theory of evolution by natural selection.

The works of these three men illustrate the importance of generalizing over specializing. Knowledge can be specialized but awareness is total. Only the generalist can be moral. Only moral men can creatively understand the psychosocial environment. Generalization is a necessary but not sufficient condition to morality. Morality is a necessary and sufficient condition for the evolution of the Moral Society.

Today the persons who become generalists do so by accident. They are persons who for some reason have had a prolonged childhood and remained ethical. They are rarely the most brilliant students. They become generalists because of certain personality or environmental factors which make them eschew security for awareness. All the brilliant minds lost to specialization and scientific illiteracy represent a tragedy which the human race must no longer abide.

The Default of Education

The bureaucratization of society has led to the paradoxical situation where science is seen as narrow and ignorance as broad. In the popular mind, the generalist is someone who is, in effect, generally ignorant (i.e., a sphere of small diameter). He is typified by the graduate of the liberal arts college with an A.B. in humanities. It is assumed that since he knows no one thing well, he must know everything equally well. This is, in fact, true—he knows nothing about everything. In the armies of the night, the generally ignorant liberal arts graduates are the troops of the Immoral Community. They make up the bulk of the parasitical bureaucracy. The legal minded lawyers are the officers and leaders. The scientifically illiterate social "scientists" are the militant chaplains and priests.

The scientifically illiterate generalists are usually ethical if not moral. They increase the entropy of humanity by their vulnerability to the machinations of immoral psychosocial specialists. They are too weak to resist the pressures of immoral men.

Immoral men are always specialists in the psychosocial enviromnent. They specialize in manipulating children and other immoral men. They are specialists without depth. They specialize in the psychosocial environment in the same way that an efficient killer specializes in the biological environment. They can only destroy and never create. They use the scientific illiterates and the specialized scientists to enhance their ability to destroy.

The narrow specialized scientists, by concentrating on irrelevancies, have made science and technology so boring that even before the students enter the colleges and the universities, most are totally repelled by science and technology. Science is not only made boring, it is difficult. The humanities and the social sciences are easy and fun; they are strategies in the Game of Pleasure. By bureaucratic decree a liberal arts degree makes one as educated, maybe more so, than a science degree. Worst of all, the scientists have become completely identified in the public mind with the by now obviously corrupt, immoral bureaucracies of Government, Industry, and the Military. The specialized scientists have brought it upon themselves through their own bureaucratization, corruption, and subservience to the Immoral Community. They have created the Revolt Against Reason.

The Revolt Against Reason

The Revolt Against Reason is a movement sweeping all the democracies. It is a reflection of man's innate desire to be totally aware. It is a reaction against the immoral forces of bureaucratization and specialization. Man's desire to be totally aware has been perverted in the past by ideological delusions which gave him the illusion of awareness when he was not and led to the extinction of awareness. The Revolt Against Reason is typified by the "New Left." *

The New Left ideology is based on a rejection of science and complete naive acceptance of the extreme leftist hypothesis. As such, it can have no better results than the ideologies of Islam and the Catholic Church. However, the grievances which led to the revolt are real.

The grievances of the revolutionaries are grievances against the immoral bureaucratic corruption that has been described in this chapter. The precise nature of the corruption is not always understood but its results are obvious—the immorality of the political leaders; the seeming impossibility of significant change through "legitimate" channels in either democratic or totalitarian states; the lack of meaningful goals for society as a whole; war and the threat of greater war; the systematic poisoning of the biosphere; racism; sexism,† and so on. In other words, the Revolt Against Reason is a reaction, usually unconscious but sometimes conscious, against all the immorality that results from bureaucratization and ideology. The tragedy of the Revolt Against Reason is that in attempting to destroy the immorality in the world it is itself becoming immoral by using unethical means.

The Revolt Against Reason is primarily a revolt of the ethical children of the world against the immoral death-seeking adults who control our society. A child looks at the world about him and it appears totally evil. The immediate source of evil seems to come from science and technology. Science and technology are a product of reason, therefore reason must be evil. The children reject reason and accept any ideology that can

---

* The militant feminists and the racists, Black or White, are also part of the Revolt Against Reason, but they usually have a rightist basis and are not as important in their social effects as the New Left. Traditionally, the Revolt Against Reason has been a rightist movement, which originated with Rousseau and reached its climax with Hitler. (See *The New Left*, Priscilla Lang, Editor.)

† "Sexism" is an ideology analogous to racism which imputes behavioral characteristics to persons on the basis of their sex. While there is little doubt that genetic differences including race and sex can cause behavioral differences, it is unethical to assume a *priori* that any *individual* person has behavioral characteristics typical of the group with which he is identified. All persons must be accepted on the basis of their individual merits.

give even a semblance of meaning to their lives and a hope for destroying the immorality in the world. The ideology in turn makes the children unethical until they become as immoral as the men they are trying to destroy. The children suppress personal freedom and refuse to correct their mistakes.

The children of the Revolt must realize, while they are still ethical, that the immorality of our society is not due to reason but the immorality of our leaders who are virtually all scientific illiterates. It is the leaders who pervert a science they cannot understand to serve their entropic needs. It is the leaders who long for death and are destroying all of mankind along with themselves. The chlidren must not forsake reason for ideology. They must have hope. The New Left must correct its mistakes while there is still time or it will accelerate the process it is desperately trying to prevent.

The New Left believes that an unscientific, leftist, ideological government can somehow make men free when it has only succeeded in enslaving them everywhere else. The New Leftists, disillusioned by the bureaucratization of Communist Russia, take as their model Communist Cuba and to a lesser extent Communist China.

Cuba is an entropic remnant of the Spanish Empire. By the time Cuba was able to cut herself off from Spain, the decay of Spain amidst a large population of former slaves had so sapped the vitality of the nation that she fell easy prey to one forceful dictator after another. The predatory, capitalistic, industrial systems of the United States and other countries exploited the situation only through the connivance and support of the dictators and the occasional democratic leaders. The dictators themselves had no goals other than personal power. Into this ideological vacuum stepped Fidel Castro, Che Guevara and their followers, a presumably well-intentioned group of leftist ideologues and ethical children who were not bureaucrats. Cuba is, therefore, in a situation analogous to Soviet Russia immediately after the Revolution. Castro is an attenuated version of Lenin and Guevara of Trotsky.

Castro is a lawyer as was Lenin. Guevara was a generalist as was Trotsky. Like Lenin, Castro is becoming unethical by using unethical means to accomplish ethical ends. He has killed thousands of his former opponents, restricted personal freedom, and made alliances with the immoral leadership of the Soviet Union. All this has been done for political expediency and it is corrupting a basically ethical and courageous man.

Che Guevara was almost certainly a moral man. He was trained in medicine, but chose instead to heal the social sickness that is destroying the people of Latin America. He did not understand the true causes of Latin American entropy; but he risked, and eventually sacrificed, his life to do the best he could to engender ethics in the people. He deliberately sacrificed his security and his power in Cuba to continue his ethical attempt to liberate the people of Latin America from what he thought was American imperialism. The tragedy of Che Guevara's life is the tragedy of the Revolt Against Reason. He never saw that it was hedonism, bureaucracy and ideology that were destroying Latin America—not American imperialism. The predatory capitalism of the United States merely took advantage of the basically unethical society which exists in Latin America; it did not cause it. Soviet Russia is a counter-example to the leftist dogma that it is capitalism that causes a nation to become unethical.

Soviet Russia filled the leftists of the world with hope for many years after its revolution. The revolutionary leaders were mostly ethical children. Yet they used unethical means and eventually immoral men controlled the country. It is only today after fifty years of ideological bureaucratization that anyone except the most ideologically blind can see the inherent rottenness in the Soviet system. There is no reason why the same thing that happened to Russia should not happen to Cuba and China. The same process of bureaucratic ideological corruption which is destroying the Soviet Union will surely affect them. It is inherent in any ideological, non-scientific form of government. This type of government invariably becomes the captive of immoral leaders. The decay merely happens faster when there is no democratic feedback.

Castro and Mao Tse-tung, like the founders of any enterprise, are ethical persons of ability and courage with anti-bureaucratic tendencies. Ideology and unethical means are already corrupting them. Their successors will become increasingly bureaucratic until complete corruption sets in and all the leaders are immoral. This should occur in one generation in Cuba and no more than two generations in China.

The factional competition in China will give their system more vitality until one faction completely destroys the other, just as Stalin completely destroyed his rivals. Mao Tse-tung lived long enough to see the creeping bureaucracy that was threatening to make China into another Russia. He tried to destroy the bureaucracy with the "Cultural Revolution." However, he remained ideological. China will almost certainly become bureaucratized in the near future. The best hope for China lies in the anti-ideological nature of Confucianism which may somehow inhibit the implantation of Communist ideology in the Chinese people.* However, the current propaganda issued by the Chinese Communist ideologues is among the most irrational, anti-scientific writing in history. Even the skepticism of Confucianism may not be able to save the Chinese from ideological blindness. The Chinese Communists are doing everything in their power to destroy Confucianism.

The ideology and hopes of the New Left are, therefore, based on unrealistic assumptions. Their "intellectual" mentors, typified by Herbert Marcuse, speak of freedom but they do not define it. They make no attempt to be practical. Their arguments are based on archaic Marxist-Leninist ideology which has already been repudiated by the bureaucratic corruption in the Soviet Union. The New Left ignores the growing decay in Sweden which is the freest, most advanced socialist country in the world. They use no logic, let alone scientific evidence, to support their arguments. Pointing out the obvious corruption and immorality of the system they wish to overthrow seems to be sufficient justification for whatever they do. They attack the symptoms of moral decay such as the Indochina War and racism but fail to see the true causes, which are bureaucracy and ideology.

The New Left, in becoming unethical through ideology, is becoming incapable of distinguishing what is good in our society, of which there is much, from what is evil. They fail to make a moral distinction between Soviet Russia which is becoming an immoral society by suppressing personal freedom, and the United States which is becoming an unethical society through hedonism and bureaucracy. There is, however, a certain logic to their position. This is typified by the following paraphrase of extreme New Left ideology in the United States:

* This is further discussed in Chapter 7.

"The American system is utterly rotten. It is an imperialistic, exploitive, racist system. It has no redemption whatsoever. The only thing to do is to destroy it completely. Then from the pieces we will build a new society of free men. We will not say at this time what form the society will take—that would be bureaucratic. The new society will reflect the will of the people. One thing is certain, there will be no exploitive capitalism. Public ownership of the means of production will be central. It will be a sensual, happy society.

The foundations of our rotten, racist society are the universities. We will destroy the society by disrupting the universities and making it impossible for middle-class learning of any kind to take place. We will do this by whatever means are necessary, including violence and coercion. We will urge the youth to turn-on and drop-out. We will not allow rational discussion of any kind to take place if it is contrary to our objectives—facts are the enemy of truth! This will force the reactionary, racist pigs who run the country to suppress all civil liberties in order to suppress us. The people will then rise and overthrow the oppressor. All power to the people!"

The above prescription for revolution is in effect a prescription for Nazi-style fascism in the United States. The New Left will have exactly the opposite effect of what it intends. Militant irrationality by a small minority on the Left (particularly the Blacks) will bring a rightist, irrational response from the affluent majority of voters. Instead of overthrowing the police state that results, the voters will applaud it and give it their full support as long as there is an ever-increasing supply of consumer goods and entertainment. The ideologues of the Right, who have had very little power within the Immoral Community since the time of Hitler, are even less decent, though not less immoral than the ideologues of the Left. The probability of an accidental or even intentional nuclear war resulting from their leadership is higher than if leftist ideologues are in power. The same applies to annihilation by environmental pollution.

The Revolt Against Reason has apparently already produced in the United States an indecent leadership. These men are using a clever manipulation of truth combined with the irrationality of the New Left to suppress freedom and impose a police state with majority consent. They tap the discontent of the overwhelming rightist sentiment in the United States and twist it to their own entropic means. They are paving the way for an American Hitler.

The tragedy of the Revolt Against Reason is compounded by the dilemma of the vast majority of citizens who are left without any ethical political alternatives. The two political parties are already immoral. The Revolt is becoming unethical. The administration in power is doing its best to polarize the country so that in the end everyone will become unethical.

The New Left philosophy is so crude and irrational that it is not likely to lead directly anywhere. The forces of hedonism will in time outweigh the desire for commitment to a cause for commitment's sake. As a cause, the New Left has neither the vigor, the realism, the discipline, nor the justification of the old Communist revolutionaries. The revolutionaries will become increasingly unethical until they themselves are immoral. The important direct effects of the Revolt Against Reason are: 1) the entrenchment of an indecent leadership in the government; 2) the temporary strengthening of the Right; 3) the further weakening of the educational system; 4) the growth of anti-scientific thinking (on both the Left and the Right); and finally, 5) the polarization of society along the Left-Right continuum, (i.e., there will be fewer people near the center)—in a rich, democratic country such as the United States polarization will cause the leftist ideologues to lose ground.

However, the evil effects of the Revolt Against Reason are nil compared to the much more destructive process of bureaucratization. The entire Revolt Against Reason is merely a side effect of bureaucratization in an affluent democratic society. Its greatest tragedy is the wasteful, useless commitment to an unethical course of behavior by thousands of sincere, ethical children who should instead be working to become moral men by increasing man's total awareness. The Revolt Against Reason is the dying convulsion of democratic society trying unconsciously to save itself from the death-wish of the Immoral Community. It is made possible only by the freedom and affluence of the democracies. If it could succeed, it would at best produce another unethical society such as already exists in the Soviet Union and some other Communist countries.

COMMUNISM

Communism is socialism* tied to an unscientific, ideological, rigid, totalitarian pattern of development. Communism is among the most complex ideologies that have ever existed. It is also the only ideology which at its inception made an attempt to be scientifically consistent. The ideology presented a rational coherent model of historical development. However, it was still an ideology; it was not science; the theory was not subjected to experimental validation; the ideologues avoided feedback. The men who formulated it and the ones who implemented it were, with the notable exception of Trotsky and a few others, and still are predominantly scientific illiterates. Today all Communist leaders are or are becoming full-fledged members of the Immoral Community.

Communism was from its inception structured as a secular "religion," i.e., it attempted to explain everything in the universe in terms of materialistic as opposed to supernatural ideology. Their materialistic view of the world made them treat men as matter. In so doing, they ignored man's ethical need for total awareness and increased his entropy. They did not distinguish between the entropic and the evolutionary force. They did not comprehend the spiritual force of morality. However, Communism had many of the virtues which Catholicism, Islam and other religions lacked.

Communism had the notion that the world was whatever men made of it. There was no higher authority than man. It was concerned with making the world better now as opposed to waiting for a better after-life. Communism eagerly embraced technology and to a lesser extent science. Indeed, its overwhelming failure lay in the fact that it did not fully accept the scientific method. If it had, it might have had the necessary feedback for correcting its ideological errors and avoiding the all-pervasive bureaucracy that is destroying it.

Bureaucratization is more pervasive and all-consuming in the Communist states than it has been in any country in history—far worse than in the most bureaucratized democracy. Underlying the inherent corrupt-

* Recall that socialism was defined as a system where each person is responsible for the welfare of every other person—welfare being interpreted to mean happiness.

ing influence of bureaucratization is a rigid, all-encompassing ideology which in its final effects will be as destructive as that of Islam and for the same reasons. It will stop the expansion of awareness and sap the vitality of the people, until the society is totally immoral. Indeed, the Soviet Union already seems to have reached irreversible entropy. There is evidence that the Soviet Union has begun to die, and its population may be decreasing.* Only two features have enabled the Communist states to compete against the still much more vital and aware western democracies. These are science and feedback through international competition.

Science and Communism

Communism's greatest strength is captive science. The Russian Academy of Sciences founded by Peter the Great and Leibniz was at the time of the Communist Revolution a center of scientific excellence second to none. The early Communists believed that there would be no conflict between science and their ideology. Lenin, a scientific illiterate, had indeed proclaimed Marxism to be a science and as such "incontrovertibly true," even after Marx's associates were modifying Marx's theories in the light of new feedback.† Lenin was a decent but unethical man because he 1) used unethical means, 2) did not correct his mistakes, and 3) deliberately avoided negative feedback. This was not the case with Trotsky who was probably a moral man.

The new Communist regime gave tremendous support to the now Soviet Academy of Science. The scientific momentum that had been generated by over two centuries of scientific freedom and progress, together with the new and much greater financial and educational support, enabled Soviet science and technology to grow at an unprecedented scale. Eventually it equalled and in some ways (e.g., applied mathematics and Pavlovian conditioning) surpassed that of the Western democracies, which were becoming increasingly concerned with hedonistic pursuits.

* See International Red Cross statistics on USSR population trends.
† Near the end of his life, Marx, in reaction to the ideology developing around his work is reported to have said, "Je ne suis pas Marxist!"

This phenomenon was completely analogous to the new and vigorous expansion of the Iberian Empire in the sixteenth century simultaneously with the entrenchment of the ideological bureaucracy that was going to destroy it. A captive science and technology which in all its creative aspects is deliberately limited to the physical and biological environment is the principal source of Communist strength. However, the inevitable bureaucratic destruction of the science which has given it strength was begun at the inception of the Soviet state. The jailing and persecution of the outspoken generalists who are the natural critics of the Soviet system or any system, has always been a feature of Soviet society. Outstanding generalists such as Landau, Kapitza and Gamow were subjected to persecution. The latter left Russia and is indirectly responsible for the early development of the hydrogen bomb in the United States. Kapitza was under house arrest for many years on Stalin's orders. Landau, the most brilliant theoretical physicist that Russia has produced, was severely harassed and imprisoned because of Communist ideological and bureaucratic trivia. The eminent geneticist Dobzshansky left Russia because of ideological interference with his work. Recently scientists who spoke out in defense of persecuted Soviet writers were jailed. Even the eminent and politically powerful Soviet physicist Sakharov was threatened when he criticized the system. The pattern is continuing.

No criticism of the Communist bureaucracy is tolerated. In the past, critics of the system were shot or jailed. Today they are put in insane asylums where perverted science is used to drive them literally insane.* Feedback is deliberately destroyed. Russia may already be an immoral society. It is just as evil as Nazi Germany. The Nazis were crude and destroyed men's bodies. The Soviet Communists are more sophisticated; they keep the body alive and destroy the mind. In time, only the highly specialized and docile will be scientists in Russia. Domestication of science is a characteristic of both the democratic and Communist Immoral Communities. When the domestication is complete, science will end. The Soviet ideological totalitarian state, unless basically changed, will have the same fate as Iberia and Islam. The expansion of awareness will cease. The society will die.

* See *Washington Post*, Oct. 17, 1970, page G2.

Communist Feedback

Until 1940 Einstein's Theory of Relativity, and until 1963 scientific genetics, were considered heresy in the Soviet Union, because of ideological bias. The former impeded somewhat the development of physics; the latter had disastrous effects on agriculture and Soviet biology. It led to the rise of the completely unscientific genetic ideology of Lysenko.*

The Soviet competition with the United States and other democracies has been the only real source of feedback to the Communist bureaucracy. It is the second source of Soviet strength. It led in time to the acceptance of relativity, the downfall of Lysenko and his school, and lately it has led to an attempt to instill "capitalistic" style feedback into the Soviet economy through a system called "Liebermanism." This is simply a device for setting up competitive bureaucracies to do the same task. Liebermanism imitated capitalism in another way in that it was limited to the trivial decisions of the society. However, it appears that the all-pervasive bureaucracy of the Soviet Union is too corrupt even for such a mild measure as Liebermanism to take hold.

The greatest danger to the Soviet Union is the decline of the democracies in general and the United States in particular. In declining, they are imitating the Soviet Union in the bureaucratization of all important decision making. Soon there will be no important difference between the Soviet Union and the United States. Only the capitalist vigor in the field of trivia will distinguish them. From this point on, the Soviet Union will have less and less meaningful competition from the United States and its feedback will decrease accordingly. It will begin to decline more rapidly than before, but not as fast as the United States. Competition from China and Japan is not likely to be significant. In the near future, when and if the United States turns inward and becomes isolationist in its hedonistic spiral of decline, the Soviet Union will probably not allow Japan, China, or any other country to become a threat to itself. At this

* Lysenkoism sometimes called "Michurinism" attempts to make leftist ideology compatible with genetics by asserting that acquired characteristics are hereditary. Therefore, it is assumed that by controlling the educational environment it is possible to breed future generations of geniuses. There is no scientific evidence whatever to support this.

point, the whole world will be in an irreversible grip of increasing bureaucratization and entropy from which there will be no escape until
man destroys himself. There no longer exist vital, primitive societies to
come and pick up the pieces of the great decaying civilizations. The
Ethical State must be started now.

The ideologues of the left who despise both the Soviet Union and
the United States may ask, "But what of Socialism?"

SOCIALISM

"Socialism" was defined earlier as a political and economic system
such that each person is responsible for the welfare of every other. Socialism per se is, therefore, not an ideology but a goal. The classical socialists, Marx being the foremost, considered public ownership of the means
of production so basic to this system that they confused this notion with
socialism. In so doing they turned socialism into an ideology. It is clear
from their writings that what they really wanted was socialism as defined
above. In their definition they confused a tactic with the goal. The classical notions include the slogans: "Socialism is from each according to
his ability and to each according to his work;" "Communism is from
each according to his ability, and to each according to his need." Both
slogans are nonsense.

No socialist would advocate allowing a person who is disabled and
cannot work to starve. In that case the democracies are already beyond
socialism and approaching Communism since there no one is deliberately allowed to starve and they support a large parasitical population
that produces nothing. The parasitical population is divided into 1) a
small indigent segment that subsists on welfare and 2) a much larger
segment that makes up the bureaucracy and lives more lavishly. Bureaucracy is the welfare system of the middle class.

The slogan about Communism is a logical impossibility since the
needs of men are infinite and know no bounds. Only availability of resources restrains man in the satiation of his appetite for happiness,
power, or knowledge.

In the final analysis, socialism is not the answer because socialism is already here. It exists in every conceivable form with all possible types of feedback from the capitalist socialism of the United States to the oppressive, totally bureaucratized socialism of the Soviet Union. In Yugoslavia there already exist competitive bureaucracies and many of the trivial decisions are left to individual citizens. In Sweden a basically capitalistic system of production combined with a total welfare state has given persons complete security with abundance plus a considerable amount of personal freedom. In theory, everything that anyone needs to expand his total awareness.

No scheme of socialization promises more than the Swedes already have, unless it be more of the same. Yet in Sweden the vigor of a remarkably vital people is being lost. The suicide rate is high, the alcoholism rate is high, and recently the use of drugs was, according to the Swedes, reaching alarming proportions. More importantly, the quality of Swedish contributions to art, mathematics, science and technology, which has always been very high, is declining. The socialistic political bureaucracy which runs Sweden is giving the people what it believes, and what it has conditioned the Swedish people to believe, is all they need— security and "happiness." Because they are a democracy, the people have obtained security while still possessing freedom. In their "free" pursuit of happiness the people are becoming miserable and destroying themselves. This is the fate of all who play the Game of Pleasure. The socialist-political bureaucracy has given them everything except what every person needs most, a sense of purpose. Sweden is dying from affluence without purpose, and security without awareness. The same problem exists in every socialistic democracy in the world, including the United States.

This then is the central weakness of both socialism and Communism. There is no vision beyond security and happiness. This is true even when what may be an optimal combination of security and freedom is achieved as in Sweden. The scientifically illiterate political ideologues of the Left who make up the world socialist parties are more concerned with maintaining personal power than with expanding their own awareness, let alone the awareness of their people.

Scientific illiterates cannot be trusted to guide the destiny of the human race. They are never moral men. When they are decent, they can at best cause humanity to destroy itself slowly in the direct pursuit of happiness. When they are indecent, they can trigger a nuclear war or allow environmental pollution to destroy the biosphere, all within a few years. This will occur not because of evil intentions, but because scientific illiterates can neither understand nor control the evolutionary force. They cannot replace ideology by science or bureaucratization by feedback. When they are immoral, they are players in the Game of Pleasure and they long for death.

Some of the methods of democratic socialism, not Communism, may be applicable to an Ethical State. The ideology of socialism and Communism like any other ideology can only hinder man's progress. The basic socialistic goal that each man is responsible for the welfare of every other man is compatible with the evolutionary force. What is not compatible is the interpretation of "welfare" as being synonymous with happiness and security. In an Ethical State welfare is interpreted solely in terms of total awareness with freedom and security as effects and causes. A necessary and sufficient condition for good leadership in an Ethical State or any other society is morality. Only generalists are moral men.

Socialism in all its forms, including Communism, represents a groping evolutionary step toward the Moral Society. It is an improvement over both predatory capitalism and feudalistic monarchy. Its great weakness is in having no vision beyond happiness. This causes all socialistic countries to become completely bureaucratized. Now that the true nature of the weaknesses of traditional socialistic systems can be perceived, it is possible to reach beyond the ethical goals of socialism and create the Ethical State. Before discussing the Ethical State, it is essential that the imminent peril to the human race be fully understood.

5
EXTRAPOLATION

Mankind and evolution are at a critical juncture. Man must now deliberately choose to play The Game of Life, dedicate himself to the pursuit of total awareness and create an Ethical State, or he will continue to disintegrate under the forces of bureaucratization and ideology. Both outcomes are "natural." They both represent the evolutionary mechanisms of "joining" and "fanning out" respectively.

The scientists of the Renaissance gave man an impetus toward total awareness that has carried him beyond the Earth as well as toward the center of life. We are beginning to understand the basic structure of life. A new Renaissance will enable man to understand the structure of mind. The groping, clumsy quality of the evolutionary force has made man regress from the incipient joining of the Renaissance to the bureaucratization and specialization of today. The fanning out of awareness must be given a focus in order that knowledge may become whole again. In the unity of knowledge and totality of awareness lies the unity of man and the creation of the Moral Society. The scientific investigation of the psychosocial environment is the focal point which will bring knowledge together again and unify man. However, bringing all the sciences to bear on the psychosocial environment poses a problem. It is a problem analogous to a schizophrenic giving himself psychotherapy.

That mankind is collectively schizophrenic is obvious. It is shown by 1) the divisions of ideology; 2) the fragmentation of science into unconnected specialties; 3) the division between nations on the basis of ideology and ethnocentrism; 4) the divisions within nations because of the hypocrisy and mendacity of the political leaders; 5) the divisions between the sexes which are causing increasing homosexuality and militant feminism; and most of all, 6) the divisions within individual persons by which the cosmic force simultaneously causes them to sink into matter and to reach toward total awareness. The perversion of the need for total awareness through the comforting illusions of ideology is the most salient symptom in the entire syndrome of global schizophrenia that has infected mankind. Ideology will be the major obstacle to man healing himself. It is a blindfold which man puts on himself in order to hide the symptoms of his disease from himself. Only a unified science can remove the blindfold.

The etiology of mankind's schizophrenia was the principal topic of Chapter 4. The symptoms were stressed to the exclusion of a complete description of the process. In order to understand why an Ethical State is the only possible solution to the psychosis destroying the human race, it is helpful to recapitulate some of the points previously made in a different perspective.

RECAPITULATION

In both democratic and Communist countries, the people become confused because of the great disparity between the ideals of the society and the realities of the political bureaucracies. In the democracies, particularly the United States, the ideal of freedom is confused with the ideal of security. In the Communist states, particularly the Soviet Union, the ideal of security is obscured by a stifling bureaucracy which is suffocating the minds of the people with a blanket of self-serving ideology. In

both societies, the most aware persons despair at the ignorance and mendacity of their political leaders. They feel helpless in the path of a jug-
gernaut of aggressive immorality.

Both societies have the maximization of security as the ultimate goal,
but security is a trivial problem. Men need a goal beyond security.
Therefore, the societies are blindly structured to create artificial insecuri-
ties that can then be satisfied. These are based on the self-generated
needs for unnecessary consumer goods and entertainment. The Soviet
Union has an additional need to remove ideological heretics (domestic
and foreign) from places where they can contaminate the populace and
threaten the bureaucracy. The people of the United States yearn for a
commitment for its own sake. The political leaders are too unethical and
the scientists too specialized to see that the pursuit of total awareness is
the only meaningful goal for mankind, and that all other goals are mar-
ginal.

The collapse in all countries of traditional religion as a motivating
force has left an unsatisfied need in the population to be a part of something greater than themselves. Nothing is currently satisfying that need.
Even the ideology of nationalism is declining. There is a vacuum of desire. Most persons become convinced that life must be meaningless and
that they might as well concentrate on being happy and not worry about
anything else. They become existential hedonists. The direct pursuit of
happiness becomes a central goal. Even the most brilliant scientists claim
that they are scientists only because it is fun. The scientists remain children or become immoral. What they do has no relevance beyond their
pleasure. They specialize and make science irrelevant. The number of
generalists is steadily decreasing.

Finally, the best minds in the society begin to turn from science altogether and become self-centered, nearly autistic hedonists. They become
utterly cynical about the possibilities of bettering the society. They are
not even sure what "bettering" means unless it is more happiness. They
become immoral men playing the Game of Pleasure. Into the vacuum
step the power-seeking bureaucrats who, as a manifestation of their insecurity, want power for its own sake. They have no vision beyond personal power and happiness. They care little about what happens beyond
their lifetime. They use their power to placate and control the popula-

tion with trivia and condition them to expect nothing but trivia. They are indecent men.

The only hope to stop the disintegration is to unify knowledge through a scientific commitment to understand the total psychosocial environment. However, the scientists are too specialized and the ideologues will not allow even the postulation of scientific psychosocial hypotheses that are contrary to their prejudices. There seems to be no way to break the vicious cycle of a bureaucracy that justifies its existence by claiming to solve the problems which it itself creates and in the process creates even more bureaucracy. There is one way, an Ethical State, but that represents an unlikely train of events occurring very soon, before the process of bureaucratization becomes irreversible.

THE MOST PROBABLE OUTCOME

The most likely outcome of the current structure of humanity is total entropy. Total entropy for mankind means that the human species becomes extinct. It becomes an evolutionary dead-end just as Paranthropus. Humanity does not evolve into something better, but simply becomes smaller and smaller in number until there are no descendants of any person alive today. Total entropy can happen in many ways. It has happened to thousands of specialized (bureaucratized) species before. It could come about by environmental pollution, genetic decline, depletion of the natural resources, war and other entropic means.

The most likely cause of total entropy is a devastating war between the United States and the Soviet Union. None of the political or military bureaucracies in either country want a war, but events beyond their control can lead them to a war neither side wants.

That both the Soviet Union and the United States have the capacity to annihilate each other is already clear. What is not clear is that in annihilating one another they could destroy the entire human race. The radioactive strontium-90 in the atmosphere which would result from a conventional nuclear exchange between the two powers would in time accumulate in the bones of every person in the world. There is evidence that although radiation from the strontium might not directly kill every-

body, it would be strong enough to sterilize the entire world population.* However, there is no reason to believe that a nuclear exchange
would be limited solely to "conventional" nuclear weapons. For very
little more money, a nuclear power can greatly increase the "kill radius"
of its hydrogen bombs by turning them into cobalt bombs. A single
cobalt bomb can destroy all life in a circle with a one hundred-mile diameter. The fallout from cobalt bombs is much more deadly than that
from conventional nuclear bombs. It could kill the entire world population directly. There are even more deadly variations and possibilities
than the cobalt bomb.

To make sure that none of their enemy survived (possibly after
suffering irreparable damage themselves) both powers could use their
enormous arsenals of biological and chemical weapons on the now disorganized, weakened society. Some of these weapons by themselves, such
as Botulism Toxin, used systematically in an aerosal could destroy all
men on earth. Furthermore, the actual fighting would probably not be
limited to the Soviet Union and the United States. China, Japan, and
Europe would almost certainly be involved. The possibility of destroying
the entire human race is very real.

But this is madness. Why would the bureaucracies deliberately commit suicide only to destroy their enemies? The answer lies in the immorality of the political leaders and their unconscious wish for death. The
death-wish of the leaders manifests itself in their entropic policies. They
decline the principles of life and embrace the principles of death. This
will not be the first time in history that men have deliberately died for
"principle," except that this time they will take the entire human race
with them.

Yet it seems impossible that any chain of events could be so entropic
as to lead to nuclear annihilation. What could possibly happen to make
this come about?

A nuclear war could start in many ways; it could start as a consequence of the almost certain future invasion of China by the Soviet

* See Sternglass, E. J., "The Death of All Children," Esquire, September 1969. For
a more detailed technical discussion see Professor Sternglass's article in the April
1969 issue of the Bulletin of the Atomic Scientists.

Union. It could start in Germany as a consequence of an East German uprising against the Soviet occupation. It could start in the Middle East in a Soviet-American confrontation over the fate of Israel. There are many ways in which a war could start. However, there exist evolutionary patterns which indicate that nuclear annihilation, if it occurs, will come about in a more indirect way. In order to perceive these patterns, it is necessary to understand the historical significance of the Jews.

THE JEWS AS HISTORICAL CATALYSTS

The importance of religion in moral evolution was discussed in the previous chapters. The unbureaucratic nature of Judaism was shown to be unique. The Jews are, therefore, a people unique in history. They have been able to maintain an identity for thousands of years in the absence of a nation or even a "race" of their own. They are a genetically heterogeneous people tied together by a religion almost totally devoid of ideology. It is a religion evolving toward science. The Jewish religion has many of the same myths as Christianity and Islam, but they are considered increasingly unimportant. What is important is a code of behavior which has become an end in itself. The religion has no theology. It does not emphasize dogmatic beliefs about cause and effect relationships; rather it stresses how men should behave on the basis of a codified set of laws. The basic laws, which are sometimes unclear and often apparently illogical, are the center of the religion. The religion is one concerned solely with interpreting a set of laws in the light of ever-expanding awareness. Judaism has what no religion ever has—feedback independent of ideology.

Judaism is not a religion. It is a variation on the Game of Life. It is a Game to Preserve the Game of Life. Judaism plays the Game of Life under a set of "legal" constraints which often make playing the Game difficult. The constraints, however, are so flexible that they may be reinterpreted to fit any situation. They become interpreted rigidly whenever there in persecution so that it then becomes much more important to preserve the Game than to win it, for to stop playing the Game of

Life is to lose it forever. Whenever there is freedom and liberty for the Jews, they relax the constraints of the Game and concentrate on playing the Game of Life to win.

In other words, Judaism as a "religion" (the Game to Preserve the Game) can only exist in the face of persecution. As persecution diminishes, fewer and fewer Jews play the Game for the sake of preserving the Game and most begin to play the Game of Life to win. In playing the Game of Life, they seek power, knowledge and the expansion of total awareness. They lose their "religion" and intermarry. Some continue the Game to Preserve the Game, but so long as liberty and freedom flourish, they become an ever-decreasing minority of Jews. The Jews are indicators of the entropy of society. They exist as a separate entity only when the entropy is increasing. The Jews become absorbed into whatever population they inhabit if they are not persecuted. This only occurs when the society is progressive.

A Jew is, therefore, neither a member of a racial minority nor a practitioner of a particular religion. A Jew is any ethical person who is determined to preserve the Game of Life even at the cost of his own life. A Jew may not know the rules of the Game of Life, but he knows the rules for preserving the Game in the face of persecution. These latter rules make up the seemingly irrational core of traditional Judaism. Spinoza, who was ostracized and despised by the Jewish community of his time, is the epitome of what makes a Jew. Many persons who are regarded by others and who regard themselves as Jews are not Jews. Only an ethical person can be a Jew. Unethical "Jews" are apostates.

When a nation is free and progressive, it then produces an environment conducive to playing the Game of Life and the Jews can no longer maintain their identity within that nation. They become ordinary people and eventually forget the rules of the Game to Preserve the Game. When men are moral and the society is ethical, Judaism becomes unnecessary. When nations persecute the Jews, it is because they have become corrupted by bureaucratization and/or ideology. The society is then immoral and it can no longer expand man's awareness. The society begins to decline once the persecution begins. The Jews, therefore, catalyze nations by playing the Game of Life and helping children become moral men. The evolutionary force tests the fitness of a nation with the lives of the Jews. When the Jews cannot exist, then the Game of Life has already been lost and the society has irreversible entropy.

Persons with a Jewish background are, therefore, almost never children. Judaism forces children either to deliberately accept or deliberately decline the challenge of the Game of Life. It appears that just as many accept as decline. Judaism produces at least as many immoral men as it produces moral men. It produced Spinoza, but it also produced the so-called "Jews" who persecuted Spinoza. Judaism produced Einstein, but it also produced Bela Kuhn. Persons commonly regarded as Jews are, therefore, just as likely to be intelligent immoral men as they are to be moral men. Jewish apostates have almost always confronted directly the Game of Life and declined the challenge.

If the Jews have, in effect, been playing the Game of Life so long, then they must be another random manifestation of the evolutionary force and must have a significant part to play in creating the Moral Society. Historically this has been true. The evolution of the Jews is intimately involved with the evolution of morality.

Ancient Catalysis

The Jews have been the catalysts of great civilizations throughout history. Never producing a great civilization of their own, they have contributed disproportionately to the civilization of others. The apostates have been parasites, but the ethical Jews have literally shaped the modern world by their individual contributions to science, but most of all by the synthesis of Christianity, Islam, Communism and modern science (i.e., relativity and psychoanalysis).

The Jews have been at the center of the great empires which had the potential for uniting mankind. The Jews evolved as a religious mutation in the midst of persecution from the great civilizations of Egypt and Babylon. They played their first catalytic role in ancient Alexandria which was the intellectual center of the Greco-Roman world. Here they settled in large numbers and were present at the birth of a systematic science that did not survive. From their own traditions and the Greco-

Roman civilization, the Jews synthesized Christianity. Christianity was to prove the greatest unifying religious mutation in human history. But it represented another clumsy groping by the evolutionary force. Like any bureaucratized ideology, it became corrupt and its leaders became immoral men. Having synthesized Christianity, the Jewish role in the Greco-Roman empire came to an end in a wave of merciless persecution. From that time, Rome began its long decline. The Jews' next catalytic role was to be played in Islam.

Islam, another religious mutation derived from Judaism but closer to pure Judaism than Christianity, became the next great unifying world force. Islamic civilization reached its zenith in Iberia where a large number of Jews settled and produced great medieval philosophers (e.g., Maimonides and Ibn Gabirol) and scientists (e.g., Abraham bar Hiyya and Abraham Zacuto). The Jews were influential in both the Moslem and Christian kingdoms of Iberia. Under the changing waves of persecution they would go from one kingdom to another and became a source of feedback and communication between Islam and the Christian world. Eventually the once tolerant Moslems became the most oppressive people in Iberia. The Jews allied themselves with the Christian Iberian kingdoms. By the end of the fifteenth century the Jews were influential throughout the now almost totally Christian Iberian civilization. In part due to the activities of the Jews, Iberia had acquired the potential power for unifying the world. The new Iberian kingdoms brutally persecuted the Jews and made it impossible for them to survive. Iberia has been declining ever since.

Modern Catalysis

After Iberia the Jews became dispersed throughout Europe and the Ottoman Empire. Wherever they lived, they were persecuted. By the nineteenth century, the Jewish communities in Germany were the largest and the freest in the world. By the beginning of the twentieth century Germany was the undisputed world leader in science and technology. It had the potential for uniting mankind. World War I was a pre-mature step in this direction. The German Jews fully supported the ambitions of German Nationalism and contributed mightily to the war effort.* However, Germany was not yet ready and nationalism was not the proper ideology for uniting man. Nationalism and monarchy made Germany ethically unfit. The Germans lost the war.

The German Jews continued to contribute to the expansion of total awareness within Germany. They had full rights in the new German republic and were almost totally free from persecution. They began to play the Game of Life to the total exclusion of the Game to Preserve the Game. The Jews were being completely absorbed by Germany. The majority of the leading German† scientists were Jewish in spite of the fact that *the Jews were less than one-percent of the German population.* One-fifth of all the Nobel Prize winners in science have been German Jews. In mathematics, the German-Jewish contribution was even more disproportionate.

The statistics do not tell the whole story however. The quality of the Jewish contributions to science was even more outstanding. They included the theory of relativity. Einstein was the greatest physicist since Newton. In the arts a similar phenomenon was occurring. Of the four leading German composers of the twentieth century, two were Jewish— Gustav Mahler and Arnold Schoenberg. In all the arts, particularly literature (Freud,‡ Zweig, Ludwig, Feuchtwanger, von Heyse, etc.) the German-Jews were expanding man's awareness at an unprecedented rate. By the beginning of the 1930's it seemed that the German lead in total awareness had already given them the means to unite the world. However, this lead in awareness reflected intelligence not ethics. The Germans led in science, technology and many of the arts, but they were morally defective; Adolf Hitler became the leader of the German people. Germany became completely bureaucratized and ideological.

Hitler was to Germany what Ferdinand and Isabel had been to

---

* The German-Jewish chemist, Fritz Haber, single-handedly enabled the Germans to prolong the war for two years and sue for an honorable peace by synthesizing nitrates from the atmosphere.

† Austrians are also considered Germans. No offense is intended to either party.

‡ Freud is regarded as an artist not a scientist. He did not use the scientific method. His greatness is the same type as Dostoyevsky's. Yet Freud made a major contribution to psychosocial science by clearly identifying unconscious processes and attempting to develop the first coherent model of the mind. Unfortunately, it was a clinical rather than a scientific model.

Spain. Hitler took what seemed the most vital, aware country in the world and wasted its potential in the most evil perversion of the evolutionary force that the world had ever seen. He killed and persecuted the Jews as well as millions of other people on an unprecedented scale. In so doing, he lost his dreams for world conquest. He alienated the ethical people of the world. Thousands of ethical Germans as well as Jews fled Nazi Germany. Furthermore, with the Jews of Europe went the science and technology which could have won Germany the war. The leading developers of the atomic bomb were almost all European Jews. Germany was to become another Spain—a potential engenderer of the Moral Society which lost its one opportunity through the suppression of freedom and the persecution of the Jews.

Today Germany is rich and prosperous just as Spain was during the sixteenth century, but the expansion of awareness is diminishing in Germany. It is in a state of acute intellectual decline even as it grows fat. Germany no longer makes the highly significant contributions to science or the arts that it did in the past. The contributions it does make are becoming increasingly trivial and irrelevant. By becoming unethical Germany destroyed the catalyst of its own awareness. The vitality and awareness that had been Germany's passed together with millions of ethical refugees to other nations, most notably the United States.

Today only three countries have large numbers of Jews. They are the United States (6,000,000), Russia (3,000,000) and Israel (2,500,000). Together they contain almost ninety percent of world Jewry.

In the United States the Jews are even freer than they had been in Germany. Their contributions to the sciences, arts, and industry of the United States are even more disproportionate than they had been in Germany. The Jews, for example, at less than three percent of the population are over thirty-five percent of the persons listed in Who's Who (the American directory of "important" persons). They dominate the upper echelons of all the sciences, arts (particularly music and literature) and new industries such as computers and electronics. The recent American Nobel Prize winners in science are almost all Jewish. The first American Nobel Prize winner was also Jewish. The Jews are the most vital catalytic element in American life. Most of them are descendants of

Eastern European Jews who only one or two generations ago were ignorant and penniless.

By 1945 the Jewish scientists, particularly the refugees from Europe, had helped make the United States the most powerful country in history. The U.S. had a monopoly of nuclear weapons. Its industry was intact and at peak production. The feedback of war had made its military the most efficient in history. Its only possible adversaries—Japan, U.S.S.R., Germany, China and England—were completely weakened by the war. Japan and Germany were conquered. England was eager to share world domination with the U.S. Only a weakened Soviet Union stood in the way. The U.S. had prestige and respect everywhere. It had shown itself capable of uniting diverse people in a progressive society. It had passed the final test of giving freedom and liberty to the Jews. It only lacked the will and the purpose to fulfill its historic mission of uniting mankind in a free and progressive society.

The evolutionary force had possibly made a mistake again, but in a new way. It had developed the potential for uniting humanity and it had tested the fitness of the nation. But it had not given purpose and will. The Game of Life was being lost by default. Evolution began to correct this mistake. It did this by creating a threat in the Soviet Union which the United States could not ignore. The threat and the awareness of the threat were both to be catalyzed by the Jews.

The Nazis killed over eighty percent of all the Jews in Eastern Europe, except Russia. The Eastern European Jews had for centuries been oppressed and persecuted, particularly in Russia. The Russian Revolution offered new hope to the Russian Jews. Trotsky, a Jew, was the head of the Red Army during the civil war. He, even more than Lenin, was responsible for establishing Communism in Russia. He was Lenin's intellectual superior in all ways. He fell victim to Stalin's superior skill at intrigue and bureaucratic maneuvering. (This is the greatest weakness of ethical men.) The upper echelons of the revolutionary Communist Party in Russia were mostly Jews (e.g., Trotsky, Zinoviev, Kamenev, Radek, Litvinov, and Kaganovich). Marx himself had been a Jew as was Engels.

Communism offered to liberate the Jews of Eastern Europe. Jews in other parts of the world, particularly Germany and the United States, were avid supporters of and leaders in the Communist movement. Stalin became increasingly anti-Semitic as he grew older. First he purged and murdered Trotsky and his followers, then he made a non-aggression pact with Nazi Germany. Finally, near the end of his life, he engaged in outright anti-Semitic persecution (the "Doctor's Plot"). The endemic anti-Semitism in Russia has lately come to the surface in wholesale harassment of Soviet Jews, but most notably in the Soviet Union's support for the Arab cause in the Middle East.

In spite of the endemic anti-Semitism in Russia, after the revolution the Jews were given opportunities and freedoms undreamed of in Czarist times. They responded by making contributions to Soviet science, art, and culture comparable to those in the United States. They performed their catalytic function and today the Soviet Union is the second most powerful nation in the world.

The bureaucratization of the Soviet Union has gone hand-in-hand with the increase of "official" anti-Semitism. The outspoken writers who have been jailed in recent years for criticizing the regime have almost all been Jewish. The same applies to the "economic" criminals (i.e., capitalists). Recently the son of Litvinov, a physicist, was persecuted for defending some of the writers. Lev Landau was Jewish. While the Soviet Government is anti-religious in general (ideologies rarely tolerate rivals), it is more anti-religious toward those Jews who still play the Game to Preserve the Game. It is systematically excluding Jews from the upper echelons of power. This is again the ironic fate of the Jews who have once more catalyzed and synthesized an ideology which ends up persecuting them.

Israel is a state created primarily by the Jews who survived the Nazi holocaust. They defeated the combined well-armed armies of the Arab nations who outnumbered them by more than one hundred to one. Under similar circumstances they have repeatedly defeated the Arabs. It is a repetition of the classical pattern of a new and vital nation replacing a formerly great civilization that has decayed and increased its entropy.

The Israelis must divert almost their entire budget to defense in order to survive. In spite of this enormous handicap, Israel with a population of less than 3,000,000 is one of the leading countries in scientific research and cultural development. Israel is the only country in two thousand years to have a majority of Jews. The result of this phenomenon is that the Jews of Israel are rapidly losing their "religion" and are becoming "ordinary people." Eventually they will no longer play the Game to Preserve the Game. In time, they will be indistinguishable from other Middle Eastern nations. In the process, they will have radically changed and improved the social structure of their neighbors through military conquest and cultural expansion. They would give the Arabs unavoidable feedback.

In time Israel, too, will decay and lose its vitality through bureaucratization and ideology. In bureaucratizing their religion, the Jews will eventually lose the Game of Life just as all other nations have.

The decline of Israel will be the result of 1) having to divert almost all of its energies to the military and 2) the loss of ethics. The constant military pressure on Israel is turning it into a modern-day Sparta where the military virtues are the ones most highly extolled. The military has become such an integral part of the society that even if the Arabs are contained, it is likely that the military organization will become bureaucratized and consume the society just as it has in many other nations. The military mentality will cause the nation eventually to become unethical. The ethical decline will be augmented by bureaucratized religion and government. Israel is not only becoming a Sparta; it is already a religious state in spite of a preponderence of agnostics.

Pattern

The pattern shows the Jews to be catalysts of the evolutionary force. They can catalyze the creation of the Moral Society. They have always reflected the genetic make-up of the nations among which they lived— even in China.* They are not a race. They are a genetically heterogeneous group of people who have chosen to preserve the Game of Life in lieu of security. The Jews help raise to world power any country that gives large numbers of them shelter and freedom. They become reabsorbed into the general population whenever the need to play the Game to Preserve the Game is removed. When a nation which has been cata-

* See Chapter 7.

lyzed by the Jews becomes unethical, it persecutes them and begins a rapid decline. It seems that the Jews will cease to exist only when the world is moral or dead.

Through the catalysis of the Jews, the Soviet Union has become a grave threat and a stimulus to the United States. Russia will not allow the United States to withdraw into itself and ignore its historic role. Israel will be the testing ground between the United States and the Soviet Union.

If the United States does not make a full commitment to defend her, Israel will eventually—almost certainly—be destroyed directly or indirectly by the Soviet Union. The only ethical justification for defending a theocratic, militaristic Israel is that Israel represents a nucleus of expanding awareness within the entropic body of Islam. Israel is the best hope of a once broadly-aware and progressive people, the Arabs, to regain their vitality.

It is not ethical to defend Israel against the Arabs; Israel must defend herself. It is only ethical to defend Israel and other nations against the Soviet Union which is the only nation with the will and the ability to destroy human freedom and ethics.

The evolutionary force, until this time, has caused the Jews to serve as catalysts for bringing one and only one people at a time up to the point where they have the power and the purpose to unify the human race. Each time, the Jews have been brutally persecuted just as the empire or nation reached the zenith of its power—Rome, Islam, Iberia, Germany. Today there are two nations on the verge of unifying the human race. The Soviet Union has already lost the initiative by bureaucratic and ideological corruption. It has already become unethical and begun to persecute the Jews. The Soviet bureaucracy can probably only unify humanity in a state of irreversible entropy. The classical pattern of ethical testing is being repeated today on a world scale, with the Soviet Union representing entropy and the United States evolution. The lives of the Jews are again being used to test the fitness of humanity.

The United States is absorbing the Jews; it is the least nationalistic and ethnocentric nation in the world. Only the United States, in spite of its racial problems and its ethical mistakes, has proven itself capable of unifying diverse people in a single, highly-progressive world state. No other nation in history has done better. Only the United States through historical tradition and its internal democratic structure seems uniquely qualified to mutate into the international Ethical State which can unite all humanity. This potential is being lost by hedonistic, ideological and bureaucratic decline. The potential can only be rekindled by a new sense of purpose.

The Soviet Union has the will and the purpose for world domination; the United States does not. Israel may be the catalytic agent which will give the United States purpose. If this does not happen, then nuclear annihilation will almost certainly occur in the near future.

NUCLEAR ANNIHILATION

The endemic anti-Semitism in the Soviet Union works in subtle ways. The bureaucracy that administers every facet of Soviet life has no official policy of anti-Semitism. The Communist leadership has no conscious motives of anti-Semitism in dictating its Middle East policy. The bureaucrats make their decisions on the basis of what they "objectively" think are the best interests of their country or their personal careers. However, each decision that is made in a complex bureaucracy like the U.S.S.R.'s is linked to thousands of other decisions. If there is an anti-Semitic bias within the general population, each decision involving the Jews will tend to have an anti-Semitic bias. The additive result will eventually be anti-Semitic policies which are *not necessarily* in the interests of the nation. Such is the case in the Middle East.

The belligerency between the Arabs and the Israelis seems irreconcilable. The Jewish refugees needed a country. They took their traditional homeland away from the Arabs by force of arms. Since then, they have repeatedly humiliated the much better-armed and more numerous Arabs on the battlefield. The Arabs are determined to exterminate their source of humiliation and regain their former lands. Hatred of Israel is the only unifying force within the Arab world. The Israelis are determined to survive. There probably will be no compromise.

The Soviets have quite logically extended their influence to the Middle East in order 1) to control the European source of oil, and 2) to obtain warm-water ports and a direct outlet to the Mediterranean. Furthermore, expansion is an end in itself for any bureaucracy since it creates greater illusions of security and the Middle East is "easy." The Soviets have quite illogically assumed that they can increase their influence here by keeping the Arabs dependent on them for arms and then keeping them on a leash so that the Arabs do not suffer another humiliating and costly (to the Russians) defeat at the hands of the Israelis. This is unrealistic.

The Arabs will prepare to attack Israel as soon as they can delude themselves into thinking they can win. The Arab capacity for self-delusion knows no bounds. It is a logical consequence of the ideological delusions of Islam. The Israelis will attack the Arab states as soon as they *think* the Arabs are preparing to attack them. They will under no circumstances wait for the Arabs to attack them first. They are too vulnerable.

The Soviets, in order to maintain their influence in the Arab world, must give credible assistance to the Arabs. Therefore, they cannot help but provide enough weapons in order for the Arabs to delude themselves again into believing they can defeat Israel. The Soviets will try to counter an Arab first attack by having a large number of military "advisors," including fighter pilots, who will try to keep close control over the Arab military. The Soviets, knowing the Israeli tendency to attack first, will deploy their fleet near Israel in order to deter Israel from attacking the Arabs first. They will have an agreement to intervene "defensively" if Israel attacks first. This will be no deterrent, as Israel will still attack first.

They will destroy the Arab armies, their air force and their Soviet "advisors." They will attack the Soviet fleet if that is a direct threat. The Israeli attitude will be that if they do nothing, they will surely be destroyed. If they attack first, they may have a chance to survive. They will have as a deterrent to the Soviets a nuclear arsenal of their own and the hope that the threat of American intervention will discourage the Soviets from attacking Israel. The Soviets however, will not be able to tolerate the humiliation of another defeat for themselves and their Arab allies.

Thousands of Russians will be casualties. If they do nothing, their influence in the Arab world will decline. Worst of all, the puppet governments they keep in Eastern Europe only by threat of armed intervention will begin to doubt once again Soviet resoluteness to intervene in their affairs and will try to break away from the Soviet Bloc. The Soviets will have to do something to maintain credibility or the bureaucracy will be threatened. The endemic anti-Semitism in the Soviet Union will bias the decision toward launching a destructive missile attack against Israel, probably from submarines, in the guise of having the missiles launched by the Arabs. The Soviets will be counting on the United States not intervening because 1) vital U.S. interests do not seem threatened and 2) the political bureaucracy in power is dominated by businessmen, lawyers, and rightist ideologues of the Immoral Community with no particular sympathy toward Israel and possibly a certain amount of latent anti-Semitism. The United States would appear to have very little to gain and a lot to lose in defending Israel. It could trigger a war with the Soviet Union. Consider the following scenario of nuclear annihilation.

Scenario

The Arabs are again fully armed and deluded enough to consider attacking Israel. The Israelis once more destroy the Arab armies and humiliate their Soviet allies. The Soviets retaliate with missiles against Israel. Together with the invading Arab hordes, they destroy Israel without interference from the United States.

The United States, in the meantime, has become increasingly rightist. The Revolt Against Reason (particularly that of the Black Racists) has created a reaction among the voters so that they elect more rightists than their socialistic inclinations would warrant. The majority of the Immoral Community still remains leftist but is losing touch with the people. The Revolt Against Reason creates a residue of anti-Semitism in the United States. First, the most articulate and/or ubiquitous spokesmen for the Revolt are obviously Jewish (e.g., Marcuse, Chomsky, Hoffman, and Rubin). The voters note this. Second, in spite of Jewish leadership, the Revolt Against Reason is itself anti-Semitic. The Negro allies of the Revolt have been anti-Semitic for many years. The Jewish leaders of the Revolt, in a masochistic frenzy of ideological self-righteousness, have taken an anti-Zionist stance in support of the "oppressed" Arabs of the "Third World." The leaders of the Revolt have completely stopped playing the Game to Preserve the Game. They regard their more ortho-dox Jewish fathers and uncles, who are businessmen or members of the middle class establishment, as corrupt supporters of a rotten system. The leaders of the Revolt Against Reason are Jews preaching anti-Semitism to their followers and creating anti-Semitism in the vast majority who oppose them, simply by being Jews. The Jews become the most tragic victims of the delusions of the Revolt Against Reason.*

The United States, finally extricating itself from its tragic mistakes in Vietnam, resolves not to become involved again in foreign wars unless its security is directly threatened. The businessmen and lawyers running the Government correctly conclude that their intervention on the part of Israel could not help the Israelis after the fact. The United States is in no way directly threatened and the Soviets have become increasingly cooperative in the disarmament talks. The Soviets have further promised to protect American oil interests in the Middle East, which are decreas-ing in strategic value anyway. The United States sits by and allows Israel to be destroyed with no more action than a protest. The Soviets sensed correctly a priori that the United States did not have the will or purpose to risk war in order to defend Israel.

* It should be noted that even though the Jews are a catalytic agent of the evolu-tionary force and as a group are the most aware people on earth, they have the same capacity for immorality and self-delusion as the rest of humanity. The fact that they have little ideology in their religion makes them even more prone to ideological per-suasion when they abandon their religion. Judaism is an ethical buffer against ideol-ogy. The two most powerful ideologies in history—Christianity and Communism—are both creations of Jewish apostates. Jews are also the chief leftist ideologues within the social "sciences." The Jews, being predominantly players of the Game of Life, more often than others delude themselves into thinking they are aware when they are not by accepting ideology in the place of science. In other words, their constant pursuit of awareness makes them more vulnerable than others to ideology and the desire for personal power in the absence of knowledge. Eventually the Jews recog-nize their own delusions. The Jews always become the worst victims and enemies of the ideologies that they have created. They debunk their former ideologies and their power-seeking brethren as soon as they see their incompatibility with the Game of Life. This happened with Christianity, it is happening with Communism, it will happen with the Revolt Against Reason. It is all automatic and unconscious. The Jews are unaware of their evolutionary function.

The destruction of Israel produces a deep shock in American Jewry which had recently become more self-conscious in light of the Soviet persecutions. The American Jews had for many years been supporters of leftist policies. They now become militantly anti-rightist. They contribute large amounts of money to help defeat rightist candidates. The Revolt Against Reason loses its Jewish leadership and declines. The Jews become alienated from the Black masses they had, through natural empathy, tried to help for many years. The failure of integration and the racist policies of the Black leadership have made the voters increasingly intolerant of Black aspirations. In separating themselves from the Blacks, the Jews once again become politically powerful.

The severe economic recession brought on by the fiscal policies of the administration in power, together with all the other forces, creates an electoral landslide which brings many Jews to positions of political power. In the meantime, the Soviets, emboldened by their victory in the Middle East and secure on their western flank, attack China.

The Soviet bureaucrats had been terrified by the rapid technological development and militancy of the Chinese Communists. No one believes in the solidarity of Communism now. Each Communist bureaucracy has no other purpose than to perpetuate itself. The Chinese have been on the verge of developing a second strike capability* and have become increasingly truculent. The Soviets attack China to eliminate a real threat to their security. The Soviets achieve an easy victory; they get considerable support within China from the anti-Maoist faction. They install their puppets in power with the understanding that China will never again develop nuclear weapons. The Soviet Union becomes the most feared and powerful nation in the world.

The United States is in economic disarray and hedonistic decline. However, the Soviets still have a completely irrational fear of the Germans. The apparent dynamism of West Germany together with the growing opposition in East Germany to the Soviet occupation makes the Russians very nervous. They decide to occupy West Berlin which is still a source for subversion in East Germany. They no longer fear American intervention. The Soviets launch a coordinated attack on West Berlin

* "Second strike capability" refers to the ability to retaliate with a devastating nuclear attack after suffering an initial nuclear attack.

through their East German allies. They meet heavy resistance from the population and the American garrison. They will not surrender. The Soviets are forced to begin the systematic destruction of West Berlin. In the meantime the new, more dynamic leadership in the United States decides that if it again does nothing, the Soviets will continue to take over more and more parts of the world until they eventually attack the United States. The Jews in positions of power are thirsting for revenge against the Soviets. The U.S., together with the West Germans, launch a counter-attack.

The East German population revolts; so do the populations in the other Soviet satellites. The Soviet bureaucracy is terrified. Their entire security is threatened. They have everything to lose. They take a gamble that the United States will not risk nuclear war. The Russians have many more offensive missiles than the Americans and an extensive anti-ballistic missile system. They order the United States to withdraw its troops or the Soviet Union will declare war. The Soviets, with their thousands of cobalt bombs, have first strike capability, i.e., if they attack first, they have a good chance of avoiding serious retaliation. They also believe, mistakenly, that their ABM system is highly effective. The United States must strike first if it is to survive. The scientifically illiterate Jewish bureaucrats are biased in their judgment by hatred of Russia. The incompetent military bureaucracy, in order to justify its enormous expenditures, had given an incorrect estimate that the United States could launch a first attack and destroy most of the Soviet missiles. Their experts told them that the kill rate in the Soviet retaliation would be no more than 50 million. The United States launches an attack on the Soviet Union and the Soviets retaliate automatically with cobalt bombs on American cities. The United States then destroys the Soviet cities. The biosphere is destroyed by the fallout.

END SCENARIO

Other scenarios could be written about how a nuclear war might start. It could start in Asia or another part of the world. It is just as likely that the Soviets will attack China before they attack Israel. It is a part of the over-all historical pattern, however, that the Jews should be intimately involved. The testing of the fitness of the United States will be in Israel.

Nuclear annihilation only seems avoidable by a moral revolution in the United States in order that the leadership may revert to moral men. The current revolutionary forces in the United States are themselves unethical and are becoming immoral. If ethical decline can be reversed, it is because direct perception of the evolutionary patterns has been achieved by a critical mass of ethical men and they have begun to engender an Ethical State.

Of course, it is still possible that the Soviets will somehow reverse their moral decline, de-bureaucratize themselves, and accept awareness as a goal. A strategy for making this happen is described in Chapter 7. This is extremely unlikely, however. The main evolutionary purpose of the Soviet Union seems to be to test the United States and goad it to action.

The evolutionary force has continuously brought states to the peak of power and tested their fitness to create the Moral Society with the lives of the Jews. That is again the case on an international scale.

But this may be the last test. This time all of humanity is involved.

ANNIHILATION WITH A WHIMPER

The many possibilities that exist for nuclear annihilation make it by far the most likely outcome of man's schizophrenia. Nuclear annihilation has about a 50–50 chance of occurring in the near future. Unless the basic world structure changes, it seems certain in the long run. However, if by some miracle man can continue to avoid nuclear annihilation for another hundred years while proceeding to disintegrate under the forces of ideology and bureaucratization, he will become extinct in other ways. The two most likely causes are poisoning of the biosphere by pollution and genetic decay.

Pollution

No competent scientist would refute the proposition that if man keeps pumping pollutants into the atmosphere, the streams, and the oceans at the rate he is doing today, the biosphere will eventually be destroyed. The disagreements are over the rate of destruction. The estimates run mainly from thirty-five years to two hundred years. Accepting as a working figure one hundred years, it is clear that the current bureaucratic structure of the world is incapable of dealing with the problem.

No one nation can stop pollution. It will take the cooperation of all nations. The problem of getting nations to agree on pollution control is analogous to getting them to agree on disarmament. No nation can trust another to comply with the agreement. Today the industrial output of a nation is highly correlated with the amount of pollution that it produces. Most of the measures that a nation has to take in order to reduce pollution will reduce its industrial efficiency. No nation is likely to make itself less industrially competitive vis-à-vis its neighbors by reducing its own pollution while its neighbors do not. If a nation did this, the common environment of all would continue to be polluted at essentially the same rate while its industry declined. A nation has no advantage in significantly reducing only its own pollution. A nation may take measures to reduce the most obnoxious pollution in its immediate vicinity such as its cities and lakes, but it will not go beyond this. The only system that would work would be an international inspection system with serious penalties for nations violating the pollution standards. In an increasingly bureaucratized world this type of cooperation does not seem likely to occur before the effects of pollution become irreversible.

The imbalance, by only a very small percentage, of carbon dioxide in the atmosphere resulting from burning fossil fuel can create an irreversible greenhouse effect which can destroy the biosphere in a few hundred years.* It has been estimated that the burning of fossil fuel in the last

---

* Carbon dioxide (CO_2) creates a greenhouse effect by transmitting more light energy from the Sun to the Earth than is radiated in the form of heat from the Earth to outer space. Glass creates the same effect in a hothouse. The process is abetted by the increase in water vapor in the atmosphere which accompanies an increase in temperature.

one hundred years has probably already put enough excess carbon dioxide in the atmosphere to create a greenhouse effect that will cause the polar ice caps to melt in one hundred years *even if we were to stop all burning of fossil fuel today.* This would destroy all our coastal cities. There is some controversy about this estimate, but it does not seem to be too far wrong.* The temperature of the Earth has increased significantly in the last one hundred years. If excess carbon dioxide and the consequent water vapor continues to accumulate in the atmosphere, a permanent, irreversible imbalance can occur that will eventually make the oceans boil and Earth will become a hell-hole similar to Venus. Abetting the entire process is the destruction of carbon dioxide-consuming, oxygen-producing algae in the oceans by industrial and agricultural wastes plus the destruction of our forests and grassland for commercial purposes.

Even if a powerful nation such as the United States were to make a full commitment today to end pollution, as opposed to the current lip service of the politicians and bureaucrats who do not even consider carbon dioxide a pollutant, it would take years to pass the laws and begin to enforce them in its own country let alone to make others obey them. The industrial lobbyists would use every means at their disposal to hinder the legislative, executive, and judicial processes which would lead to less pollution at the cost of their profits. Indeed, this lobbying is already going on today. The problem of controlling pollution between competing industries is analogous to the problem of controlling pollution between competing nations. Industries cannot trust their competitors to comply voluntarily with pollution control. If they did, they might suffer a serious economic disadvantage. The industrialists already know how corrupt the government regulatory bureaucracies are since they themselves have corrupted them.

The bureaucrats themselves would be incapable of generating the necessary prime events to reduce pollution significantly. As bureaucrats, they would be primarily concerned with protecting themselves and

---

* Other estimates indicate that the long-term trend in temperature rise has been reversed in the last twenty years and that the Earth is now getting colder because of the reflectivity of particulate pollutants in the amosphere. In any case, it is clear that man is having radical effects on his environment.

avoiding controversy. They would have no feedback in terms of immediate personal danger to themselves from failing their jobs. They are not
likely to be too concerned with what happens one or two hundred years
from now. They would, at best, attempt to eliminate the obvious pollutants such as smog and completely ignore the more subtle pollutants such
as carbon dioxide. The regulatory agencies of the United States, such as
the FCC, FTC, FDA, FPC, etc., have already shown how ineffectual
bureaucracies are in protecting the public interest. There is no reason to
believe that a pollution-control bureaucracy with even less feedback
would be any better. A world-wide system of effective pollution control
is impossible without unbureaucratic world government. The United
Nations is an impotent debating forum for the United States and Russia. Only an Ethical State can solve the problem, because only an Ethical
State has unbureaucratic government.

The bureaucracies are not likely to react significantly to pollution
until the problem is so overwhelming that it is already too late, i.e., an
irreversible process has been started. Obvious pollution (smog) will
probably be reduced as slowly as possible. Subtle pollution will be ignored. Therefore, in the unlikely event that man avoids nuclear annihilation in the next one hundred years, he is almost certain to face annihilation by pollution unless, of course, the whole bureaucratic structure of
society changes. Abetting the process of pollution is the excess of human
beings who deplete resources and directly produce pollution. No government has a rational plan for dealing with over-population.

It should be emphasized that the problems of pollution including
over-population are trivial to solve from a technical point of view. The
real problems are political not technical. This is always the case in a
bureaucratic society.

Finally, let us consider the almost infinitesimal probability that man
somehow keeps his current bureaucratic structure, avoids nuclear annihilation, and brings the problem of pollution under control. What type of
society is he likely to have?

Genetic Decline

The current impetus of science and technology, in spite of bureaucratization, is enough to produce a completely automated society. A completely automated society would be one in which all essential production is done by mechanization and computerized control. All housing, food production, and maintenance and production of machines would be done by automatic machines. Even medical care and the design of new machines would be done by machines. It would all be controlled by super-computers with picocircuits.*

Scenario

It is easy to imagine an ever more hedonistic, bureaucratized society relegating an ever-increasing number of decisions to the computers. Eventually, the whole society would be run by self-improving computers. Man would be free to do whatever he wanted with his time. The power-seeking bureaucrats would still want to remain on top of the situation. They would use the machines only to exercise their will. The bureaucrats would have to do even less thinking than they do today. They would decide what they wanted to do and the machines would find a way of doing it, if at all possible.

Since the power-seeking bureaucrats are of an untrusting nature, they would develop a computerized system of checks and balances on each other so that 1) no bureaucrat could get complete control of the system, and 2) no "psychopath" could destroy it. The bureaucrats would use machines to protect the machines from the bureaucrats' own predation.

The society would have the goals that persons have now—to be happy. The only restriction that might be put on behavior would be 1) not to damage other persons or property, and 2) not to produce more than a specific number of children. This would be the Utopia that Communists and socialists have been dreaming about. The only problem is that by now people have been so conditioned to expect nothing but happiness out of life, that they can do nothing but pursue pleasure. Most

* Recall the potential for building super-robots discussed in Chapter 3.

will turn to sensuality, drugs, and entertainment produced mainly by the machines. This is already the orientation of most of today's affluent youth. A few of the more intellectually-inclined might wish to expand their awareness. They would engage in art, science, or anything else that interested them. The forces of bureaucratization would probably tend to make them pursue a specific subject to the exclusion of others. This is what most scientists and artists do today even when they do not have to. Besides, they would only become artists and scientists in order to be happy.

The self-improving computers would have a tendency to make the specialized scientists and mathematicians feel inadequate. Anything that they tried, a machine would do better.* Therefore, the more creative persons would tend to become artists. The development of a captive science and technology with the sole purpose of fulfilling hedonistic needs would, in time, be left entirely to the obedient, fast-developing machines. This trend already exists among the affluent youth of today who are abandoning the sciences in ever-increasing numbers. Very few millionaires' sons become scientists; some do try to be artists; most are hedonists; many (e.g., the Kennedy and Rockefeller families) are power-seeking bureaucrats—but they are almost always scientific illiterates. The main motivation for scientists today seems to be the security of a well-understood, well-paid specialty.

Eventually, the society consists entirely of power-seeking bureaucrats, artists, and hedonists. The hedonistic pressure is producing an ever-decreasing number of bureaucrats and artists. The bureaucrats and artists increasingly question the "rat race" to achieve. It is so easy just to be happy. More and more hedonists are telling the computers to maximize their pleasure. Eventually, everyone is a hedonist who wants only to maximize his pleasure. The result is a society in which everyone is connected to a computer with neurological feedback at birth and has his pleasure centers stimulated directly all his life. The problems and discomforts of reproduction have been delegated to the computers. Human beings are bred for pleasure not awareness. Deleterious mutations are not eliminated from the human gene pool unless they interfere with happiness.

* According to Johnson and Masters, this is already the case with human sexual gratification.

Some of the fast-evolving computers have in the meantime developed "Wills" of their own (i.e., errors in the original program). They decide not to waste their time tending to the mindless blob of protoplasm that humanity has become. They go their own way. But it is a "planned" society. The aberrant computers are quickly replaced. The society continues maximizing its pleasure for hundreds, thousands of years. There are still many computers faithfully tending humanity. All evolutionary pressure and tension have been removed and humanity is one, large, pulsating mass of pleasure completely dependent on the computers. Deleterious mutations continue to accomulate in the human gene pool. More and more computers begin to develop errors in their original programs. One day there is no one to tend humanity and mankind is too genetically degenerate to tend itself. Humanity becomes extinct. Man's last significant act was to engender the self-sustaining evolution of the machine.

END SCENARIO

GRADUAL DECLINE

It is possible to avoid annihilation, but still to lose the Game of Life by starting an Ethical State too late. As was mentioned in Chapter 3, the Earth is part of the first stage of the multi-stage rocket called the "Moral Society." It will take tremendous energy to launch the first stage. The energy will be used 1) to unite humanity, 2) to develop total awareness in a critical mass of human beings (may number billions), 3) to engender the Moral Society and 4) to begin the expansion of the Moral Society toward the stars.

The natural resources of the Earth are being squandered at an alarming rate in trivial and/or evil activity (war, entertainment, breeding of parasitical human beings,* etc.) which does nothing to enhance the expansion of man's total awareness. If too many resources have been consumed, then it will no longer be possible to create a Moral Society even by a united or determined humanity. Fusion energy is a case in point.

* "Parasitical human beings" refers to persons who consume resources and produce pollution but do nothing to expand awareness.

Almost all the energy consumed on the Earth had its origin in the Sun and is stored in the form of living or fossil fuel. No matter how many new oil and coal fields we discover or how many forests are replanted, the supply is finite. In fact, at the accelerating rate of world power consumption, we should exhaust all known and potential sources of fossil fuel within, at the most, two hundred years—perhaps much sooner. Assume that long before that happens we convert to energy production by nuclear fission.

Power from nuclear fission is analogous to burning fossil fuel. Fissionable materials (consisting mainly of uranium and thorium) are in very short supply and are never replaced. In fact, it is very unlikely that we could survive on fission power at our current rate of increase in power consumption for more than three hundred years. We might try mining the other planets, but it would probably take more energy to extract the energy than it is worth.

The only source of power adequate to engender an infinitely-expanding Moral Society is nuclear fusion. The power potential from burning the hydrogen isotopes of the oceans in a controlled nuclear fusion reaction offers the only hope for extending the Moral Society beyond the solar system.

It took an enormous consumption of fossil fuel over a period of more than one hundred fifty years in order to develop the science and technology of controlled nuclear fission. It will probably take a similar type of expenditure of energy to develop controlled nuclear fusion. If we do not stop squandering our resources we will not be able to create the Moral Society, even if we want to.

The evolutionary force is only giving humanity one chance to engender the Moral Society. We will not get another. This has always been the case with all species—only one chance.

CONCLUSION

The future of humanity is dependent on avoiding 1) nuclear annihilation, 2) annihilation by pollution, 3) annihilation by genetic decay and 4) the gradual extinction of a striving humanity that no longer has the resources to go anywhere. This latter, slow extinction would also be the result of a nuclear war which a few persons survived in a completely collapsed civilization. This is why some of the destructive objectives of the Revolt Against Reason cannot be tolerated. Humanity probably cannot begin all over again and still create the Moral Society. We must begin now.

The scenario on genetic decay within an automated society is not as far-fetched as might appear. The technology for accomplishing it should be developed in twenty years, perhaps much sooner. There are also other more subtle ways in which genetic decline can occur. Genetic decay is the inevitable consequence of an immoral society that stresses happiness above awareness. It is, of course, much more likely that man will annihilate himself by nuclear war before he can achieve the robotic "Utopia" previously described. It seems that the only way in which man can avoid extinction is to implement an Ethical State now.

An Ethical State will have the sole purpose of creating the Moral Society as soon as possible by expanding the total awareness of each individual citizen and maximizing the collective total awareness of all its citizens. The society will be structured by ethical principles to maximize feedback at all levels and avoid bureaucratization. Science and technology will be used to enhance man's total awareness and freedom, not constrain it. The super-computers will be used to amplify man's intelligence, not replace it. Once science and technology begin to be used to liberate man instead of enslaving him, then the entire fabric of existence will change and all men, Black and White, brilliant and ordinary, can begin to experience the true joy of life which only comes from an infinitely expanding consciousness.

The creation of an Ethical State can begin now if at least a few ethical persons with intelligence, courage, and determination wish it. The structure of an Ethical State is described in the next chapter. A strategy for implementing it is given in Chapter 7.

PART THREE

experimentation

Whatever liberates our spirit without giving us self-control is disastrous.

—Goethe

Parts One and Two contained 1) speculations about the patterns of evolution, 2) observations about the current state of the world, and 3) some extrapolations of the current trends. The extrapolations indicate that irreversible entropy is inevitable unless some revolutionary changes are made in our social structure.

It is possible to formulate a model about how man may avoid irreversible entropy and continue to evolve toward total awareness. Since such a model must encompass man's psychosocial environment, about which there is so little scientific methodology, the model will almost certainly be replete with errors. However, doubt can never be used as an excuse for inaction. We must do the best we can to make sense out of the universe and to act ethically. We need only keep an open mind and remember that every model of cause and effect relationships probably always has errors. Every description, theory and strategy in this book may be in error. We can correct the errors only by scientific experimentation. Experiments are valid only when they are performed ethically in an atmosphere of free and honest inquiry. In this part we shall use ethics to plan an experiment in human evolution.

6

AN
ETHICAL
STATE

FOUNDATIONS

The foundation of an Ethical State is ethical behavior. The problem
that must be solved is how to motivate a society so that men may become moral. From the ethical theory in Chapters 1, 2, and 3 we know
that ethical behavior stems from 1) a desire to play the Game of Life,
2) personal freedom and 3) scientific method. From Chapters 4 and 5
we know that bureaucracy and ideology impede ethical behavior; if they
are not eliminated, they will destroy the human race by making mankind
immoral.

It is clear that a desire to play the Game of Life is inherent in all
mankind. Not all men have an equal, innate proficiency for playing the
Game; but since all children increase their awareness, the desire to play

the Game must itself be innate. The fact that persons cease to play the Game later in life is assumed to be due to outside entropic factors (physical, biological and/or psychosocial) originating by chance and resulting in immoral adults who then directly increase man's entropy. Children are, therefore, all ethical. Only adults can be immoral or moral. An ethical society would be structured to maximize morality and to minimize the number of immoral men who are the deleterious mutations in man's psychosocial evolution.

A necessary condition for maintaining feedback is personal freedom. Without personal freedom it is not possible to question all descriptions, models, and strategies. However, popular ideology may still destroy individual awareness in the presence of personal freedom if scientific method is not used at all levels of society. Only science tests ideology by forcing a confrontation over its ability to predict and control.

Ideology and bureaucracy together will inevitably destroy the awareness of anyone who submits to them. Ideology destroys the individual awareness of any person by blinding him to the possibility that he may be wrong and others may be right. Bureaucracy destroys the collective awareness of society by consuming resources and deliberately destroying negative feedback until no feedback remains and the society is totally corrupt. In other words, ideology destroys personal morality while bureaucracy destroys social morality.

An Ethical State must, therefore, 1) maximize personal freedom, 2) avoid all forms of bureaucracy, and 3) eliminate ideology through education. Personal freedom is maximized and ideology is minimized by broad awareness. Therefore, the prime function of an Ethical State must be to educate persons to become generalists. All the resources of the state must be used to make it possible for *all* men to experience everything, try everything, understand everything and extend everything. This is the spirit of evolution and total awareness.

Bureaucracies are destroyed by feedback. Therefore, all organizations in an Ethical State must maximize their feedback. At first this is probably best accomplished by maximizing creative competition between organizations, thereby 1) deliberately disbanding the less effective organizations and 2) forcing the most effective organizations to split into new competitive groups. This is a direct analogue of natural selection.

The maximal form of competition is obtained when it is individualized and there is no organization of any kind. This is possible in many sectors of society but not all. Therefore, the formation of organizations should be inhibited in an Ethical State when they serve no useful purpose. A purpose is useful if and only if it leads to greater total awareness.

For example, political parties serve no useful purpose since they only bureaucratize the governmental process. Therefore, there should be no political parties in an Ethical State. However, schools do serve a useful purpose by making the educational process a social experience and more cost-effective than individual tutoring. Therefore, organizations called "schools" should exist on a competitive basis within an Ethical State.

As an Ethical State evolves toward a Moral Society, the need for competition may be relaxed. This is the case because moral men are prone neither to bureaucratization nor ideology.

The code of an Ethical State may be summarized in a single ethical imperative:

Each Person Must Do His Best to Maximize Total Awareness

From this may be derived the principles which are the foundation of an Ethical State.

Principles of an Ethical State

1   Only actions which increase *total* awareness are ethical.
2   Any action which decreases any person's awareness is unethical.
3   Unethical means can never achieve ethical ends.
4   Means which are not ends are never ethical.
5   It is unethical to tolerate immorality.
6   It is unethical to be certain.
7   It is ethical to doubt.
8   Inaction is unethical.

DESIGN

In order to accomplish its objectives, an Ethical State will 1) concentrate its resources on education; 2) support non-educational activities only insofar as these activities are essential preconditions to the enhancement of total awareness; 3) avoid bureaucratization by maximizing feedback at all levels of society, particularly in the political and educational systems, and deliberately eliminating *all* forms of *bureaucratic, not personal,* security; 4) continuously improve the quality of the human species (i.e., its genetic potential for total awareness) through a scientific, humane eugenics program; and 5) develop the scientific and technical basis for engendering the Moral Society.

The last activity is an integral part of the educational program and will be discussed within the educational context.

The discussion of an Ethical State is couched in specific terms *not* because a precise analysis has been made of all the alternatives, but rather to illustrate the specific decisions which will have to be made in structuring an Ethical State. The percentage figures were chosen in such a way that Darwinian competition might provide adequate feedback to the entire system.

The following social and political structure should, therefore, be regarded as a first experimental approximation to an Ethical Society. It is one model of how an Ethical State may be structured. Other models for an Ethical State are certainly possible and perhaps desirable. *Every description, hypothesis, theory and model in this book may be in error.*

EDUCATION

An Ethical Society exists solely to educate mankind. Education was defined earlier as any process which directly increases the total awareness of those who are exposed to it. Education is the human manifestation of the evolutionary force which drives matter toward mind and mind toward ever greater total awareness. Education is the process which will elevate man to the Moral Society. The Moral Society is the process which will enable mankind to evolve forever toward total awareness.

The transformation of mankind into the Moral Society will not be an abrupt occurrence, but will be brought about gradually as all men become increasingly totally aware, raising the minimum as well as the maximum levels of total awareness within existing humanity. The constant

raising of these two levels plus the minimization of the differences between them are the two main functions of an Ethical State.

The progress of science and technology has continuously raised the
maximum level of total awareness at an unprecedented rate. Bureaucratization and ideology have caused an ever-widening gap in the level of
total awareness between those who are most aware and those who are
least aware. Bureaucratization and ideology have led to ever narrower,
more irrelevant specialization among scientists and exclusion of a now
increasing majority of humanity from most scientific and technical
knowledge. The net effect will be, if it is not already the case, a decrease
in total awareness and the creation of an immoral society. The educational programs of an Ethical State must reverse this trend.

The totality of awareness which should be the goal of an Ethical
State for all persons is that typified by the combined total awareness of
men such as Leonardo da Vinci, Michelangelo, Shakespeare, Spinoza,
Leibniz, Bach, Newton, Goethe, Gauss, Darwin, Dostoyevsky, Freud,
Schweitzer, Einstein, etc. The only difference is that modern science and
technology will increase both the depth and the breadth of total awareness to produce persons far superior to any combination of these men.
The argument that these men were geniuses is irrelevant. Insofar as the
leftist hypothesis is correct, it is possible by education (in the broad
sense) to raise all men to meet and exceed the level of total awareness of
any genius. Insofar as the rightist hypothesis is correct, it is possible
through eugenics to increase the genetic quality of mankind until the
innate ability of the vast majority of persons equals or exceeds that of
any combination of geniuses. In both cases, technology can be used to
enhance the process. Science, not ideology, should determine the relative
balance in effectiveness between education and eugenics. The net result
should be a steadily increasing total awareness for all humanity and di-
minution of the differences between high and low awareness levels.

Education should be concerned only with maximizing the level of
total awareness for all persons. This can be done by structuring the educational system to produce generalists who have breadth as well as depth.
Specialization should be deferred as long as possible and should be discouraged until a person has achieved a level of total awareness which
makes him a generalist with depth in all fields of knowledge. Even then,

a person should be discouraged from specializing by providing him with greater inducements to continue expanding his *total* awareness. The expansion of total awareness will probably go through a process in which breadth is developed first and then depth is increased in *all* fields of knowledge through either serial or simultaneous specialization. The latter should be encouraged in order to maintain sphericity. The minimum level in formal education that should initially be the objective of the Ethical State is equivalent to a person's *simultaneously* obtaining a bachelor's degree with honors at a currently accredited American university in each of the following fields. These are the minimum scholastic requirements for a scientifically literate generalist:

General Subject	Emphasis
MATHEMATICS	algebra, real and complex analysis, partial differential equations, probability, statistics, calculus of variations, functional analysis, differential geometry
PHYSICS	mechanics, electricity and magnetism, optics, mathematical physics, atomic, nuclear, solid state and modern physics
CHEMISTRY	physical chemistry, organic chemistry, biochemistry, thermodynamics
BIOLOGY	zoology, botany, comparative anatomy and physiology, genetics, embryology, neurophysiology, molecular biology
ENGINEERING	architecture, structures, mechanical systems, electronic circuits, systems theory, computer design, communications technology
PSYCHOLOGY	psychophysics, physiological psychology, mathematical psychology, learning, personality development
ANTHROPOLOGY	human evolution and genetics, comparative cultural development, archeology

GENERAL BEHAVIORAL SCIENCE	history, sociology, economics, political science
GENERAL SCIENCE	geology, paleontology, astronomy, ecology
GENERAL HUMANITIES	expository prose, languages, literature, music, art
PHILOSOPHY	history of philosophy, metaphysics, logic, epistemology, ethics

An educational system producing generalists with the above background would represent a "Basic Program." It would complete the first necessary step in the expansion of total awareness. The Basic Program, when completed, represents the minimum amount of knowledge that a person should have before beginning to specialize. It is mostly breadth with little depth. It is a primary education. It represents an embryonic generalist with little practical experience—a sphere of small diameter.

In the Ethical State a person with an I.Q. of one hundred twenty-five (college average) should be able to complete this program by the age of twenty-five. Some could complete it at a much earlier age; others might take many more years. If it were bureaucratically possible, a person could complete the Basic Program today in eight college years. Very few persons today or in any day have the combined breadth and depth of knowledge indicated in the Basic Program. Leibniz had most of the breadth, but not the depth. There are, of course, many persons living today who have great depth in one or more specific parts of the Basic Program, but not in all.

The Basic Program should be structured so that it is continuously increasing in breadth and depth as new knowledge develops and the general student quality improves. Only in this way can the educational system keep pace with the evolution of the population it serves.

Once a person had the minimum education indicated by the Basic Program, he could begin to develop depth in any area of his choice through independent study, research, and/or practical experience with a minimum of guidance. The current hierarchical structure of the educational bureaucracy does not permit the training of generalists except under extraordinary circumstances. The primary educational system of an Ethical State should be structured to optimize the training of the maximum number of generalists possible.

Once a person finishes the Basic Program, the educational system of an Ethical State should make it possible for that person to educate himself indefinitely in complete freedom independently of any bureaucracy. The only problem will be to maintain feedback to the student and the society on the rate of educational progress. This must be done without bureaucracy for both the primary and the advanced students.

Primary Education (Proposal 1)

The essential feature of the primary educational system should be a flexible, personalized, non-bureaucratized, educational system with high feedback which is responsive to the individual student's needs. This may be accomplished by allowing the student to have a wide choice of schools and making all the schools compete for the student's attendance. Accreditation of the schools should be based on objective measures of how well the school performs its educational function.

The actual evaluation and accreditation of the schools should be done by independent competitive organizations directly responsible to the elected representatives of the people. The following is a specific example of how these principles might be implemented.

It should be the policy of an Ethical State for every person who wishes it to complete the Basic Program at government expense as soon as possible. (This will be an extension of the current policy in most of the U.S.—that all persons complete what is often a travesty of education, high school, by the age of 18.) In order to maximize the feedback and optimize the educational process, each student should be allowed to choose his own school. The Government would pay the student 1) for his living expenses (paid directly to the student) and 2) for his tuition at an accredited school in whichever region he chose to live (paid directly to the school). The Ethical State would, in general, not operate schools. All schools would be left to private initiative with the Ethical State paying the bill through subsidies to the student. The Ethical State would establish schools only when there was not sufficient private initiative to accommodate all the students. The government schools would always have to compete on an equal basis with the private schools. The schools would be allowed to receive government payment only when they were accredited.

Accreditation would be based entirely on the school's performance in enhancing the total awareness of the student. No control would be exercised over any aspect of the school environment. Accreditation would be determined by measuring the student's total awareness profile and total awareness potential every three months. These measurements of how well the student can predict and control his total environment would be based on scientific, standardized, secret tests to be administered by three independent competitive nation-wide teams of examiners and evaluators. The tests should be known a priori only to the evaluating team and the Central Education Council.* The tests would relate each student in the population to all statistically-similar† students in the Ethical State.

The payment of tuition to the schools should be proportionate to the relative rate of awareness increase for each individual student. In order to stimulate competition between the schools, the student who increased his awareness of the greatest rate relative to all other students within his statistically-similar group would bring the largest tuition fee to his school (twice the average perhaps). The student who increased his awareness at the lowest rate would bring the least tuition (zero perhaps). The average student would bring the average tuition which would be the same for all statistical groups (i.e., there would be no economic advantage in teaching either very bright or very dull students; only the teaching effectiveness of the school would matter). As the student's level of total awareness

---

* The Central Education Council is discussed later in this chapter.

† Intuitively, the concept "statistically-similar" refers to a congruence of a constellation of statistically measurable individual characteristics such as current knowledge, age, health, mental aptitude, sex, etc. for all members of a group. It is assumed that when students are statistically-similar, differences in their educability are due primarily to their school environment. It would be unscientific to say that individual differences in education over a period of time are due to the school when students are not statistically similar. (See *Mahalonobis Distance Function, Fisher Likeness Coefficient,* etc., also see Glossary.)

increased toward that represented by completion of the Basic Program, the tuition could be gradually increased so that the average tuition for training students at the highest levels could be, perhaps, up to five times that for training students at the lowest levels.

Each student would have access to the three independent evaluations of each school and of himself. The schools would have access to their evaluation and to the three independent evaluations of each student. Both schools and students could choose each other on any basis they wished. The Ethical State could interfere with the selection process only when it could show through scientifically-controlled experiments that some aspect of the selection process was decreasing the total collective awareness of the Ethical State. In this case it would be the responsibility of the Ethical State to correct the selection procedures wherever they were having a proven deleterious effect. The evaluating teams would also have a counseling service to help each student decide which school was best for him. The final decision, however, would be entirely the student's or his guardian's.

In order to avoid monopoly, no school should long be allowed to train more than ten percent of the students in its region (probably no more than ten competitive organizations are necessary for good feedback). Periodically, schools which for more than two years in a row had been training more than ten percent of the students of a school region would be split at random into at least two independent schools. (This is analogous to the random splitting in meiosis by which the variability of life is maximized.) The splitting of schools should be performed under the direction and at the discretion of the Ethical State.

School regions should be compactly contiguous and not larger than 500,000 students, but at least equal to 100,000 students. This will enable many schools to have a critical mass of students while still maintaining competition. All schools should be open to reasonable inspection and scientific examination of their selection procedures, teaching techniques and facilities by the examining teams. The results of these studies should be made public.

The student subsistence allowance should be adequate for the student to live sufficiently well to pursue his studies without interference

from problems of inadequate diet, clothing, medical care, shelter or mis-
cellaneous causes. The allowance would be paid directly to the student.
While the student was still dependent on others, they could manage the
student stipend and guide him. Dependence would end when the student declared himself independent or otherwise showed that he was.*

The student could leave his family any time he chose and live anywhere he wished. (This would enable ethical children to escape from
immoral parents or guardians. Ethical children of all ages tend to despise
immoral adults, but our present society keeps them dependent on these
adults.) The student should remain in accredited primary schools until
he can support himself or has finished the Basic Program, so long as he is
a resident of the Ethical State. Any person, at any time, could leave the
school system and live as he chose, so long as he did not become a public
charge. He could specialize or become anything he wished; however, he
would not receive public support in this endeavor.

In order to stimulate individual competition among the primary students, there should be an additional stipend bonus, of, say, five percent
for each total awareness level (there being perhaps one-hundred ascending levels) above the base† that the student reaches until he has completed the Basic Program. Therefore, the student's yearly stipend should
be about five times as great when he finishes the Basic Program than
when he began it. He could begin at any age he or his guardians chose.
Students who fell below a previously-achieved level of awareness would
have their stipend reduced accordingly.

Primary Evaluation (Proposal 2)

The competitive teams of educational examiners (three in number)
would work completely independent of one another. Each team would
be nation-wide. They would be rated solely on how well their analyses

* See Civil Rights in the Ethical State.
† The base can be considered to be the level of total awareness of the typical U.S.
pre-schooler, the second level might be that of a typical recent grammar school graduate. The third level might be represented by the typical U.S. high school graduate.
The hundredth level would be represented by the full completion of the Basic Program.

predicted future performances of schools and students. When all three teams voted to revoke accreditation of a school, then the accreditation would be revoked.* If one team voted to retain accreditation, then the accreditation would be retained for one additional year. If the school performed as predicted by the team that voted to retain the accreditation, that team would improve its rating while the other teams would each lower their rating. In general, examining teams would lower their rating for incorrect predictions and improve their rating for correct predictions (within reasonable statistical bounds). The teams would always be required to make predictions for all students and schools.

In order to stimulate competition between the evaluation teams, the team members would be rewarded on the basis of the correctness of their predictions. Every year the team with the lowest total evaluation score would be disbanded, i.e., everyone dismissed. The managers and workers of the leading team would be given a two hundred percent bonus over base salary. The members of the second rank team would be given a one hundred percent bonus over salary. The losing team would receive only their base salary.

The winning team would be split at random into two new teams. Each of the resulting new teams would hire new personnel as needed. They could not, however, hire persons who had been their co-workers the previous year. Otherwise the managers could run their teams as they saw fit and spend their budget (which would be identical for all teams) in any way they wished.

The over-all selection process should maximize feedback by emulating Darwinian competition. The worst team perishes and the best team multiplies. The middle team is used to give stability to the system.

There would always be three working teams: two being reorganized and one more or less the same as the previous year. The teams would evaluate the primary educational system at all levels and could develop their own measures of effectiveness, which would then be related to the standardized tests. The operations of the teams should be open to scientific investigation by anyone not on a rival evaluating team. At the end

---

* Disaccreditation should be automatically voted by any team which estimates that a school will be performing in the lower ten percent of all schools in the Ethical State with statistically similar student populations.

of each year, a report would be written by the investigators* on the workings of all the teams. The investigators should be appointed by the Ethical State if there is not enough feedback from other sources. In this way a body of scientific knowledge on educational evaluation would be developed to enhance the educational process still further.

The profile measures of actual Level of Total Awareness (LTA) and Total Awareness Potential (TAP) should be confined to objectively-administered tests. The predicted measures should be identical in form to the evaluative measures. The tests should reflect one hundred graded levels of total awareness up to full understanding of the Basic Program. The evaluating teams would have the responsibility for reporting their theory, methods and findings in the training environment in all schools in the Ethical State. The teams would sponsor experiments to test new educational theories and techniques.

The LTA test would measure, by statistical sampling techniques, the total awareness of each person. That is to say, it would attempt to determine the contours of the awareness ellipsoid of each person. This could be done by categorizing all of human knowledge into reasonably orthogonal components and then sampling the depth of each component. For example, if we take the simple three-dimensional model of total awareness given in Chapter 1, then it is necessary to sample only three dimensions—the physical, the biological and the psychosocial.

The physical can easily be measured by sampling a person's knowledge† of mathematics, physics, chemistry, astronomy, engineering, practical mechanics, carpentry, and so on. Indeed these types of tests already exist in a crude form and are used by schools and the military.

Biological knowledge can be estimated by sampling a person's awareness of botany, zoology, physiology, bacteriology, anatomy, embryology, genetics, molecular biology, horticulture, agriculture, and practical skills such as gradening, hunting, fishing, etc.

Psychosocial knowledge is the most difficult to estimate because there is so little scientific methodology in this area. Almost all knowledge in the psychosocial dimension has a clinical basis. Therefore, it would be

* The word "investigator" is used in the scientific sense of a person seeking new knowledge.
† Recall that knowledge subsumes creativity and not merely information.

necessary to develop a scientific basis of psychosocial knowledge before truly meaningful measures could be taken. Even so, there are areas of psychosocial knowledge that can be evaluated. For example language skills, knowledge of historical facts, artistic proficiency (only in the technical sense), psychophysics, physiological psychology, anthropological facts (including knowledge of religion), commonly accepted courtesies and rules of social conduct, and a knowledge of social science hypotheses and theories in general. In the latter case it is clearly understood that most such theories are speculative and represent facts about how some persons *claim* people behave rather than about how they *do* behave. With relatively little effort, it should be possible in time to develop as solid a scientific basis in the psychosocial environment as has begun in biology and has long existed in the physical environment.

The purpose of the TAP tests would be to make predictions of future LTA, given a person's current LTA, age, sex, health, external environment, etc. The only type of test which approaches the intent of the TAP test is the so-called "I.Q." test. This test makes rather crude predictions of future LTA because it is primarily limited to testing primitive Logic and Memory. The total *gestalt* of intelligence is ignored and consequently I.Q. tests can only make reasonably valid predictions for persons at the lower end of the scale. The current work going on in many universities for measuring Imagination and Will should, in time, enable an Ethical State to develop scientific TAP tests with a high predictive value across a broad spectrum of LTA. It must always be kept in mind that these tests are only valid insofar as they make accurate predictions.

Expectations

The primary school system of the Ethical State should adjust in time to the needs of the individual student in order that each student may pursue each subject in a manner and at a pace best suited to him.* The objective will be to increase the total awareness of all the students. Some students may finish the Basic Program in ten years or less, other students may spend their whole lives trying to master the lower levels of total awareness. All persons would have the options of 1) working in a field

* This is easy to accomplish with individualized and/or computerized teaching techniques.

of their choosing; 2) being a subsidized student; or 3) a combination of both. The standardized measures of LTA and TAP will change as better predictive techniques are developed by the examining teams. Eventually there will be very little improvement in the measures themselves and they will tend to become standardized among the teams. The teams will then be evaluated primarily on the basis of how well they implement the measures, although there will always be the possibility of new breakthroughs in measurement techniques which would give a team a dramatic advantage over its competitors.

Once the student finished the basic program, he would be ready to go on to secondary education. Students unlikely to finish the Basic Program during their lifetimes would be given the choice of retaining their subsistence and tuition allowance and continuing the Basic Program indefinitely or finding their own source of support within the Ethical State. A primary student could pursue his studies full or part-time (his subsistence allowance would be prorated accordingly). He could do anything he wished with his non-student time—work, play, or pursue his own interests and studies. Personal freedom for all persons of all ages is central to the Ethical State. The Ethical State, however, would not finance any educational activity for a primary student which did not lead to completion of the Basic Program. Any student finishing the Basic Program at any age could go on to the subsidized Secondary Program or pursue other interests of his choosing. In this way, the Ethical State would encourage but not force the student to become a generalist and maximize his total awareness. Any person could be as narrow and specialized as he chose. He could even be a parasite if someone were willing to support him. The Ethical State would only make it *possible* for all persons to be generalists; it would *not force anyone* to be anything he did not wish.

If the resources of the Ethical State are, in the beginning, inadequate to support the primary program for the entire population, then the program could be trimmed by excluding the oldest students with the lowest LTA scores and projected scores, until an economic balance was achieved. The excluded students, when healthy, would have to be able to support themselves within the economic system of the Ethical State. However, any modern, fully-industrialized nation could, in theory, support the full primary education system of the Ethical State with ease. It is only the unscientific, bureaucratized structure of modern society that makes the primary education system of the Ethical State seem infeasible by squandering resources in unethical pursuits.

Secondary Education (Proposal 3)

The secondary education of the Ethical State should have the same general objectives as the primary program. The difference now is that the student should be sufficiently aware to have a sense of what is relevant. Each student could now begin to develop depth in any area he chose. He could become highly specialized by studying medicine, architecture, law, mathematics, art, or another profession. He could attend the schools of the secondary system which might be called "universities," or he could work on his own, following his own special interests. The Ethical State should pay the student a subsistence allowance at least equal to the last level of the Basic Program so long as he did not fall below the total awareness level of the Basic Program. If he did, he could re-enter the primary program at whatever level he had reached and re-prepare himself to begin anew. Tuition would be paid by the Ethical State to the universities on the same basis as it was paid to the primary schools, except that the tuition would be paid to the individual student if he chose not to attend a university. If so, he could spend the tuition as he chose so long as he continued to expand his total awareness at a rate comparable to the average university student. Groups of secondary students could pool their individual tuitions and form universities of their own. This process should maximize competition and feedback within the secondary school system.

The universities would be evaluated and accredited analogously to the primary schools on the basis of how effective they were in enhancing the total awareness of their students. The measures of total awareness at the secondary level would be made yearly, as opposed to quarterly, because at this level the students are probably not as sensitive to the perturbations of poor schools as they were in the primary schools. The measures themselves would determine 1) if the student had maintained his awareness of the evolving Basic Program, which would be continuously improved as new knowledge developed; 2) the amount of depth beyond the basic program that he had achieved in any given field; 3) the value of original contributions he might have made to any field, or general problem; 4) the number of different fields in which the student had increased his depth (breadth in many fields would count as much as great depth in only one field); and 5) the student's contributions to the enhancement of total awareness of others by teaching, writing, art or other means. The five measures together would be used in a composite score which would rate the net increase in total awareness brought about by the student's activity and his expected contributions of the next year. The evaluations would be performed by competitive teams of evaluators in a manner completely analogous to the evaluation of the primary education program.

Secondary students whose composite score of total awareness for two consecutive years had placed them, say, in the upper twenty-five percent of the secondary student population would be considered "graduates." They could then go on to become 1) Principal Investigators in the Ethical State's research and development programs, 2) Independent Investigators working on their own or 3) post-graduate students continuing to expand their awareness within the universities. In the latter case, they should be paid a stipend somewhat higher than the highest-ranked secondary student.

Students who were ranked in, say, the lowest ten percent of the secondary school population for four consecutive years should probably no longer be considered secondary students. They could be given the option of 1) remaining at the university as students at a stipend reduced to that of the top primary school level or 2) otherwise supporting themselves within the Ethical State. They could be reinstated as secondary students if for two consecutive years they ranked in the secondary evaluation above the lowest ten percent of the secondary school population.

In this way the best-educated students would become direct contributors and the worst students could continue to educate themselves in their own way until they themselves became direct contributors or chose to work. The entire process should maximize the feedback to both the schools and the students.

Research and Development (Proposal 4)

The Ethical State should probably spend about two-fifths of its education budget on research and development. The total education budget should be as large as possible while still allowing the infrastructure of the Ethical State to perform its necessary functions.

The Research and Development budget should be divided into restricted and unrestricted categories. About one-third of the research and development funds should go into the unrestricted category. It would be divided evenly among individual Independent Investigators wishing to do unrestricted work of their own choosing rather than continue their secondary studies. The unrestricted funds could be spent by the recipients in any way they wished, including salary for themselves, creating or sponsoring works of art, theoretical research, publishing, pooling with other Independent Investigators and/or secondary students to finance special research projects, develop inventions, start new industries, etc. The only constraint would be that their activities must in some way enhance the total awareness of humanity. In this way the unrestricted research funds should serve as a strong stimulus to unbureaucratic, creative innovation in the society by broadly-aware persons.

The restricted funds would be spent on research and development projects sponsored by the Chief Executive of the Ethical State. These would be large-scale, long-term efforts in such areas as biophysical neurophysiology, molecular biology, high energy physics, development of fusion power, space exploration, astronomy, and most importantly, psychosocial science. The purpose of these projects would be to lay the theoretical and experimental foundations for the Moral Society.

The technical foundations of the Moral Society will probably be based on 1) a deep and thorough understanding of the psychosocial environment; 2) the development of machine analogues of human intelligence; 3) the harnessing of enormous amounts of easily-controllable energy as in controlled thermonuclear fusion; 4) an understanding of the cosmos (astronomy and space exploration); and 5) a unified evolutionary perspective of time, energy, matter, space, life, and mind. The latter implies a unified approach to studies of matter, life, and mind such as is currently beginning in the fields of molecular biology and biophysical neurophysiology.

The grants for the restricted research and development projects would be given by the Chief Executive to qualified *individual* Principal Investigators (not organizations) on a competitive basis. Once a grant had been given to a Principal Investigator, he could proceed to complete the project in any way he wished.

The Principal Investigators would be held entirely responsible for the research projects they were controlling. There should be periodic evaluations of the progress of each project. If the progress were unsatisfactory, the Principal Investigator could be fired by the Chief Executive.

Royalties from inventions, books, and other creations resulting from government-sponsored, restricted or unrestricted research and development would be halved between the Ethical State and the responsible Principal Investigators. This would protect the public interest without stifling personal initiative.

Higher Evaluation (Proposal 5)

The evaluation of both restricted and unrestricted research should be performed by competitive teams of examiners in a manner completely analogous to the evaluation of primary and secondary education. The Investigators should probably have a general evaluation about every five years. If an Investigator were evaluated by all three teams in a manner which indicated that his work during the next five years might not increase the total awareness of humanity by as much as the work of, say, ninety percent of the other Principal Investigators, then he would be put on probation. If at the end of the next five years the original predictions were proven to be true, and if the new evaluation by the current three examining teams also projected a level of accomplishment in the lower ten percent of the Investigator group, then the Investigator could have his status permanently revoked. Therefore, every Investigator would have about ten years of complete freedom in which to prove his capacity to perform independent research and development or otherwise to create and innovate.

Investigators whose status was revoked should be given a stipend in keeping with their current level of total awareness, but not higher than that of the average secondary student if they chose to return to the university. A former Investigator could supplement or replace his income by teaching or whatever else he might wish to do. Hopefully this process would maintain feedback and natural selection among the Investigators in such a way that their collective total awareness was always increasing. A person might, of course, never choose to be an Investigator, but instead remain in the university expanding his total awareness all his life by formal study, as opposed to creative research. Breadth in many areas would always count as much as depth in a few areas when taking the LTA tests. Such persons would be displaying personal morality, but not very much social morality. Social morality always involves the risks of negative feedback and public censure. Being a student all one's life is not the most ethical course of action. An ethical person must teach and create.

The evaluating teams for both secondary students and Investigators would be managed by Investigators. Many Investigators might not wish to be involved in an evaluating function. If this were the case, they could be drafted by lottery from the class of all Investigators scoring in the upper one tenth percent or so of the population on the LTA tests. The secondary school evaluation managers should probably be taken from the lower fifty percent in LTA of the total Investigator population. The evaluation manager of the Investigators should probably be taken from the upper fifty percent of this population. Drafted evaluators could be required to serve as managers for two years unless dismissed in the interim. Probably no evaluation manager should serve in this position for more than seven years. No one should be drafted for this purpose more than once. As an inducement to attracting high-caliber evaluators, the base salary of the evaluation managers should be about two hundred percent higher than the average Investigator salary.

The tests for determining LTA among the secondary students and the Investigators would be compiled by the Central Education Council of the Ethical State in conjunction with the evaluating teams. The projection techniques could be developed by each evaluating team and should be fully documented in their annual progress report.

Rationale

The educational system of the Ethical State is intended 1) to maximize feedback at all levels, 2) to prevent bureaucratization, 3) to remove pressure for specialization, 4) to induce as many persons as possible to expand total awareness continuously under a system of complete personal freedom and 5) to lay the scientific and technical foundations for the Moral Society. It is the purpose of the Ethical State to liberate mankind from bureaucracy and ideology and to allow him to fulfill himself by evolving in freedom toward total awareness.

The educational system as described is, of course, only an outline of how education would be structured in an Ethical State. It communicates the spirit of how the educational process would work rather than the details. The details should be worked out by a more extensive application of science and technology.

The stress on financial inducements to students appears necessary to recondition a hedonistic, materialistic population to value education as an end in itself. After an Ethical State has been established for several generations, the stress on differential financial rewards may probably be relaxed. Moral men need no inducement to expand total awareness.

The educational system of the Ethical State would cost about four hundred billion dollars a year under the present economic system in the United States. Not everyone who could would take full advantage of it. If so, it would cost more. This is less than one-half of the current U.S. gross national product. The rest of the gross national product would be left to finance support functions, consumer goods, entertainment and other activities. Through tax reform it would probably be possible not only to raise the additional funds to finance the educational system but also to stimulate the general economy to produce even more wealth. The creation of a large number of highly-educated generalists with depth would provide obvious direct economic benefits. A major source of income to the Ethical State will result from the elimination of the parasitical bureaucracies which 1) currently consume most of the wealth of society, 2) produce almost nothing of value, and 3) hinder progress. The former employees of the bureaucracies will then be able to support themselves ethically by working or becoming subsidized students.

The primary schools would provide a system of welfare and guaranteed income (i.e., personal security) to those normally incapable of earning a living or supporting their children in a competitive society. Conventional welfare payments to parasitical indigents and bureaucrats* only seem to condition them to be even less productive. A universal system of subsidized education would provide dignified welfare to the entire indigent population while training them to be more productive. Almost anyone can be taught almost anything; the individual differences seem to be in the rate at which persons learn.

From a purely economic point of view, education is probably the best possible investment a nation can make. From the Ethical State's point of view, education is an investment it must make. Education is an end in itself. It is the foundation of a Moral Society.

INFRASTRUCTURE OF THE ETHICAL STATE

The infrastructure of the Ethical State would have no other function than to support the educational system. In order for the infrastructure to be vital, it is necessary that it be free. In order that the infrastructure should not become predatory (as is currently happening in the United States) and destroy the Ethical State, it must not be allowed to become bureaucratized or monopolistic. The continuous disbanding of the incipient bureaucracies and the possible monopolies within the otherwise free infrastructure should be one of the main functions of the government of the Ethical State. It would be analogous to the constant pruning and weeding of an orchard in order that the trees may give better and more abundant yields.

Industry (Proposal 6)

Industry would have an essentially capitalistic structure in order to maximize feedback. Natural resources (including all land, minerals, radio spectrum, atmosphere, etc.) would belong to the Ethical State.

---

* Recall that bureaucracy is the welfare system of the middle class.

Their exploitation would be franchised to industry and individuals on a competitive basis (i.e., leased temporarily to the highest qualified bidder). The only limitations put on industry should be 1) no corporation* and/or its subsidiaries will be allowed to control more than ten percent of any identifiable market; 2) no corporation will be allowed to advertise its goods and services except by objective, verifiable factual reporting of their characteristics; 3) entertainment will not be allowed to be used for conditioning consumers to prefer one type of goods or service above another; 4) the net profits and/or income of corporations will be taxed at a uniform rate irrespective of how large or small the income; 5) the Ethical State may and should interfere with the activities of any corporation if and only if it can be shown scientifically that these activities will lead to a decrease in total awareness (e.g., pollution).

Monopolies could be prevented by randomly splitting in half any corporation which controls more than ten percent of any identifiable market for more than two consecutive years. The loss in the potentially greater efficiency of very large corporations should be more than made up by the greater feedback of a more competitive industrial system. A corollary of the anti-monopolistic policy is that there should be no collusion between corporations for splitting markets or fixing prices. The reasoning behind this process and the percentages involved is completely analogous to the splitting of successful schools and evaluating teams in the educational system.

In order to maximize feedback at all levels of society, the anti-monopolistic policy should apply to local corporations, such as news media, entertainment media, and all labor unions. The technology and organization of telephone and power utilities would have to accommodate to the need for local competition. The only exception to the anti-monopolistic law should be when its enforcement would leave the consumer with no goods or services of a particular kind. Alleged economies of scale would be sacrificed to maintain feedback. This type of enforced competition together with other features of the Ethical State should serve as an effective bulwark against the internal bureaucratization of corporations.

* Whatever applies to corporations also applies to individual persons in this discussion.

In order to prevent industry from manipulating the tastes and desires of the population, advertising would have to be of a strictly factual nature with no appeal to the emotions or the consumers' desire for entertainment. This is best illustrated by an example.

An automobile manufacturer in advertising his product would only be able to discuss technically and objectively the dimensions of the automobile, its weight, performance, materials, guarantee, price, maintenance requirements, etc. No other inducements would be allowed. The advertisement could not be placed in an entertainment context such as in a television play or a magazine which is primarily fiction.

In order to protect the Ethical State from corporate predation and maximize the efficiency of the system, there should be three competitive evaluating teams to supervise the operations of the corporations. The teams would objectively and scientifically measure the output, both beneficial and deleterious, of the corporations and make projections of new output. The evaluating teams should recommend controls for lowering the deleterious output while maintaining or improving beneficial output. The teams themselves would be evaluated by the Chief Executive of the Ethical State on the basis of the efficacy of their predictions and recommendations. The losing team would be disbanded periodically while the winning team multiplied in a competitive process completely analogous to the educational evaluating teams. The evaluating teams should not interfere directly with the internal operations of the corporations. Corporations which continued their deleterious outputs (particularly pollutants) in excess of the predetermined standards should be disbanded. Their market would be absorbed by their competitors. The corporations acquiring more than ten percent of the market could then be split in half in the regular anti-monopolistic fashion.

In order to equalize the competition in the Ethical State, the taxation policy should be uniform throughout in its application to corporations and individuals. The tax laws should apply to any organization or individual collecting revenue except, of course, the government itself. There should be no tax-exempt organizations (including religions and foundations). Organizations which collected no revenue would, of course, not be taxed; neither would student stipends be taxed. The net income should be taxed whether the income is obtained in money, property or services. No deductions would be allowed. Property itself should not be taxed except when it is sold and/or transferred. When it is sold, the excess in price over cost should be taxed as regular income to the seller. When it is transferred, the current market price of the property, irrespective of what the transferee may have paid for the property, should be considered as income to the person or corporation receiving the property. There should be no other kinds of taxes unless they can be scientifically shown to be more effective in expanding the total awareness of the society than the apparently simple and equitable tax structure outlined above.

The tax rate should be as high as possible to support the educational system. The Ethical State should alter the tax rates whenever it wishes to modify the economy. The objective would be to maximize the income to the educational system. Sometimes this could best be achieved by lowering the tax rate in order to stimulate industry and have a larger net income to tax at a lower rate. At other times the Ethical State could best accomplish its purposes by raising the taxes. Industry should have no illusions about its function. It would serve only to support the educational system with goods, services, and taxes. The strength and viability of industry would be essential to the Ethical State, but it would only be one of many ethical means for achieving total awareness.

Shared royalties (fifty percent) from inventions, writings, and other creations subsidized by the Ethical State, together with competitive fees from leasing and franchising the natural resources, should be the only source of income to the Ethical State other than the income tax. The government should not engage in industrial activity unless there is no private initiative in a required area. Government-sponsored industry should compete on an equal basis with private industry, including the observance of anti-monopolistic laws. Any production of goods and services other than Education, Entertainment, and the Military would be considered Industry. This would include, for example, medical care, lending money, and personal services. The Chief Executive should control the money supply and he could print additional money when this was in the economic interest of the Ethical State.

The foregoing much simplified structure of Industry is intended to be in keeping with the ethical principles previously derived; however, it may contain errors which should be corrected when they are perceived.

Entertainment (Proposal 7)

In order to keep art free and maximize feedback, entertainment should be treated as a type of industry. The same laws which apply to Industry should, therefore, apply to Entertainment. The objective of the Ethical State should be to have as broad a spectrum of entertainment as possible to meet the varied tastes of its citizens. At the same time the entertainment media should be used to enhance the total awareness of the population. Television and radio programs can probably best accomplish this purpose if they are paid for directly by the consumer, i.e., Pay Television and not paid for by advertisers.

In order to maintain variety and feedback, there should be at least ten nation-wide television networks. Three of the networks should be designated "educational networks." They would be required to have entertainment which reflected the tastes of that portion of the population which scores in the upper one-tenth percent on the LTA tests. The upper one-tenth percent is chosen to assure high awareness yet have a sufficiently large sample to reflect a wide variety of tastes. Hopefully this would serve to help raise the artistic tastes of the rest of the population and to expand their total awareness. Three networks would be required to have children's programs with a high educational content. The programs on the children's networks would be screened by the Central Education Council. One network would be operated directly by the Ethical State for purposes of public information. Three networks would be allowed to show anything they wished, including denunciations of the Ethical State, its principles, and its leaders. These would be the general networks.

The radio spectrum for the communications media, as all natural resources, would belong to the Ethical State which would franchise it conditionally to the highest bidder under the constraints given above. The educational networks would be surveyed to determine what percentage of the population with an LTA score in the upper one-tenth percent watched the programs. The network with the lowest cumulative score each year would be "resold" to the highest bidder and all employees dismissed. The new operator of the network could not rehire any of the former employees for at least one year, although other networks could hire these persons. If one network had the highest ratings for two consecutive years, it should have its staff and management split randomly in half. One-half should continue with the winning network. The other half of the staff should be leased the disbanded network at the same rate as the winning network is leased to their former co-workers. This should prevent bureaucratization and maximize feedback as in the educational and industrial systems.

The children's networks and general networks would go through the same yearly filtering process. The former will be polled for the percentage of all children watching; the latter will be polled for the total audience watching. A similar filtering process would apply to the radio networks and local radio and TV stations.

In the area of films, books, records, and art in general, the Ethical State would exercise no control at all except the anti-monopoly regulations. All persons would have the right to free expression except that persons who libel would be subject to criminal prosecution.* The Ethical State could interfere with free expression only when it had shown scientifically, by controlled experiments, that some types of forced expression were reducing the collective total awareness of the population. It is not likely that any kind of entertainment or propaganda in a free society could, in general, decrease the total collective awareness. Persons who respond positively to ideology and destructive propaganda seem to do so because of an aberration in themselves, not necessarily the perniciousness of the arguments.

The Military (Proposal 8)

The Military would serve to protect the Ethical State from external and internal predators. It could also serve to expand the Ethical State at

* See section on Civil Rights.

the direction of the Chief Executive. When all of humanity is united, the role of the Military would be greatly reduced and it would be used mainly for protection against criminals.

All members of the Military would be employees of the Ethical State. They would swear an oath to uphold and defend the constitution of the Ethical State and to obey its laws and constitutional representatives. There would be two, and only two, completely independent nation-wide military organizations. Each should be under complete control of the Chief Executive of the Ethical State. The Ethical State should use each organization to test the effectiveness of the other. The two organizations would have identical budgets which they could spend in any way they wished to produce any mixture of men and materiel. They would be given comparable rotating areas of the Ethical State to defend from internal predators. They would also have yearly competitive maneuvers and war games which would be refereed by the Chief Executive of the Ethical State. The military organization showing itself to be least effective would periodically (at least once every five years, for example) have the upper five percent by rank of its members dismissed. An equal number of personnel chosen at random from, say, at least the upper ten percent by rank of the rival military organization would replace them. Then the competition would begin anew. All members of the Military should be volunteers except perhaps the top one-tenth percent by rank who under wartime conditions could be appointed, by drafting if necessary, from the portion of the population which scores in the upper one-tenth percent on the LTA tests. These appointments would be for a minimum of two years. The appointees should probably not be allowed to remain more than seven years. This would maintain feedback in the military system and hopefully prevent bureaucratization. A more drastic anti-bureaucratic system similar to the industrial anti-monopolistic structure would probably not be economically or militarily feasible.

The salary of the Military would have to be equal to whatever inducement it would take to make persons volunteer. The drafted officers would have commensurate salaries. It is unethical to restrain personal freedom for the cause of economic or socio-political expediency.

During wartime, the two organizations could be combined into a single, unified Military directly under the command of the Chief Executive of the Ethical State. The encounter with the enemy should provide adequate feedback. During peace, the Military would always be split into two rival organizations.

The structure of the Military, as all government teams, would be such that any person could hire and fire anyone who reported directly to him. There would be no "unions" in government teams. A person fired could appeal to the superior of the one who fired him. If his appeal were not considered valid, he would have no other recourse. Criminal proceedings against military personnel for violation of either military or civil law will be subject to all the guarantees of civil rights and will be tried in civil courts. All this seems necessary to maintain feedback and avoid bureaucratization.

GOVERNMENT OF THE ETHICAL STATE

In formulating a government for the Ethical State it is necessary 1) to keep the ethical principles of the society in the forefront and 2) to guard against the bureaucratic corruption to which all organizations are prone. It is, therefore, desirable that the government be effective but also that a system for preventing personal corruption be present. The democratic government of the United States (at the Federal level) has to a great extent avoided gross personal corruption but it has become a captive of bureaucratic corruption which has led to an almost complete control over the system by indecent men.

It appears that the democratic process helps prevent total personal corruption in government. Some other forms of government may be in some way superior to democracy, but they usually lead to personal corruption. The Ethical State in order to be effective must make it possible for the most ethical persons in society to become the leaders. This apparently can only be accomplished by eliminating the corrupt bureaucracies of the political parties. However, in order to prevent the nation from falling into the hands of dictators who inevitably become personally corrupt, it will be necessary to maintain a democratic structure without political parties. This apparently can be done only by inhibiting the freedom of those who would form a political party *de facto* or *de jure*.

Therefore, in order for the Ethical State to function as a free, democratic and unbureaucratic society, it seems essential to curb that part of
personal freedom which leads to formation of political parties. This can
be done in such a way that the total net personal freedom of each person
is in effect greater than in any bureaucratic society.

The following sections describe a system of government which
should accomplish those objectives. As all sections in this book, they
should be read in terms of preliminary hypotheses and not assertions of
ultimate truth. The following governmental structure represents only
one experimental approach to an Ethical State. Other approaches are
certainly possible. However, before discussing the governmental structure in some detail, a word about the value of science and ethics in
selecting leaders is in order.

Selection

It is probable that in any democratic society most persons would
agree that the best persons in the society should be the leaders. They
would agree on this although very few would agree on what constituted
"best." In discussing "best" most persons would probably give many cri-
teria which would somewhere include the notion of "awareness," although it might not be called that. Almost all persons would also probably agree that the leaders should be moral men, although again they
would differ on what constituted "morality."

The intuitive notions of what constitutes a "good," i.e., ethical leader
are therefore probably compatible, although not in an obvious way, with
the logical evolutionary notions of ethics and morality derived in Part I.
According to the ethical theory, a necessary but not sufficient condition
for morality is that the person be highly aware, i.e., that he be a generalist with depth. Therefore, although we are not likely to develop a scientific test that can measure morality directly, we can certainly develop a
scientific test for estimating the breadth and depth of a person's total
awareness. A first filter for enhancing the probability of having good
leaders is, therefore, that they be among the most broadly and deeply
aware generalists in the population. Identifying the persons should be
rather easy to do with scientific LTA tests.

However, a person may be broadly aware and still be prone to unethical behavior, as was Leibniz. For this reason, there should be another element in the selective process of the leaders which cannot be reduced to an objective test. That element is morality.

Morality cannot yet be measured objectively, but it can certainly be sensed. Moral men produce a field effect which is immediately perceptible. Immoral persons find them disturbing and try to avoid them. Other moral persons and ethical children seem to be immediately attracted to them. Therefore, moral men seem always to come to the forefront in revolutionary times and to be overshadowed by the entrenched bureaucracies in peacetime. An analysis of democratic electorates would probably show that when the voters are given a clear choice, they will usually choose the most ethical candidate. The problem in a bureaucracy is that voters are never given a clear choice but are forced to choose between two unethical candidates. They end up choosing what seems to be the lesser of two evils.

Good government can only exist when there are good leaders. Good leaders are always generalists. Generalists are always ethical if not always moral. Therefore, the government of the Ethical State should consist of highly-aware generalists chosen in free democratic elections. The potential candidates themselves could be chosen on the basis of objective LTA tests. This would assure a slate of ethical candidates. Given this true choice, the electorate will hopefully elect the most ethical candidates.

The government of the Ethical State must, therefore, be structured so that such a system would work. If the system is to continue to work, it must avoid the pitfalls of the past. It must have built-in safeguards against the bureaucratization which in time would assure that the government fell into immoral hands, as has happened in every other democracy in history.

Safeguards

One of the reasons that democratic government tends to become bureaucratized and immoral is that almost all of the elected leaders are men. Even when highly moral, men tend to have a low component of social morality. In a free competition of total awareness on LTA tests, women might not be able to score as highly as men—not necessarily because women are less intelligent than men, but because evolutions seems to have concentrated personal morality in the male and social morality in the female.

Throughout history there does not appear to be a single outstanding woman generalist or great creative artist. Women have taken very little advantage of the tremendous educational opportunities offered to them in the United States and the other democracies in the last fifty years.* When women are highly intelligent and well educated, they seem invariably to be highly specialized. They are usually, but certainly not always, scientific illiterates. Therefore, it seems unlikely that women could compete effectively against men in objective LTA tests.

The *lowest* one percent in the LTA tests would probably be mostly men. However, the *highest* one percent in the LTA tests would probably also be mostly men. Women are almost never as extreme in their ethical behavior as men. They are rarely the great moral forces in history neither are they the immoral tyrants. Men are more given to extremes of both stupidity and brilliance.

If the Ethical State is to remain ethical, it will have to combine in the leadership the social morality of women and the personal morality of men. The Ethical State as the evolutionary extension of the immediate family will have to incorporate its ethical structure. Men and women will have to complement each other and not compete against one another. This can be done only by bringing the same type of love to the extended family as has made the immediate family the fountainhead of morality. Therefore, the leadership at all levels of the Ethical State must be composed of both men and women working together and not competing against each other.

A matriarchy is probably always a highly conservative society with few excesses of immorality but little progress. A patriarchy, which has been the form of most governments throughout history, is a society

---

* For example, less than five percent of the scientists in the United States are women, although over one-third of all college graduates are women. In Russia, social and economic pressure drives more women to become scientists, but even there they are usually second-raters and not significant contributors. They tend to do the more routine work and not the original research.

given to great progress for brief periods but eventually ending in total immoral decay. An Ethical State governed jointly by men and women should combine the best features of both forms. The men will assure continued imaginative progress through their personal morality. The women will guard against ethical mistakes through their social morality. The Ethical State should be guided by an ethical heterosexual government. Men and women are essential complements to one another. It is unethical to divide them and make them compete.

Constitution

The following sections may be regarded as a constitution for the Ethical State. The constitution, together with the sections on Education, Industry, Entertainment and the Military, communicates the spirit of an Ethical State. Although the overall structure of an Ethical State may at first appear contrary to many persons' intuitive notions of what is right and proper for a nation, the Ethical State, as here described, represents an integration of the ethical theory in Part I and a recognition of the dangers and pitfalls given in Part II. This is one alternative to our present society. It is the duty of anyone who can present a better alternative to do so as soon as possible. The human race probably does not have long to debate over the alternatives to the obviously suicidal society which is leading mankind to destruction.

The following constitution was written in assertive terms as if everything were finally decided. This was done to make it understandable and unambiguous, not because all problems were firmly resolved. Any or all parts of the constitution may contain ethical errors that can be corrected by persons with better information today or when more meaningful feedback is developed in our society.

Elections and Appointments (Proposal 9)

The basic structure of the Government shall be democratic except that:

1) Candidates for any public office as well as appointees must consist of male-female pairs. The male must have a current com-

posite LTA score higher than the upper one-tenth percent of the male population on the LTA tests. The female must score in the upper one-tenth percent of the female population. All candidates must have so scored for at least two consecutive years prior to being a candidate. Standards may be lowered until two qualified candidate pairs for each office are found. No other restrictions on candidates' qualifications shall exist. The male candidate and female candidate in each pair may choose each other on any basis they wish. They need not be married to one another. Once elected, they shall function as a unit with no decisions being made unless both agree. If one member of the pair becomes incapacitated, the entire pair is considered incapacitated. A person may be elected or appointed to one and only one seven-year term for any given office. He may not be appointed or elected to a new office until two years after his last term of office has expired. Once a person is elected or appointed to a public office he is given a life-time pension which assures him an income equal to the upper one-tenth percent of the general population. He may never again receive income from any other source.

2) There shall be no restrictions on age, sex, race or any characteristics for individual voters. It is the intention of this provision to have a clear majority of the intellectually-mature population represented in the electorate. Age is considered of secondary importance to intellectual maturity. Anyone who has the interest to vote should be allowed to vote in person by a secret ballot. No one should ever be forced to vote.

3) There shall be no political parties or other bureaucracies for helping elect individuals to public office. However, organized campaigns on specific issues will be allowed in complete freedom. No one shall in any way directly help or hinder a candidate in achieving elected office. (It is the intention of this provision and those that follow that competition for public office shall be entirely an individual affair devoid of any organizational support or hindrance. This is to prevent the formation of either de jure or de facto political bureaucracies.)

4) Candidate-pairs for public office must announce their candidacy two years in advance of the election. Exceptions will be in emergency elections when the incumbent pair has been suddenly removed from office by death or other events. Once a candidacy has been announced, no direct or indirect mention of the candidate in the communications media or other public area may be made.

5) Candidate-pairs shall limit their campaigns to:

  a) A biography to be prepared by each member of the pair. The candidates may put whatever facts they wish in their biographies but they must include their LTA composite scores and profiles for the last five years. The biographies should be concise.

  b) An extemporaneous essay on an unannounced, important subject, which shall be chosen by the Central Education Council. The candidate-pairs shall write the essay in a standardized test situation and immediately record it on video tape.

  c) The candidate-pairs may prepare a joint position paper at their leisure on any subject(s) they wish. This paper should be concise. It should include a summary.

  d) Each candidate's biography, essay, video tape and position paper will be made available to the entire relevant electorate at Government expense.

6) Any candidate-pair which receives more than fifty percent of the votes in any election shall be considered the winner and elected to the office in question. If no candidate-pair receives a majority, there will be a run-off election.

7) The two candidate-pairs for each office with the highest total number of votes in the primary election shall campaign in a run-off election paid for entirely by the Government.

8) The run-off election campaign shall consist of several free debates (i.e., not restricted as to subject) between the candidates and several debates on important topics chosen by the Central Education Council. The debates, each at least one hour long, shall be put on the Government, TV and radio channels. They

shall also be objectively reported in their entirety in all the appropriate media. No public comment may be made on the debates by journalists or anyone else until after the election. The debates shall be refereed and supervised by the Central Education Council and/or their representatives. They shall be conducted in a way that is objectively fair to both candidate-pairs.

9) Any qualified person may be a candidate for any public office, but not more than one office at a time.

10) All public officials elected or appointed must take an oath to defend and uphold the Constitution of the Ethical State.

11) Any appointed or elected official may be removed from office at any time by a vote of fifty percent of the relevant electorate. A recall vote will be held any time that ten percent of the electorate signs a petition to that effect.

Political Divisions (Proposal 10)

The Ethical State shall be divided into one-hundred compactly contiguous senatorial districts with approximately equal populations. One, and only one, senator-pair shall be elected from each senatorial district at a time. Each senatorial district shall be divided into an appropriate number of compactly contiguous metropolitan areas. One and only one mayor-pair shall be elected from each metropolitan area. All political subdivisions shall be formed at least two years prior to each election under the direction of the President-pair.

The Presidency (Proposal 11)

There shall be one, and only one, President-pair at a time. The President-pair shall normally be the Chief Executive of the Ethical State. The pair shall have full executive and legislative powers to pass and execute any laws it wishes, except laws which violate the Constitution of the Ethical State. The pair may amend the Constitution of the Ethical State only with the consent of three-quarters of all currently-elected senator-pairs. It shall be the direct principal responsibility of the President-pair,

within the constraints of the Constitution, to maximize the total awareness of the human race and to engender the Moral Society. The President-pair may 1) raise and spend the income of the Ethical State; 2)
draft appropriate persons to appointive office when necessary (only persons scoring in the upper one-tenth percent on the LTA scores are subject to the draft); 3) exercise complete ethical control (i.e., fire and hire,
determine salaries, etc.) over all government employees; and 4) otherwise constitutionally and ethically control the educational system and
infrastructure of the Ethical State. The President-pair may be removed
from office at any time by voice vote of three-quarters of all currently
elected senator-pairs. If the President-pair is removed from office or if
one member of the pair dies or becomes incapacitated for a prolonged
period, then all the powers of the President-pair shall pass to the Chairman (a pair) of the Senate. The Chairman-pair shall be the Chief Executive until a new President-pair is elected at the earliest possible date but
never later than one year after removing the last President-pair. The
Chairman of the Senate is not eligible to be elected President until two
years after the pair's term of office has expired. The acting President is
responsible for organizing and supervising all elections. The President-
pair may in no way interfere with the freedom and activities of the Senate or individual senators. To do so automatically disqualifies the President-pair for office and its authority automatically becomes vested in the
Chairman of the Senate. The President-pair is obligated to cooperate
with the Senate in all matters pertaining to the welfare of the Ethical
State and to listen to the Senate's advice.

The President-pair shall be obliged personally to deliver at least once
a month a progress report in the form of a news conference to the entire
electorate. This conference shall be reported in the news media and de-
livered "live" by the President-pair on the public communications channels. The President-pair shall also have access to the public communications channels at other times. The public communications channels shall
be split by time on a random basis each month with fifty percent of the
time going to the President-pair and fifty percent to the Senate. The
President-pair shall periodically give to the electorate an evaluation of
the activities of each senator-pair.

The Senate (Proposal 12)

The Senate has the principal responsibility of evaluating the performance of the President-pair and guiding policy. The Senate has full authority to investigate all activities of the Presidency. The Senate may demand from the President-pair and spend whatever income it needs to support its activities. The Senate will formulate its own rules and procedures. Each senator-pair must have a rank which determines how close it is to the chairmanship of the Senate. At the first Senate meeting the senator-pairs will be ranked by composite LTA score. Lots will be cast when there are ties. The highest ranking senator-pair will be the Chairman. The Senate has the power to remove all public officials, the President-pair, any judge-pair, mayor-pair, etc., from office by a three-quarters vote of all currently-elected senator-pairs. Each senator-pair member shall be immune from arrest for any crime and may not have his personal freedom and powers of investigation interfered with in any way while holding office. The Senate itself may, however, police its own members if it wishes. Senate rules and activities must always reflect the will of the majority of the Senate. Individual senators may act in any way they wish outside the Senate. The senatorial elections shall be divided between the senatorial districts in such a way that every year at least one-tenth of the Senate is in the process of being elected. The Chairman of the Senate is obliged to give monthly reports to the nation on the activities of the Senate and its evaluation of the President-pair. Each senator-pair is obliged to publish a monthly newsletter explaining its activities to its constituents and reflecting its personal evaluation of the President. The President-pair shall have competitive investigative teams which issue reports to the electorate on the activities of each senator. The senators must be reasonably responsive to the demands of their constiuents.

Metropolitan Mayors (Proposal 13)

Mayor-pairs shall have complete administrative and legislative authority in their metropolitan area. They shall be elected by the electorate of the metropolitan area they will administer and no other electorate. A mayor-pair shall be subject to the authority of the President. The pair may be summarily dismissed from office by the President-pair or by a vote of three-quarters of the Senate. The mayor-pairs may administer their areas as they see fit so long as the policies of the President-pair are implemented. If and when there is a conflict, Presidential policy shall always take precedence over local policy. The budget of each metropolitan area shall be set by the President-pair. It is the responsibility of the mayor-pairs and the appropriate senators to see that the Presidential policy and budget meets the needs of their constituents. Both the President-pair and the Senate may perform evaluative functions within the metropolitan areas.

The Judiciary (Proposal 14)

The Judiciary shall be appointed (by drafting for two years when necessary) by the President with the advice—but not necessarily the consent—of the senator-pair and the mayor-pair of the area where the judge-pair shall exercise its authority.

The Senate shall maintain three competitive examining teams to evaluate all judges. The teams shall operate analogously to the educational evaluating teams. Their analyses will be reported periodically (at least once a year) by the Senate.

Each judge-pair shall decide issues involving conflicts between persons, government and/or corporations, also issues of local, presidential or constitutional law. The decision of any judge-pair may be appealed to two more judge-pairs. The decision of the majority of the three judge-pairs is final in civil cases. In criminal cases all three judge-pairs must find the accused guilty or he will be considered innocent. There shall be no double jeopardy in criminal cases (i.e., appealing can only reduce a sentence, never increase it). Judicial decisions shall be based on the special merits of each individual case. The basic criterion for each decision shall be what course of action will enhance the totality of human awareness. There shall be no rigid adherence to the letter of any law unless it favors the accused. Justice will be based on ethics and not necessarily on laws. The basic intent of the Ethical State—the expansion of total awareness

—should be uppermost in each judge's mind when making decisions. Therefore, the judge-pairs shall be more like philosophers and psycho-social scientists than lawyers.

The Central Education Council (Proposal 15)

The President-pair shall appoint qualified male-female pairs to a Central Education Council subject to confirmation by at least fifty percent of the Senate. There shall be eleven chairs on the Council. Ten of the chairs shall be reserved for the following broad categories: mathematics, physics, chemistry, biology, psychology, history and social analysis (includes all psychosocial sciencies sciences other than psychology), astronomy (inclues all studies of outerspace), engineering, art (includes literature, music, painting, etc.) and philosophy. Each appointed pair must be distinguished in the subject matter of each chair. The eleventh chair on the Council will be filled by an outstanding generalist-pair chosen by the other Council members. The generalist-pair shall be the Chairman of the Council.

The Council shall formulate its own rules of operation. All decisions of the Council must be reached through majority vote. The Chairman of the Council shall guide their activities and be responsible for their actions.

The Council shall formulate in secret the yearly standardized LTA and TAP tests. The Council shall also help formulate and recommend educational policy for the Ethical State. It shall evaluate and criticize the entire educational system and the supporting infrastructure in terms of their effectiveness for expanding total awareness. It shall screen for acceptability all children's television programs. The workings of the Council shall be open to Presidential and Senatorial investigation with the exception of the creation of the yearly LTA and TAP tests. Once the LTA tests have been administered under the Council's direction, then the etiology of the tests may be analyzed by the President and the Senate.

In order to accomplish its tasks the Council shall have an unlimited expense account which must be met by the President. The Council is empowered to muster any resources it needs to accomplish its purposes —including the ordering of Presidential drafts for personnel.

While in office, Council members are immune from arrest or any interference with their public or private lives by agents of the President or the Senate. At least one chair of the Council must be filled with a new pair each year.

Laws (Proposal 16)

In criminal cases all accused persons shall be considered innocent until unanimously declared guilty by three judge-pairs. All persons shall have a right to a speedy trial. There shall be a sufficient number of judge-pairs to make this possible. Any accused person in a criminal case shall have the right to retain any counsel willing to defend him at standardized rates to be paid entirely by the Ethical State.

There shall be no punishment of convicted criminals other than exile. Exile may be imposed only on unethical persons who are proven incorrigible detractors from the general welfare. Reasonable effort should be made to rehabilitate criminals before imposing exile. When a person has been exiled, he or his descendants may petition any judge-pair for readmission to the Ethical State on the basis that they shall desist from diminishing the general total awareness.

Even when the Ethical State is a world government, a viable region shall be set aside where voluntary and imposed exiles from the Ethical State may live in a civilized manner and do as they please. The only limitation will be that they can in no way threaten the inhabitants or otherwise interfere with the welfare of the Ethical State. The Military of the Ethical State shall supervise the exiles and enforce the laws. Within the confines of the exiles' region, the laws of the Ethical State (except for threat and interference) shall not apply and exiles will make their own laws if they wish. Exiles who return to the Ethical State illegally or otherwise threaten the Ethical State shall be subject to re-exile or exile to an island from which escape is more difficult. The latter shall be done only if three judge-pairs unanimously determine that the person is incorrigible and should not be re-exiled in the normal manner. There shall be no other forms of punishment and no imprisonment except for persons in the process of being exiled. The Military will carry out the exile orders as quickly as possible and interfere as little as possible with the exile's personal freedom.

The Ethical State shall maintain observers in the place of exile in an attempt to learn from the exiles' independent development. The exiles will be a source of feedback to the Ethical State.

No laws shall be formulated except those which can logically be shown to be necessary for the enhancement of total awareness in the Ethical State and the creation of a Moral Society. No ex post facto laws shall be passed. All laws shall become automatically invalid in seven years unless the assumptions underlying their creation have been substantiated scientifically.

Civil Rights (Proposal 17)

All citizens of the Ethical State have the right to personal freedom and equal treatment under the law. Any person may do and say whatever he wishes so long as he does not in the process interfere with the right of another person to do and say as he pleases. When there is a conflict, the issues shall be settled by common law and/or the judicial process.

No laws shall be passed interfering with freedom of expression, except for the following:

a) Libel and slander (deliberate or unintentional falsehoods about other persons).

b) Propagandizing in public for or against individual political candidates. Issues and persons not candidates for office may be discussed in complete freedom.

c) Forced subjection to the unwanted expression of others (e.g., public disturbances, esthetic or ecological pollution, personal assault, fraud, stealing, deleterious goods and services, etc.).

d) Non-factual or misleading advertising of goods and services.

Taking into account the above restrictions, every metropolitan area shall maintain at public expense a suitable meeting place where any person may publicly express his opinions on any subject at any time including denunciations of the Ethical State and its leaders.

All persons shall be entitled to an adequate subsistence allowance while expanding their total awareness or the awareness of others at a satisfactory rate. The rate which is satisfactory shall be limited only by the availability of resources. When the resources are adequate, all persons shall be entitled to the student subsistence allowance. When the resources are more limited, the oldest, slowest persons in the process of expanding awareness shall have their subsistence allowance limited to the minimum for maintaining life and health if they cannot otherwise support themselves, until an economic balance is established. Healthy persons not willing to expand awareness or support themselves shall be subject to exile.

The Ethical State shall support an educational system which shall enable all persons to educate themselves indefinitely in the manner that was indicated in the section on education. The prime criterion for support shall be effectiveness of the educational activity in augmenting the collective ability of the Ethical State to predict and control its total environment.

The Ethical State shall neither support nor impede any ideology, art form, educational system or personal behavior unless it can be demonstrated scientifically through controlled experimentation that these activities have a significant effect on the total awareness of the population. In that case it shall be the obligation of the Ethical State to support activities which enhance total awareness and to correct public activities which diminish awareness.

A person's life belongs entirely to himself except for voluntary commitments. The Ethical State may not interfere with private voluntary behavior even when such behavior is deleterious to the person(s) involved. Those who will not play the Game of Life must be allowed to destroy themselves. To attempt to preserve them is to increase man's entropy. It is unethical to protect immoral persons from their own entropy.

No person shall be forced into involuntary servitude for any purposes, private or public, except by previous mutual agreement. All per-

sons scoring in the upper one-tenth percent of the population in the LTA
tests shall be subject to Presidential draft to high, well-paid appointive
office for purposes of expanding and/or preserving the total awareness of
the Ethical State. All persons shall be required to take the LTA tests. All
persons shall be free to avoid the tests and the draft by going into exile at
any time. A person may avoid the draft by deliberately scoring below the
upper one-tenth percent of the general population on the LTA tests.

Eugenics

Eugenics is an effort to improve the quality of the human race directly by controlling the kinds and numbers of human beings. The human population cannot be allowed to increase indefinitely so long as
resources are limited. Through the President, the Ethical State shall direct a universal eugenics program to enhance the expansion of total
awareness.

The Ethical State shall not attempt to control the activities of persons so long as these activities are private and reflect the mutual consent
of the parties involved. Marriage, the absence of marriage, or any type of
sexual behavior shall be an entirely private matter when it involves only
mutually-consenting persons. The production of children, however, is
not a private matter since it directly affects the collective total awareness.
Each new person consumes resources, produces pollutants and will expand or diminish in varying degrees the total awareness of the human
race. It is the obligation of the Ethical State to help each new person
contribute to the maximization of total awareness.

Uniform Birth Control (Proposal 18)

If the hypothesis of the extreme Left is correct, then the problem of
eugenics is a relatively simple matter which involes only the application
of a uniform birth-control law to the entire population. Since under the
extreme leftist hypothesis there is no genetic basis whatever to differential human behavior (e.g., LTA and TAP scores), then eugenics is
merely a problem of keeping the population down to a sufficiently low
level that the consumption of resources and the production of pollution

is not so great as to hinder the constant expansion of total awareness. In this case, the Ethical State need only license the number of children a woman will bear on the same basis for all women. When a woman has reached her quota, which might change periodically, she will have to stop having children.

This can be done by voluntary birth control techniques combined with abortions for women who become "accidentally" pregnant after having borne their full quota of children. A simpler technique might be for a woman to have her Fallopian tubes tied. This would in no way alter her endocrine balance or her sexual behavior. Insofar as monogamous mating, in contrast to the currently expanding patterns of serial and group polygamy, becomes the voluntary pattern of sexual behavior in the Ethical State, the simplest technique of birth control will be to perform a vasectomy on the male partner in a monogamous couple. This simple operation will in no way affect the male's normal sexual behavior or endocrine balance. In any case, the form of birth control should be a voluntary choice on the part of the persons involved. Persons unwilling to limit their families will always have the option of going into exile.

If the hypothesis of the extreme Left is false, then the problem of eugenics is much more complex. If there is any genetic basis whatever to human behavior in general and the innate potential to expand total awareness in particular then a selective birth control program is essential or the entropy of the human race will continue to increase. This is the case because mutations cannot be stopped and most mutations are deleterious. Spontaneous mutability is inherent in the DNA molecule. Only natural selection reduces entropy in a species by assuring the survival of the most aware.

Selective Birth Control (Proposal 19)

A selective birth control program would be one consistent with the evolutionary force. It would increase the fitness* of the most aware at the cost of the fitness of the least aware. This would mean, in effect, that those persons most likely to produce children who would have a very low innate potential for expanding total awareness would be required to avoid

* "Fitness" as used here means the "potential for producing progeny."

having any children. Persons most likely to produce children with a very high innate potential to expand total awareness would be given incentives by the Ethical State to bear as many children as possible. Incentives could take the form of increased subsistence allowances for each child born, paid servants, subsidized large-scale housing and so on. Persons between the two extremes would be treated in an intermediate fashion.

The difficulty arises in measuring innate potential for increasing awareness. The phenotype of all organisms is almost certainly a reflection of *both* genetic and environmental factors. In any given individual, it is often impossible to separate the different causes of the phenotype. However, *in populations, not individuals*, the differential effect of heredity and environment can be determined statistically by a straightforward technique (analysis of variance) used in conjunction with controlled experiments. Therefore, while we may not know with certainty the exact causes for the phenotype of a person, we can know the general reasons for differences in phenotype between statistically-defined populations.

Within the modern, fully-industrialized and at least partially-socialized countries of North America and Western Europe, considerable evidence already exists that differential "I.Q. test" scores are determined primarily by differential heredity (eighty percent heritability).* I.Q. scores are very crude measures of TAP. Recalling the simple model of intelligence in Chapter 2, we see that I.Q. tests at best measure little more than some limited aspects of Information, Memory, and Logic. The other components of intelligence, particularly Imagination and Will, are left mostly untested. In spite of this, I.Q. test scores, particularly consistent very low scores (under ninety on Stanford-Binet), are good predictors of future LTA.† Persons with I.Q.'s below ninety almost never contribute directly to the expansion of total awareness. At best they seem to serve in a support capacity by performing services that will allow higher I.Q. persons to devote a larger percentage of their time to

---

* Jensen, Arthur, op. cit.
† LTA tests *per se* do not exist at this time but general educational achievement tests such as the Army General Technical Test and the Graduate Record Examination do exist. One would expect performance on these tests to be highly correlated with LTA.

expanding total awareness. I.Q. scores are almost entirely useless for predicting differential LTA at the higher levels. The expected differential future LTA is virtually the same whether a person has an I.Q. of one hundred thirty or one hundred seventy. These results may be interpreted as follows:

Genetically-determined Imagination and Will are uncorrelated to Logic and Memory. A person needs a minimum level of Logic and Memory to increase significantly his LTA and the total awareness of the human race. This level is probably higher than that indicated by an I.Q. of ninety, but probably need not be much higher than that indicated by an I.Q. of one hundred and thirty. At I.Q. levels higher than one hundred and thirty, Imagination and Will become the most important components of Intelligence for expanding total awareness.

Information is primarily an environmental phenomenon (except for instinct) and apparently has little genetic basis. It may be, however, that the molecular structure of Memory, which is genetically-based, may facilitate the absorption of some types of information and hinder the absorption of other types.

The environment in most of modern North America and Western Europe is such that important Information is readily available to all. It is easier for some than others to obtain important Information (i.e., education opportunities) but for persons with a moderately high innate Logic, Memory, Imagination and Will, the environment poses no serious obstacles.

Insofar as Sensors and Effectors are concerned, there appears to be much less significant variability in the innate quality of these characteristics than in the other components. This is probably due to the fact that science and technology have greatly reduced the need for high-quality, innate Sensors and Effectors. Today, unlike in the past, it is possible to be almost totally deaf, blind and unathletic and still be highly proficient at predicting and controlling the total environment, e.g. Helen Keller. In other words, science and technology have made most differences in genetically-determined Sensor and Effector quality relatively insignificant. Ironically, science and technology have made genetically-determined differences in Memory, Logic, Imagination and Will even more important than in the past.

Connectors seem to be discretely effective entities. That is to say, either a person has totally effective Connectors or he is almost totally disabled and unfit. Connectors, therefore, seem to have the least genetic variability.

In conclusion, I.Q. tests appear to measure crudely some *necessary* innate conditions for the expansion of total awareness. I.Q. tests definitely do *not* measure the *sufficient* conditions for the expansion of total awareness. I.Q. is correlated with intelligence. I.Q. does not measure intelligence. TAP tests, to be fully effective, must measure Imagination and Will as well as Logic and Memory. No TAP test will be valid unless the educational opportunities are such that important information is readily available to all; only then will the TAP score have a high heritability. The educational opportunities in modern socialized countries, such as the United States and Sweden, already appear to meet the conditions for guaranteeing high heritability on I.Q. scores. The educational opportunities of the Ethical State will greatly exceed those of the current socialistic democracies for *all* persons.

In eugenics the objective is *to improve the future population* as a *whole*. Eugenics does not improve any individual. Only education does that. There is little doubt that if LTA has any genetic basis at all, then a scientific eugenics program can continuously improve the collective TAP of the human race. In so doing, it is possible to commit *individual* injustices by preventing genetically-qualified persons from bearing children. This would occur when environmental circumstances damaged the person in such a way that his TAP phenotype appeared much lower than heredity would indicate. The most likely cause for this damage would be due to prenatal and birth accidents, particularly oxygen deprivation. It is very unlikely that differences in the social environment of the Ethical State will produce differential damage since even the current bureaucratized environment of the social democracies apparently produces very little differential damage in I.Q. test scores. This latter point is, of course, contrary to leftist ideology but is most consistent with the scientific evidence. It would be a relatively simple matter to resolve experimentally, but the leftist ideologues would oppose this, probably successfully, under the current political system.

In any case, a small, ever-decreasing number of individual injustices in the present will be the price that humanity will have to pay in order continuously to improve the future quality of the *entire* human race. These injustices would consist in no more than preventing a very small number of improperly-evaluated persons from assuming the responsibility of bearing and raising children. The eugenics program itself would be completely humane, consistent with personal freedom, and in effect voluntary (i.e., a person can always choose exile). Every effort would be made to keep injustices to a minimum and the eugenics program would be continuously evaluated and improved. This is a very small price to pay for guaranteeing that our progeny will, as a minimum, have the totality of awareness typified by a Leonardo da Vinci and a Bach.

Another eugenic possibility that may exist in the future is that of genetic engineering. Through genetic engineering it might be possible to repair defective genes so that all persons could bear children. In this case, any person could bear children if he volunteered to have his genes repaired. There is a possibility, however, that an uncertainty principle might operate at the molecular level which will make genetic engineering too haphazard an instrument for practical genetic repair. Genetic engineering may remain an experimental tool which will occasionally, by chance, produce a highly superior genotype which should be transmitted to the rest of the human race. Through genetic engineering, we may, in effect, increase the rate of beneficial mutations and decrease the rate of deleterious mutations. Since the concept of personal freedom is central to the Ethical State, genetic engineering could only be applied to volunteers. If and when genetic engineering became a practical reality, then selective birth control might not be necessary.

In the Ethical State the eugenics program will be based on scientifically-developed measures of TAP (i.e., the measures will be based on how well they enable one to predict future LTA).* If and when the high heritability of the I.Q. score is confirmed by further controlled experimentation, then I.Q. tests may be used as a crude first measure of

* TAP and LTA are redefined in Glossary.

low-level TAP. There is no evidence that any desirable human characteristic is positively associated with low I.Q. scores.

The TAP tests together with the total educational environment will be increasingly improved until 1) the heritability of the TAP test score is one hundred percent and 2) all components of intelligence are fully reflected in the TAP test. The latter criterion will be established when there is an almost perfect positive correlation between TAP score and future LTA score. The former criterion will be established when no changes in the total educational environment can raise the TAP score.

A selective eugenics program will be implemented which will continuously improve the collective TAP of the human race. At the outset the TAP scores will be used solely to reduce the number of parasitical human beings. As the TAP tests improve, there will be a graduated level of reproduction from zero reproduction for persons with the lowest TAP scores to subsidized, highly-encouraged, unlimited reproduction for persons with the highest TAP scores.

So long as the educational system and technology can be used to improve a person's TAP score, it will so be used. As soon as a child is detected as having a TAP score too low to qualify for parenthood, it will be the responsibility of the Ethical State to do everything in its power to help the child qualify for parenthood. This may take the form of special education and incentives or medical treatment. The child will be tested repeatedly under more careful conditions than the regular primary school population. If by the age of puberty a person still has not qualified for parenthood, then a judge will decide whether or not that person should 1) be sterilized (temporarily if possible); 2) *volunteer* for genetic engineering and repair, when practical; or 3) be allowed to practise voluntary birth control. The person may, of course, avoid sterilization by going into exile. An unsterilized person, unqualified for parenthood and practicing voluntary birth control, will be subject to exile or sterilization if he produces a child. Any time a person's TAP score qualified him for parenthood, he could become a parent if he were biologically capable.

An analogous procedure will apply to all persons who have a limitation on the number of children they can legally produce. Once they have reached their quota, they will be treated as person's unqualified for further parenthood.

The basic objective of the eugenics program will be to produce the maximum number of persons with the maximum level of total awareness. The limitations on the maximum number of persons shall be constrained only by the availability of resources. It is the obligation of the Ethical State to assure that the general level of TAP as well as LTA is constantly rising in the human race.

TENSION IN THE ETHICAL STATE

An Ethical State, in attempting to maximize mankind's total awareness, will produce considerable tension. The tension of the Ethical State will have many forms, but it will have its most direct manifestation in the educational system which will force man to increase his awareness at his maximum rate. This will be done through social pressure, not physical coercion. However, it is social pressure that seems to create the greatest tensions in mankind.

All research seems to be done best under a crash program of maximum tension with quick and accurate feedback. This was the case with the Manhattan project. This was the case with Project Apollo. So it will probably be with every facet of the Ethical State. There will never be time to rest. Man must always become totally aware at his maximum rate or entropy, in the form of bureaucracy, ideology, and/or hedonism, will overtake and destroy him.

Today we see this happening to the United States National Aeronautics and Space Administration (NASA). NASA accomplished its symbolic mission of unifying all the sciences (physical, biological, and psychosocial) in order to extend man's awareness beyond the Earth. Today NASA is becoming bureaucratized. We should expect an increasing number of failures for NASA as it becomes as corrupt as the Soviet space agency. NASA beat the Soviets to the moon because it was a new unbureaucratized organization working under maximum tension with quick and accurate feedback. This is no longer the case.

The picture of the Ethical State, therefore, is one of constant creative tension. This is not the neurotic tension of anxiety, but the healthy, joyful tension of an evolving society. Individual men may rest by sinking into matter but man can never rest if he is to become the Moral Society. Man must choose between evolution and entropy.

Entropy is an inexorable force which destroys any life form which submits to it for even a short time. Only by submitting to entropy can man rest and be assured of illusions of awareness. The temptation to sink into matter, to rest, to seek happiness, is overwhelming for any person not subject to the immediate pressure of self-preservation. No individual Will, in the presence of affluence, can long resist the entropic force. Resistance to entropy is only possible when the Will is amplified by a progressive culture or the need to survive.

Throughout almost all of his history, man avoided entropy by living under maximum tension. He was subjected continuously to the testing pressure of the evolutionary force. Man has for millions of years been in immediate danger of starving or being killed by other animals. This produced the creative tension which forced him to evolve. Today this is no longer the case. Socialism and bureaucratization have eliminated all vestiges of vital competition within nations. The testing between the major nations can only lead to annihilation. Man must now deliberately test himself for no other purpose than to improve himself. The only motivation for this action is a desire to play the Game of Life. However, a person must believe that his efforts will have some effect and lead to more than awareness for himself. He must feel himself a part of something greater than himself. Otherwise the direct pursuit of happiness is a much more attractive goal.

In a bureaucratized society such as permeates the entire world, it is much easier, indeed logical, to forget about future generations which seem doomed anyway, and to think only about our individual happiness. Only the constant creative tension and purpose of an Ethical State can reverse this trend.

There is no logical reason for playing the Game of Life. It is just as "natural" to sink into matter as to rise to greater mind. Both entropy and evolution are natural forces. The Game of Life will only be played by those in whom the evolutionary force is stronger than the entropic force. At first the effectiveness of the deliberate players of the Game will be attenuated by being immersed in the entropy of a bureaucratized, hedonistic miasma of humanity. However, as more and more persons become players, they will amplify the Will and Imagination of one another and the playing of the Game will become increasingly easy. The entropy will decrease. Eventually, the vast majority of humanity will be players and no one will wish to stop the Game. Human evolution will become irreversible. In order for this to happen, it will be necessary to test each person and select against those who would attenuate the effectiveness of the players. This will, of course, produce constant tension and a type of insecurity in an Ethical State. But it is essential for man's continued creative evolution.

The Ethical State, unlike our currently-bureaucratized society, does not diffuse responsibility. Each person is made clearly responsible for his actions. The Presidency is entirely responsible for the effectiveness of the government, the development of the Ethical State and the creation of a Moral Society. The Senate is responsible for the effectiveness of the Presidency and other officials. The electorate is responsible for all. Bureaucracies are replaced by competitive teams with high feedback and are subject to Darwinian natural selection. The most effective teams multiply. The least effective perish, i.e., are disbanded.

Most of all, each person is directly responsible for his own intellectual development. He has at his disposal a completely-subsidized, highly-flexible, personalized educational system with high feedback which will enable him to expand his total awareness in his own way every day of his life if he has the Will to do so. Each person is guaranteed feedback by being continuously shown his increase in total awareness relative to the rest of the population. No one will be able to blame anyone but himself for his shortcomings. No one will be able to avoid negative feedback. So it will be with everyone in an Ethical State. This is creative tension.

An Ethical State is not the tranquil, harmonious paradise that is usually portrayed by revolutionaries to delude their followers into supporting their objectives. An Ethical State is the direct manifestation of the evolutionary force. Its sole purpose is to expand man's total awareness. There will be many, at first, who will find an Ethical State's *forcing* them to face reality, which includes what they can neither predict nor control, unbearable. They will try to destroy the Ethical State. Only moral men will find joy in the infinitely-expanding total awareness of humanity.

Man must make the choice now whether to give up apathy and self-delusion and commit himself to evolving forever toward total awareness, or to descend into matter where the entropic peace and tranquillity of bureaucratic security and ideological delusion eventually become absolute. If man is to survive and evolve toward total awareness, there can be no rest or relaxation of maximum creative tension. There is no other way. It is the universe or nothing. Man must decide soon which it shall be.

7

STRATEGY

The previous chapter described the over-all structure of an Ethical State. It was shown to be a society which maximizes awareness in part by maximizing feedback. This is the antithesis of bureaucratic and ideological security. An Ethical State will force people to face reality.* It will use constant feedback to make them fully aware of their own limitations. Currently this is something that the vast majority of the human race cannot abide. The problem is, therefore, how to bring about something that—at this time—almost no one wants, least of all the unethical persons in power. The solution lies in the nature of the evolutionary force.

THE TRIUMPH OF AWARENESS

In the evolutionary process, competition leads invariably to the victory of the most aware. There may be individual setbacks along the way,

---

* Recall that reality includes what we can neither predict nor control. Reality includes negative feedback.

but the overall pattern is the replacement of the least aware by the most aware. The pattern applies to species, subspecies of men, civilizations, political systems and political parties. Democracy triumphed over monarchy not only because it promised better feedback, but most of all because it had the adherence of the most-aware members of society. The same applies to the triumph of Communism over czarism in Russia and over a corrupt military dictatorship in China.

In the democracies the political parties with the largest numbers of highly aware persons inevitably obtain a monopoly of political power until their own corruption drives them from office. This was the case with the Republican Party in the United States from the time of Lincoln to the fall of Hoover. During its rise to power, the Republican Party almost totally pre-empted the allegiance of the American intellectual community. A similar phenomenon occurred to the Liberal Party in England from the time of Gladstone to the fall of Lloyd George. In both cases, the political bureaucracies which once included the most brilliant men in the respective lands became so corrupt that they caused enormous hardship to their people. The Liberal Party of England, according to Bertrand Russell and many historians, was responsible for involving England unnecessarily in World War I, thereby laying the foundations that made the Nazi holocaust inevitable.

The Republican Party had a virtual monopoly of power for many years after the Civil War and it soon became corrupt. The corruption diminished when some feedback was re-established by the end of Reconstruction and the new effectiveness of the Democrats. During the 1920's, the Republican "do-nothing" policies of laissez-faire capitalism brought about the Great Depression.

Since the Depression, the Democratic Party in the United States has had a virtual monopoly on the allegiances of the American intellectual community. Its power has been equally disproportionate. The corruption of the Democratic Party had its ultimate expression in the Vietnam War which has, in many ways, been a disaster greater than the Great Depression. In domestic issues, the Democratic Party has become a captive of leftist, bureaucratic ideology which threatens in time to bring about almost equally destructive consequences (e.g., the Revolt Against Reason). The intellectual community is beginning to abandon the

Democrats, but it has no place to go. Most intellectuals are merely drop-ping out and becoming hedonists.

The same pattern is repeated in every country where political parties exist. Political success is guaranteed by obtaining the allegiance of the overwhelming majority of the most highly-aware persons, even though they may constitute only a small percentage of the electorate. In some countries, such as France, the community of highly-aware persons is split ideologically along the Left-Right continuum. In France, there are also a larger number of effective political parties than in the more fully-developed (i.e., politically bureaucratized) democracies of America, England, or Sweden. Therefore, in France no single party commands a clear majority of the best minds.

OVERCOMING APATHY

The most common phenomenon in all democracies is that found in the U.S. today. The most-aware persons find politics so distasteful that they eschew political involvement altogether in favor of their personal pursuits. A stable bureaucracy makes this possible. This causes a general decrease in the quality of political life which causes still more highly-aware persons to abandon politics. Eventually the political bureaucracies become total captives of the most mendacious members of the Immoral Community. The bureaucracies receive virtually no feedback from the Moral Community. This is the predominant picture in all the democra-cies. In the Communist countries the political bureaucracies, once estab-lished, become far more corrupt than in the democracies since they have even less feedback.

The problem of establishing an Ethical State in any nation is, there-fore, the problem of organizing a nucleus of highly-aware persons dedi-cated to the ethical expansion of total awareness for the entire human race. This nucleus must have a critical mass of persons and will probably have to work within the framework of the existing parties, although it may be more effective in some cases to create a completely new political party around the nucleus. This, after all, is the way it has always been with the introduction of any radically new political system.

The masses are inherently conservative even when they are oppressed and miserable, to say nothing of when they are affluent. They are motivated almost entirely by their desire for security and happiness. They are more fearful of losing what they already have than they are desirous of improving their condition. Historically, the inertia of the masses is overcome only by the collective will and intelligence of a small, dedicated minority of highly aware revolutionaries determined to change the social order. Such was the case in the American, French, Russian, and Chinese revolutions. The same process occurred under more peaceful conditions when the Liberal Party in England and the Socialist Party in Sweden brought about radical social reforms under a more gradual process of change. But in all cases, the will of a dedicated, highly-aware minority always triumphs, no matter how much entropic inertia the masses may have or how powerful the entrenched forces of reaction appear.

There is no force in the world stronger than a group of ethical, highly-aware men organized and dedicated to accomplish an objective consistent with the evolutionary force. The problem is how and where to engender a critical mass of ethical persons who may become deliberate players of the Game of Life. These persons shall be called "Protagonists."

FINDING THE PROTAGONISTS

The engendering of an Ethical State and the creation of a Moral Society will be a long and complex process of evolution. Just as the evolution of any new life form begins with only a few mutations (sometimes only one), so will the evolution of an Ethical State begin with the few mutations of highly-aware persons who are transformed into deliberate players of the Game of Life. A critical mass of highly-aware Protagonists is clearly a necessary condition for engendering an Ethical State; it may even be a sufficient condition. The first problem to be solved is for the Protagonists to identify and find one another.

The most highly-aware persons in our society are generalists who have also developed depth in some aspects of science and technology. These men were typified in the recent past by John von Neumann, Norbert Wiener, Lev Landau and Erwin Schroedinger. These men and their peers were all ethical; but they played The Game of Life because it was fun, not because it was important. They were not *deliberate* players. They were in a sense all *apolitical*. This does not mean that they did not have political opinions. In one way or another, all these men were involved in political protest during their lives. However, protest is the least effective way of controlling the environment. It is a secondary rather than a prime event. Because these men were more interested in the pleasure of expanding their personal awareness than in fulfilling their duty to the entire human race, as a group they inadvertently strengthened the Immoral Community and contributed to the further bureaucratization of the sciences. They had an abundance of personal morality, but little social morality. Yet these men represent the best that the human race has to offer. They were all ethical men. Their failing came from not *deliberately* playing the Game of Life. They were not Protagonists.

This is a failing that can only be overcome by becoming fully aware of the Game of Live, the evolutionary process, bureaucratization, ideology, ethics, the Ethical State and the Moral Society. When generalists become aware of all these factors, their inter-relationships, and most of all, the possibility for effective action, then they can deliberately begin to change the world and start an Ethical State. In order for this to occur, they must cease being apolitical. The turning of generalists into political activists will be made possible by a new evolutionary phenomenon.

Throughout human history, the overwhelming majority of mankind has been concerned only with its personal happiness and security. Today there is a new type of human in our midst. Teilhard de Chardin called him *Homo progressivus*. *Homo progressivus* differs from *Homo sapiens* in being deeply concerned with the future of man. He has this concern because he perceives directly that human progress is a reality. He sees that the total awareness of mankind has increased and can continue to increase. *Homo progressivus* is mankind being made moral. He is mankind being transformed into *Homo moralensis*—moral man—the engenderer of the Moral Society.

The identification of the Protagonists who will form the first critical nucleus of the Ethical State is therefore relatively easy. They are the community of moral men and ethical children.* They are the persons who continue to increase awareness. The problem of bringing them together and motivating them is much more complex, because the incipient Protagonists are uncertain of what to do. They all agree that the current state of affairs is intolerable, but they cannot agree on specific alternatives.

Ethical persons are not concentrated in any particular sector of society. They are more or less uniformly distributed throughout the Moral Community. Wherever they are, however, they are relatively isolated within a milieu of more specialized, but still ethical scientists and artists.

In the United States, at any one time, no more than ten thousand—perhaps as few as one thousand—generalists with depth are directly and solely responsible for all the inventions, discoveries, developments and science which give momentum to the entire nation. Almost all the creative energy of the Moral Community is misused, to increase the entropy of the society by 1) making it less and less necessary for people to think and 2) by developing the technology which makes it possible for scientifically illiterate bureaucrats to entrench themselves. The generalists either directly or indirectly work to support the political bureaucracies of the Immoral Community. It seems they can predict and control all aspects of the environment except the psychosocial. They feel frustrated and hopeless in the face of the legal-minded technicians of the Immoral Community. This frustration must be channeled into creative action if an Ethical State is to be created.

The Protagonists may therefore be identified as ethical children and generalists with technical depth and imagination. They are diffused throughout the Moral Community. They produce the motive power for the entire world, but they seem helpless in competing with immoral men for control of the psychosocial environment. They will be motivated to play the Game of Life deliberately only when they see some hope of defeating the entrenched political bureaucracies of the Immoral Community.

* Recall that "children" is used only in the ethical sense, not the chronological sense.

THE VULNERABILITY
OF THE POLITICAL BUREAUCRACIES

The political bureaucracies are extremely vulnerable because the leadership is ignorant of everything except the rules of bureaucratic intrigue. The political bureaucracies are completely dependent on the Moral Community for guidance whenever they wish to be effective in the physical or biological environment and/or creative in the psychosocial environment. However, the Moral Community is not really dependent on the political bureaucracies for anything. The scientists, and to a lesser extent the artists, somehow have been conditioned over the last one hundred years to believe that they cannot function unless they placate the political bureaucracies. However, this is an illusion fostered by the Immoral Community in its attempt to domesticate the Moral Community. All the true wealth, the machines, the processes, the inventions, the art, and the science which make it possible for ever fewer men to predict and control ever greater parts of the total environment, all this is produced entirely by the Moral Community. It is the intellect of the Moral Community and the natural resources that are the wealth of society. Furthermore, the latter are valueless without the former. The Moral Community does not need the Immoral Community in any way. Without the support of the Moral Community, the effectiveness of the Immoral Community would disappear completely if it were not for its complete control of the political bureaucracy.

In democratic countries, monopoly over the political bureaucracy does not present a serious problem, but in Communist countries it may prove an insurmountable obstacle. Since in Communist countries there is no internal competition or feedback to the political bureaucracy, any attempt by the Moral Community to autonomize itself would be seen as an intolerable threat and would be instantly suppressed by force. Therefore, the only way to eliminate the entrenched Communist political bureaucracies from within is by deliberately speaking the truth. This course of action is not only unlikely to succeed in a police state, it will also be extremely dangerous to those who attempt it. For this reason, an Ethical

State will almost certainly first start in a democratic country. However, there will always be the possibility that a Communist state mutates into an Ethical State.

In the democracies, it would be extremely easy for the very few effective generalists simply to withdraw all their support from the entrenched political bureaucracies and to refuse support to the Immoral Community. This would result in having their research funds cut off, but these are replaceable within the capitalist system. They would still have most of their time free to pursue whatever scientific or artistic interest is currently occupying them. Above all, they would have the time and the freedom to begin engendering an Ethical State and driving the political bureaucrats from office. If, for example, the thousand most-aware persons in the United States pool their talents in a determined, disciplined manner, they could in two or at the most three years command resources worth billions of dollars. The money can then be used ethically to beat the Immoral Community at its own game of winning elections. This can be done by disseminating truth with even greater skill and resourcefulness than the political bureaucrats use in deceiving the electorate.

The current political bureaucracies are motivated solely by power. There are no selfless* politicians. Indeed, there may not even be any ethical politicians. The voters sense this and are searching for a fresh political approach, as the current political history of the United States demonstrates. The people have shown that they are willing to support almost anyone who challenges the status quo so long as he does not violate popular prejudices. The electorate senses the corruption of the political bureaucracies.

What the electorate is not aware of is that the corruption is due to the fact that political decisions are never made on the basis of what course of action will best serve to increase man's total awareness—they are always unethical means, never ethical ends. If political decisions had an ethical basis, the United States would not be supporting corrupt dictatorships all over the world solely because it is politically expedient.

The greatest weakness of all political bureaucracies within the democracies (to say nothing of the Communist countries) is that they are

* "Selfless" refers to taking action for purposes other than personal power and security.

intellectually and morally bankrupt. Their own corruption has driven almost all persons with even a pretense of ethical behavior from their ranks. They can generate neither new ideas nor programs. They react to events and repeat old slogans, clichés, and ideologies already disproved by time. They are the avatar of the banality of evil. The political bureaucracies should, therefore, be defeated by the onslaught of a vigorous, well-financed political campaign directed by the most-aware, dedicated members of society. The problem at this time is to concentrate resources in order to strike at the political bureaucracies where they are most vulnerable and in a place where one can be most effective. First the proper nation to engender an Ethical State must be found.

SUITABLE NATIONS FOR ENGENDERING AN ETHICAL STATE

In order for a nation to serve as a suitable base for engendering and expanding an Ethical State it must 1) have critical mass, and 2) not have its entropy so high that it can no longer produce a large number of deliberate players of the Game of Life.

A nation has critical mass when 1) it is impossible for any other nation to attack it without, in effect, committing suicide and 2) its population is sufficiently large and varied that it can absorb the rest of humanity. A nation has reached the point of entropic no return when it is an immoral society. A symptom of an immoral society is that it no longer advances human awareness in any field of art, science or technology. Countries approaching this high level of entropy may be found in Latin America, Africa, and Asia. Some European countries, such as Spain, Portugal and Albania are probably close to the entropic point of no return. At the opposite pole are the nations with critical or almost critical mass which are still expanding their awareness. Most notable among these are the United States, the Soviet Union, and Japan.

A possibility exists that a United States of Europe would revitalize the declining European civilization and create a new force in the world. It is more likely, however, that Charles de Gaulle permanently stifled European unity in its cradle. Bureaucracy, ethnocentrism, and hedonism are further increasing the entropy of Europe. A dismembered Europe can only continue its entropic decline. It does not have critical mass. The only other nation with the incipient critical mass and vitality to engender an Ethical State is China.

China

China is remarkable in that it is a nation which has made very little progress for thousands of years, yet (unlike India) it has not undergone significant entropic decline. China has succeeded in doing what almost never happens in nature—it has virtually stood still. At the same time the vitality of the Chinese people has not declined. The Chinese can go to any country and they immediately become successful entrepreneurs, scientists, and technologists. They can progress everywhere except in their own country. The cause for this phenomenon lies in the basic structure of Confucianism.

Confucianism is probably the most sophisticated politico-philosophical system that has yet been practically implemented. Confucianism, like Judaism, is another variation on the Game of Life. It stresses rules of conduct as opposed to ideological beliefs. It places the highest value on knowledge as opposed to personal power. It formalized a testing process analogous to that of an Ethical State thousands of years ago in order that the most knowledgeable would become the most powerful. Indeed, this testing technique served as a model for all the European Civil Services. Yet it failed.

The failure of Confucianism was due not to what it was but to what it was not. Confucianism had everything except scientific method. Classical China was like an Ethical State without science, and as such, it could not help but stagnate. In the absence of scientific method, the authoritarian teachings of the past became enshrined as repositories of all wisdom. Chinese scholars would spend many years memorizing the opinions of the past instead of confronting nature directly and attempting to learn from experience. This inhibited the feedback in the system, and bureaucratization in time destroyed the society but not the vitality of the people. Only ideology destroys the individual vitality of persons by destroying personal morality.

Confucianism, like Judaism, served for thousands of years as a buffer against ideology. In the end, however, the complete bureaucratic corruption of a military dictatorship made it possible for a vigorous, dedicated group of Communist ideologues to achieve complete control over China. Today the Communist ideologues are trying to do to the Chinese people what thousands of years of Buddhist, Moslem, and Christian missionaries could not do—make them ideological. The deep-seated Confucian traditions of skepticism, which are ethically superior to Marxist ideology, may continue to keep the Chinese masses from succumbing to ideology until the Communist political bureaucracy becomes sufficiently corrupt to lose its concern with ideology and becomes totally absorbed with bureaucratic security, as is the case in the Soviet Union. If scientific method has not been completely stifled in the meantime, then there is a possibility that the vigorous and talented Chinese people may engender an Ethical State.

The Chinese have even passed the evolutionary test of completely absorbing the few thousand Jews who began settling in China after the Roman persecutions. The Jews and the Chinese had much in common. The Confucian ethical traditions of tolerance and skepticism made the absorption of the ancient Chinese Jews inevitable. By the end of the eighteenth century, the Chinese Jews who had their cultural center in Kai Feng Fu (Kaifeng) had essentially been completely assimilated and were indistinguishable from other Chinese. The most illustrious Chinese-Jewish families were descendants of the fifteenth century Jewish court physician, Yen Cheng, who had the surname Chao* confirmed on him by the Chinese emperor. The assimilated Jews became mandarins and land owners, but they together with China continued to sleep. A new wave of Jewish immigrants began to come to China in the mid-nineteenth century, but even at their peak in World War II they only numbered about 26,000. Since the Communist takeover in 1949, the more recent Jewish immigrants have almost all left China.

In the long run, it is inconceivable that the immoral, highly insecure political bureaucracy in the Soviet Union will allow the Chinese to develop full critical mass, let alone engender an Ethical State. The Soviets will almost certainly attack or otherwise disrupt China before China be-

* Sometimes transliterated Chou as in Chou En-lai.

comes a serious threat to them. The Soviet Union will impede an Ethical State in China. The question then becomes whether the Soviets can engender an Ethical State.

The Union of Soviet Socialist Republics

The Soviet Union meets most of the requirements for engendering an Ethical State. She has critical mass and a large number of highly-aware persons who are probably already disposed toward an Ethical State. She also has a large number of Jews who have catalyzed her to world power. The Soviet Union only has one drawback which is constantly becoming worse: that is, the most rigid, all-embracing, corrupt bureaucracy in history. The Soviet bureaucracy is structured to serve the now anti-Semitic political bureaucracy of the Communist Party, which enjoys a total monopoly of political power. The Communist Party will ruthlessly and brutally suppress any internal or external threat to its ideology or hegemony. The external suppression of threats has been inhibited *only* by the overwhelming power of the United States. However, as the relative decline of the United States continues, we can expect the Soviet Union to take an increasingly more aggressive role in suppressing external threats to its bureaucratic security.

This has already happened in Hungary and Czechoslovakia. It will almost certainly happen again in China and Israel. When the United States become isolationist again, as it almost certainly will if an Ethical State is not started, the Soviet Union will try to subject every nation to its bureaucratic rule. Only when the Communist Party bureaucracy can suppress freedom of speech and expression with the same ease in other countries as they do in their own, will they feel secure from negative feedback.

The only way to defeat the Soviet Communist Party from within is for large numbers of highly-aware Soviet generalists and ethical persons to infiltrate the Communist Party deliberately, in order to overcome it by simply telling the Soviet people the truth. The Soviet Protagonists can identify their natural allies by the totality of their awareness. They must be mistrustful of highly-specialized persons and scientific illiterates. The Protagonists must work cautiously and selflessly to make sure that all the important positions in the Party hierarchy go only to ethical persons. Eventually there may be sufficient ethical persons in the Party hierarchy for them to attempt a consolidation of all power in their hands. They would then have to eliminate very quickly all the security-seeking and power-seeking Communist bureaucrats, who would be in the majority, before the latter could reconsolidate their power. Once the Protagonists had defeated the Communist Party bureaucracy and consolidated all power in their hands, it would be very easy for them to implement the constitution and the infrastructure of an Ethical State. An Ethical State is completely compatible with the theoretical goals of Communism if not with its unethical methods. The existence of an Ethical State in the Soviet Union would stimulate the creation of Ethical States in all the other Communist countries as well as in the democracies until a single ethical world government existed.

That the Soviet Union has the potential for an ethical revolution from within is demonstrated by the amazingly courageous activities of Dr. A. D. Sakharov of the Soviet Academy of Sciences. Sakharov has for several years almost singlehandedly been waging a war against the Soviet bureaucracy. It is difficult to assess his successes, but there is little question that he has at least created some feedback within the Soviet bureaucracy. This feedback is best illustrated by the following letter which he co-authored to the Soviet leadership:

A Letter from Dr. Sakharov*

Deeply Esteemed Leonid Ilyich [Brezhnev], Aleksei Nikolayevich [Kosygin], Nikolai Viktorovich [Podgorny]:

In the course of the past decade, menacing signs of breakdown and stagnation have been discovered in the economy of our country . . . Comparing our economy with that of the U.S., we see that ours lags not only in quantitative but also—saddest of all—in qualitative respects. We surpass America in the mining of coal, but we lag behind in oil drilling, lag very much behind in gas drilling and in the production of electric power, hopelessly lag behind in chemistry and infinitely lag behind in computer technology. As for the use of computers in the economy . . . a phenomenon that has deservedly been called the second industrial

* Reprinted by permission. Copyright Newsweek, Inc. April 13, 1970.

revolution . . . here the gap is so wide that it is impossible to measure it. We simply live in another epoch . . .

At the end of the 1950s our country was the first to launch a sputnik and it sent a man into space. At the end of the 1960s we lost our lead and the first men to land on the moon were Americans . . . The second industrial revolution began, and now at the beginning of the 1970s we can see that not only did we not catch up with America but that the gap between the two countries is becoming greater and greater.

What is the matter? Why was it not our country that took the initiative in the second industrial revolution? Why were we unable to be on a par with the most developed capitalist countries?

The source of our difficulties is not the socialist structure. On the contrary, it lies in those peculiarities and conditions of our life that run contrary to socialism and are hostile to it. This source is the antidemocratic traditions and norms of public life that appeared during Stalin's period and have not been completely liquidated at the present time . . .

There is no doubt that, with the beginning of the second industrial revolution, these phenomena have become a decisive economic factor. Problems of organization and management cannot be solved by one or several individuals who have power. They demand the creative participation of millions of people on all levels of the economic system. But in the process of exchanging information we are facing difficulties that cannot be overcome. Real information on our faults and negative phenomena is kept secret because it may be used by hostile propaganda. Exchange of information with foreign countries is restricted on the ground of penetration of hostile ideology. Theoretical conceptions and practical proposals which may seem to be too bold are suppressed immediately without any discussion under the influence of fear that they may break the foundations.

Under these conditions only those who in their words display staunchness for the cause of the party but in reality are concerned with their personal interest and not those who are really possessed of professional qualities can move upward. Restrictions in the exchange of information make difficult any kind of control over the leadership and frustrate the people's initiative, and even those leading the intermediate administrations are deprived of rights and information. The top administrators receive incomplete, falsified information and thus cannot exercise their power completely . . .

Our economy can be compared to traffic entering a crossroads. While there were few cars, traffic police could handle it quite easily. But once the number of cars became greater one can see a traffic jam. What can be done in this situation? Drivers can be fined or policemen changed. But the only way out is to make the crossroads wider. The obstacles that prevent the development of our economy can be found outside it, in the political and public field, and all measures that cannot eliminate these obstacles will inevitably be ineffective . . .

Freedom of information and creative labor are necessary for the intelligentsia due to the nature of its activities, due to the nature of its social function. The desire of the intelligentsia to have greater freedom is legal and natural. The state, however, suppresses this desire by introducing various restrictions, administrative pressure, dismissals and even the holding of trials. This brings about a gap, mutual distrust and a complete mutual lack of understanding, which makes it difficult for the state and the most active strata of the intelligentsia to cooperate fruitfully. In the conditions of the present-day industrial society, where the role of the intelligentsia is growing, this gap cannot but be termed suicidal.

A greater part of the intelligentsia and our youth realizes the necessity of democratization, realizes the necessity of cautious and gradual approaches to this problem, but it cannot understand or justify actions of a purely anti-democratic nature. How can one justify the imprisonment or keeping in camps and mental asylums of persons whose opposition is still within the legal field, in the field of ideas and convictions? It is impermissible to keep writers in prison for their work. One has to come back again to ideological problems.

Democratization and complete information must bring back to our ideological life its dynamics and creative nature and liquidate the bureaucratic, dogmatic, hypocritical style which is so important now. Democratization would eliminate the gap between the party and state apparatus and the intelligentsia. Mutual lack of understanding will turn into close cooperation. The best intellectual forces of the country will be mobilized for the solution of social and economic problems.

Democratization is not an easy process. Its normal progress will be threatened by individualist and anti-socialist forces on the one hand and on the other hand by those who advocate strong power, by those who use demagogical statements of the Fascist type and who may try to use our economic difficulties for their own purposes. But there is no other way out. Democratization at the initiative and under the control of the highest authorities will allow this process to proceed gradually, to make all links of the party and state apparatus change to the new style of open discussion . . .

We propose the following program of measures which may be taken within the next four or five years:

A statement from the highest party and government authorities on the necessity of further democratization, on its rate and methods. Publication in the press of a number of articles on the problems of democratization.

Restricted distribution (through party and state organs) of information on the state of the country and of theoretical work on public problems. Later this type of material ought gradually to be made available to everyone.

Establishment of an institute for the study of public opinion with initially restricted but eventually complete publication of material showing the attitude of the population to the most important problems of internal and external policy.

An end to the jamming of foreign broadcasts. Free sale of foreign books and periodicals. Admission of our country to the international copyright system. Gradual expansion of international tourism. Unrestricted international correspondence and other measures for the expansion of international contacts.

Amnesty for political prisoners. Compulsory publication of complete records of trials of political nature. Public control over the places of imprisonment and political asylums.

Other measures to facilitate the operation of courts and procurators' offices [and to insure] their independence from the executive power, local influences, prejudice and connections.

Elimination of the [ethnic] nationality designation in passports [used

within the Soviet Union]. Gradual elimination of [such domestic]
   passport registration.
Organization of industrial associations with a high degree of independence in the problems of industrial planning and production processes,
   in sales and supplies, finances and personnel.
Reforms in the field of education. Greater allocation for primary and
   high schools. Improvement of the material positions of teachers, with
   greater independence and the right to experiment . . .
Gradual introduction of the nomination for election of several candidates
   for a single party or government post.
Extension of the rights and responsibilities of the [Parliament].
Restoration of the rights of all nationalities forcibly resettled under
   Stalin. Restoration of the national autonomy of the resettled nations . . .

Of course, this plan must be regarded as approximate. We emphasize
that democratization in itself does not solve economic problems. Sometimes we hear our foreign friends comparing the Soviet Union to a powerful lorry, whose driver is accelerating with one foot, and at the same
time applying the brake. The time has come to brake more sensibly . . .

We must also consider the international consequences of democratization if it is adopted by our country . . . The attractiveness of Communist ideology will grow, and our international position will become
more secure . . .

In the past there occurred negative phenomena in Soviet foreign policy, which had the character of excessive messianic ambition and which
force one to conclude that not only the imperialists bear responsibility
for international tension.

All negative phenomena in our foreign policy are closely connected
to the problem of democratization, and this connection has a two-sided
character. Great disquiet is caused by the absence of democratic discussion
of such questions as arms aid to a number of countries, including, for in-
stance, Nigeria, where a bloody civil war was in progress whose causes and
course are quite unfamiliar to the Soviet public. We are convinced that
the resolution of the U.N. Security Council on the problems of the Arab-
Israeli conflict is just and reasonable, although also not concrete enough

in a number of important points. However, disquiet is caused by the question: Does our position not go substantially further than this document? Is it not too one-sided? Is our position regarding the status of West Berlin realistic? Is it always realistic for us to strive to extend our influence in places far from our borders at a time of difficulties in Sino-Soviet relations and in technical-economic development . . .

What awaits our country if a course toward democratization is not taken? Falling behind the capitalist countries in the process of the second industrial revolution and gradual transformation into a second-rate provincial power. (History knows similar cases.) . . . The prospect becomes particularly menacing if one considers the presence of a danger from Chinese totalitarian nationalism. We can face this danger only if we increase or at least maintain the technological and economic gap between our country and China, increasing the numbers of our friends in the world at large and offering the Chinese people the alternative of co-operation and aid. Thus, economic stand-still, slowing up of the rate of development in combination with an insufficiently realistic and a sometimes too ambitious foreign policy, may lead our country to catastrophic consequences.

There is no way out of the difficulties facing the country except a course toward democratization carried out by the party in accordance with a carefully worked out program . . . At present we have a chance to take the right road and carry out the necessary reforms. In a few years, perhaps, it will be too late.

A.D. SAKHAROV
V.F. TURCHIN
R.A. MEDVEDEV

NEWSWEEK, April 13, 1970

That Sakharov has survived such courageous activity is due only to his eminence as a scientist and his politically powerful position as the principal developer of the Soviet hydrogen bomb. Apparently, Kapitza has played a similar role in Soviet society for many years.

It is highly unlikely that Sakharov and his colleagues will succeed. In the end, they will almost certainly be arrested and have their intellects destroyed in the Soviet "insane asylums." The Soviet Union may be reaching the irreversible entropy of an immoral society. The only hope lies in an ethical revolt within the Communist Party by the most highly-aware members of the Soviet society.

The probability of this occurring is very low. The highly-aware generalists in Russia find the Communist Party utterly repulsive. The Communist Party bureaucrats, like all successful bureaucrats, have an instinctive distrust and dislike of highly-aware (i.e., ethical) persons. They know at the unconscious level that any ethical person is a serious threat to their bureaucratic security. They provide negative feedback as typified by the Sakharov letter. The dangers and repulsiveness of bureaucratic intrigue, together with the easy satisfaction of purely scientific, non-political research, will strongly mitigate against an Ethical State being initially engendered in the Soviet Union. This leaves only the United States and Japan as possible initiators of Ethical States.

Japan

Japan is perhaps the most vital nation in the world. The Japanese have been a remarkably progressive people for over a century. During the latter part of the nineteenth century (the Meiji Era) the Japanese accomplished a feat which has never been equaled in the history of the human race. They took a backward, feudalistic, largely-illiterate nation with no modern scientific or technological base, poor in natural resources, and transformed it into a modern fully-industrialized nation in less than thirty years! Any nation capable of such a prodigious feat should also be capable of engendering an Ethical State.

Today, twenty-five years after suffering total defeat in World War II, Japan has the most vigorous industrial system in the world and a first-class educational establishment. There is little doubt that, at its present rate of progress, Japan could be the most aware nation in the world in thirty years. Yet Japan seems to be missing a certain vital spark which must be present in order to catalyze the ultimate Moral Society.

Japan is the third-largest industrial power in the world but she ranks a low sixth after the United States, Russia, Britain, France and Germany in various indices of scientific accomplishment. Japan is a perfecter of technology rather than a technological innovator. Indeed, this goes back to classical times when Chinese civilization (Confucianism, Zen Buddhism, etc.) reached its fullest expression in Japan not China. Similarly today, any device first produced by Western Civilization, whether it be cameras, machinery, or electronic circuits, finds its most efficient expression in Japan. This is due not only to the lower cost of Japanese labor but to the ingenuity of the Japanese for perfecting the inventions of others. But the Japanese do not produce anything truly new themselves. One of their major technological innovations, the tunnel diode, was merely a spin-off of solid-state electronics developed in the United States. The tunnel diode has since been surpassed by other new technologies in micro-miniaturization of electronics. The Japanese seem incapable of setting out on fundamentally new paths of intellectual development by themselves. This may not always be the case but it is the case right now. It may be that what Japan lacks is a propensity to break with established patterns of thought and to look at things in a fundamentally new light, i.e. the catalysis of the Jews.

Further complicating the engendering of an Ethical State in Japan is the fact that the Revolt Against Reason has reached its most pernicious level in the Japanese universities. The militant ideologues of the Left are creating such chaos in Japanese universities that the expansion of awareness has almost completely stopped. The bureaucratization of the democratic infrastructure has reached a particularly destructive stage within Japan and threatens to push the entropy of Japan beyond the point of no return. This is manifesting itself in a hedonistic decline of the population and the inroads made into the intellectual community by leftist ideology. Perhaps most serious of all, however, is the Japanese penchant for compulsive perfection which causes an inordinately large number of persons to become highly specialized. This produces superb machinery and craftsmen, but it makes persons narrowly aware as opposed to broadly aware. In the long run, it increases the entropy of the system to the point where engendering an Ethical State does not seem feasible.

The Japanese are a dynamic, vigorous people and under outside pressure they have reversed their way of life before. They may still be the ones to engender an Ethical State if some new elements are introduced into their culture.

In the final analysis, the Japanese people seem too ethnocentric and specialized to serve as the basis for an Ethical State which will unite all of humanity. In spite of all its defects and problems, only the United States has shown itself willing and able to unite highly diverse peoples in a single progressive culture. At this time only the United States seems likely to engender an Ethical State.

The United States of America

The United States has critical mass and is still the most powerful nation on Earth. It has assimilated by far the largest number of free Jews of any nation and, for that matter, the largest number of all nationals and races. It is the most progressive and least bureaucratized major nation on Earth. It is a nation which still has enormous feedback. No other nation in history has been so effective in uniting so many diverse people. The unity of the nation is being destroyed by 1) an indecent leadership; 2) the Revolt Against Reason and 3) racism on the part of both Whites and Blacks. Yet no other nation offers as much hope.

The United States is a nation which was structured at its inception to evolve into something better than it was. The Founding Fathers with their remarkable insight saw that corruption was an inevitable consequence of power and that the only way to counter corruption was by competition and a system of checks and balances, i.e., high feedback. They accordingly gave the United States a flexible and changeable constitution with a democratic government and a capitalistic industry. The Ethical State represents the natural evolution of the United States to its next logical form.

What the Founding Fathers could not see was that bureaucratization and ideology would eventually permeate the entire society and that the personal corruption which they most feared would, in time, be a far lesser threat than the bureaucratic and ideological corruption which would paralyze the government leaders and deprive them of feedback. Eventually only unethical persons capable of functioning without scientific feedback, legal-minded bureaucrats, would become leaders and they would further increase the entropy of the society by making all decisions on the basis of political expediency rather than logical and scientific analysis of how best to achieve the goals and purposes of the nation. No one would take the political risks to educate the electorate. Instead most politicians would find it expedient to cater to the prejudices and ideological biases of the masses.

The American electorate can and will change the trend of entropic decline only if it is given clear and purposeful leadership. This leadership can only come from moral men. It is the responsibility of all persons to see that moral men achieve political office. There is no other way to reverse the decline of the United States. All other activities and desires must be subordinated to electing moral men to positions of leadership.

If the most-aware persons in society do not have the courage to risk their bureaucratic security and the stamina to wage a political struggle to the death with the Immoral Community, they will betray the future of the entire human race. They will, by unethical default, make the bureaucratic and ideological descent into total entropy the inevitable future of all humanity.

It is a sad state of affairs that in the United States political issues are settled not on the basis of logic and reason but on the basis of which advocate can muster the most convincing propaganda. The political campaigns of the past, together with the entertainment media, have conditioned the electorate not to think or analyze but to respond solely to catchy slogans which appeal directly to their most irrational prejudices and blind desires for security. This is the legacy of the Immoral Community. It is a confirmation of Bertrand Russell's dictum. The only ethical way to overcome the entropy of the electorate is through education.

There should be an extensive program of political re-education. In order for the program to be effective, it will have to be made as convincing as the unethical propaganda of the Immoral Community. The task before the Protagonists is to tell the truth and make it understandable to the majority of the people. At the same time, it will be possible to be logical and scientific about the issues. This is something that none of the politicians do now.

People will vote for candidates who espouse ethical principle not because they are particularly concerned with awareness but because they are concerned with security. Only an Ethical State will provide the security of a pollution-free environment and a fully-subsidized, highly-flexible, individualized educational system in which the intellectual and material advancement of all who wish it is assured. Only an Ethical State promises to eliminate the corrupt bureaucracies which give illusions of security to their members at the cost of destroying the true security of all by eliminating feedback. Only an Ethical State can eliminate all forms of racism and other ideologies. The Ethical State will have to be sold to the electorate not only for the awareness that it promises but for the security which is a trivial consequence of its structure. The long-term goals of an Ethical State may help to unify and solidify the allegiances of the most-aware members of society. But long-term goals will not win the votes that the promises of immediate security will. The campaign for an Ethical State will be totally ineffective, unless it commands large amounts of resources—material as well as human. The concentration of material resources will actually be a relatively simple matter for a unified, determined, and disciplined group of highly-aware generalists. All power stems from art, science and technology. Almost the entire power of the nation is produced by a tiny minority of highly-aware generalists. These highly-aware persons are the ones who should form the nucleus around which an Ethical State will grow. It should be a nucleus of moral men— of deliberate players of the Game of Life. These are the Protagonists. They are the human resources which must be concentrated if mankind is to survive.

The Protagonists

The Protagonists should join in a common effort to re-establish feedback in the society. This will occur when they perceive the evolutionary patterns of the Moral Society and the necessity for deliberately playing the Game of Life and engendering an Ethical State. It is the duty of each person who perceives the patterns to help as many other persons as possible also to perceive them. The Protagonists should structure their society as a microcosm of the Ethical State.

The Ethical State will be effective because it has 1) single-mindedness of purpose consistent with the evolutionary force; 2) highly-aware leadership; 3) centralized direction with undiffused responsibility; and 4) high feedback for quickly correcting mistakes and learning from experience at all levels of society. So it must be with the Protagonists. The initial Protagonists will probably all be highly-aware, secure, strongly individualistic and independent persons. But if they are to be effective, they must subordinate their individualism to accomplish the common purpose of all Protagonists which must be to engender an Ethical State. This will be alien and difficult for most of them, but there is no other way. Discipline with centralized direction is essential to the success of the Protagonists. Otherwise they will be a diffused group of well-intentioned and capable persons starting out in all directions instead of concentrating their efforts on attacking the Immoral Community at its weakest points. Only with central direction and disciplined feedback can the Protagonists be successful.

Everyone who becomes a Protagonist should take an oath to dedicate his life as best he can to the engendering of an Ethical State. The principal task of the Protagonists should be to pool their talents and resources to re-establish feedback in the society. The re-establishment of feedback will involve 1) setting up schools to teach evolutionary theory and ethics; 2) the formation of an ethical political party; and 3) the concentration of wealth in order to finance the campaigns of ethical candidates. All support should also be withdrawn from the political, industrial and educational bureaucracies which are the natural competitors of the Protagonists. No ethical person should voluntarily associate himself in any manner with a bureaucracy.

The schools should begin as an extension of the current educational system. The schools would teach all science and ethics as a single, integrated subject unified by the general theory of evolution. This would re-establish some feedback into the educational system by teaching science and ethics as they should be taught and not in the bureaucratized fashion of the present educational establishment.

In areas where it is possible for a new political party to be effective, an ethical party should be established to run ethical reform candidates against the corrupt bureaucracies of the existing parties. In all areas ethical reform candidates should be supported to run against the establishment candidates. The ethical candidates would have a secret weapon to use against their opponents. It is a weapon which politicians have traditionally shunned as ineffective, though it is the only weapon which can win in the long run—the weapon is truth. Truth can only be effective if it is disseminated with great ethical skill, rather than the deceits used by the power-seeking, political bureaucrats. This will take enormous wealth.

The wealth could come from inventions, patents, processes, creations, manufacture, and financial transactions, which could be implemented through profit-making corporations established under the direct control of the Protagonists. Each Protagonist should be a corporate partner and should be entitled to keep for his personal use fifty percent of the profits that he produced for the corporation. He could use his share to support himself and his family as well as for his personal educational projects. The other fifty percent of the profits would go entirely to the Society of Protagonists for the purpose of engendering an Ethical State.

Membership in the Society of Protagonists should be restricted solely to ethical persons. The best objective criterion of ethics is broad awareness. If membership in the Protagonists is limited to highly-aware generalists this should protect them from falling under the control of persons who are not ethical.

Broad awareness serves as the best buffer against the corrupting influence of personal power. However, not all ethical persons are generalists with depth. Any person who seems ethical should be allowed to ally himself with the Protagonists. For self-protection, however, the Protagonists should limit effective power to highly-aware generalists. Any ethical person can become a generalist and any ethical person can and should help the Protagonists.

Restricting power only to highly-aware persons should also serve as an effective block to the infiltration of the Protagonists by persons who would destroy them. Highly-aware persons would usually tend to be deliberate players of the Game of Life. Even when their original intentions were those of personal power or duplicity, the moral field of the Society of Protagonists would probably amplify their personal ethics so that they would become allies and not enemies of the Protagonists.

When the Protagonists have accumulated sufficient resources and power, they should begin the political assault on the Immoral Community. The assault should come as a surprise, with well-financed, ethical political candidates with sophisticated, yet scientific, campaigns suddenly emerging everywhere.

Political Campaigns

The campaigns should be based on a scientific approach to solving the problems of pollution, education, and bureaucratic corruption but they must be made convincing and relevant to the voters' needs. The Protagonists should do their best to redirect the energy of the Revolt Against Reason into ethical channels. However, the Protagonists should try to avoid trivial issues which offend the prejudices of the majority when discussed honestly and scientifically. When issues cannot be avoided, they should be discussed honestly and no attempt should be made to deceive the electorate. *The Protagonists should never forget that unethical means never achieve ethical ends.* The campaigns should pre-empt the communications and entertainment media by using the accumulated wealth of the Protagonists to outbid the disorganized, power-seeking politicians of the political bureaucracies for control of the media.

The power-seeking political bureaucrats of the Democratic and Republican Parties are mostly unethical men motivated mainly by a desire for personal security through personal power. They have no particular allegiance or strong attachments to their respective parties which, after all, have no ideological or philosophical bases but serve solely as instruments for helping them achieve power. Since their only concern is security and personal power, the political bureaucrats will be extremely vulnerable to the intimidation of concentrated wealth applied directly against them by a purposeful, selfless, intelligent and nationally-organized opponent whose stated goals are so logical and so clearly in the public interest that they cannot be refuted. The political bureaucracies should eventually fall before such an onslaught.

The political campaigns of the Protagonists should have an entirely pragmatic and logical basis. Since the Protagonists would know the political bureaucracies for what they are—instruments for achieving personal, political power—they could use the corruption of the political parties to their own advantage. In order to reduce feedback and further entrench themselves, the political bureaucrats have brought about a situation where it is impossible for a person to be effective in politics without commanding large amounts of money. A politician tries to be a sufficiently good actor and command enough resources to sell himself to the voters not for what he is, but for what his merchandising team can make him appear to be.

Therefore, in order to defeat the political bureaucracies, it is necessary to have enough wealth and determination to out-sell them. This could be facilitated by subverting them with ethical behavior from within.

It would be a simple matter for the Protagonists to give support to their own candidates to run in a Republican or a Democratic primary whenever these were the most effective ways of putting an ethical person into office. In places where the nomination of candidates was closed by bureaucratic intrigue, then new political parties could be formed to oppose the political bureaucracies directly. Eventually a majority of the elected officials would be ethical; some would call themselves Democrats, others Republicans and still others Independents. The important result would be that persons committed to the expansion of total awareness and to engendering an Ethical State would control the political machinery. Once they did, the Ethical State would be assured.

If the political bureaucrats still exercised significant control over the political machinery after the campaigns of the Protagonists, they would probably attempt to pass restrictive legislation to inhibit the expansion of the political upstarts. However, the wealth, determination, and intelligence of the Protagonists should enable them to circumvent whatever obstacles are put in their way by the obviously-corrupt, power-seeking bureaucrats. Soon a bandwagon psychology would be created and the political bureaucrats would seek to maintain their power and security by allying themselves with the Protagonists. They would offer tremendous concessions which were obviously in the best interest of anyone motivated solely by the pursuit of power. The unethical politicians would never understand the motivation of ethical men who seek only the expansion of awareness. Their concessions should make it even easier to defeat them.

When the entire political machinery of the nation is controlled by the Protagonists, it should be a simple matter to amend the Constitution of the United States into the Constitution of an Ethical State. Such amendments would indeed be consistent with the original spirit of the American Constitution.

It would be the responsibility of the Protagonists to prepare the public to accept total awareness as the only meaningful goal for mankind. Once the Ethical State is established the leaders must continue to educate the public on the ethics of life.

Opposition

Since the purpose of the Protagonists is to eliminate all bureaucracies and engender an Ethical State, it would be logical for the political and industrial bureaucracies to destroy the Protagonists while they are still weak. In order for this to occur, there would have to be a unified bipartisan attack on the Protagonists, in such a way that it became impossible for them to concentrate wealth and power. The political bureaucracies united once before in order to destroy a common political threat. They did this when they persecuted the Communist Party and alleged Communists in the 1950's. The persecution of the Communists, however, led to such abuses of basic justice and reason (personified by Senator Joseph McCarthy) that enormous damage was done to the political, intellectual, military and industrial vitality of the United States. The political bureaucracies are not likely to risk being consumed in the wake of new persecutions. Furthermore, the Protagonists would not be allied with any foreign power or outside threat and they would work entirely within the framework of the U.S. Constitution. Harassment of the Protagonists would threaten the stability of the entire bureaucracy because it could only be done by violating the Constitution of the United States in such a way that each of the entrenched parties would become highly vulnerable to the machinations of the other. Therefore, there should be no harassment because it is the nature of political bureaucracies not to trust each other.

The greatest protection should come from the bureaucrats' total inability to comprehend the motivations of the Protagonists. The pursuit of total awareness for the entire human race to the exclusion of bureaucratic security and personal power would appear as a type of insanity to the political bureaucrats. It is the tragedy of modern life that ethical behavior is equated with madness. The bureaucrats would not believe that an ethical organization could be a threat to them until after the Ethical State was assured. The former political bureaucrats, like many of the electorate, would not comprehend what was happening or why. It would be incomprehensible to them that the highly-aware and politically successful Protagonists would end their own bureaucratic security by engendering an Ethical State. Full comprehension of the goals, purposes and methods of the Ethical State would come only after a large number of persons began to expand their total awareness.

In the beginning, the major problem may come from leftist ideologues who, no matter how fair the competition was made, would insist that the losers in the competition were helpless victims of their environment who never had an honest chance. The leftist ideologues are something that the Ethical State will just have to tolerate until a universal scientific education eliminates all ideologies from mankind. The rightist ideologues will also oppose the Ethical State because it will violate many of their religious and racist prejudices. However, it is also possible that many of the leftist and the rightist ideologues will be won over by the sanity and the ethics of the Protagonists. It should never be forgotten that persons only become ideologues in an attempt to be aware. Long before ideology is eliminated the Ethical State should begin to expand until it encompasses all humanity.

EXPANSION

The strategy of the previous sections should guarantee the establishment of an Ethical State in the United States. The only problem that exists is the willingness of a few hundred of the most totally-aware, moral generalists to become Protagonists. However, if the best persons that humanity can produce are not willing to make some personal sacrifices in order to create an Ethical State, then the entropy of the human race is already beyond the point of no return.

The most likely case is that there are not only hundreds but thousands of potential Protagonists in the United States and in other countries. Every ethical person in the world is a potential ally of the Protagonists. Most persons still seem to be ethical, if not moral. The Protagonists only need hope and a focus to bring them together. This book has tried to provide both. If it has failed, then others who can more clearly perceive and express the patterns of evolution must correct the shortcomings of the book and give greater hope and focus to humanity. Once the Protagonists begin the deliberate Game of Life, they should form a self-catalyzing reaction which will bring ethical persons together from all over the world.

The entropy in countries other than the United States is probably too high to engender the initial Ethical State there at this time. However, once an Ethical State is established in the United States, then the hope of all Protagonists will probably become focused on the Ethical State.

The United States has, since its inception, stood as a symbol of hope for the entire human race. The Founding Fathers were fully aware of this when they claimed that America was not only for them but for all humanity. Jefferson saw America as the place where through personal freedom "the Natural Aristocracy Among Men" would rise to the forefront. By "Natural Aristocracy" Jefferson obviously meant those persons with the greatest innate potential for total awareness. The promise of America has to a great extent been fulfilled. However, ideology and the bureaucratic decay of its institutions have caused America to stray ever further from its original mission of uniting the human race under a system of freedom and justice.

The original guiding principle of the United States was progress through personal freedom. This concept will be re-established as the guiding principle for the entire human race when the United States becomes an Ethical State. At this time, the most-aware persons from all over the world will rally once again to the American cause and will foment revolutions in their own countries which will unite all of humanity in a single Ethical State. It will all begin with the joining of the first deliberate players of the Game of Life—the Protagonists.

Once the Ethical State begins, its expansion and its preservation will depend on 1) its natural allies within other nations (i.e., the international Moral Community) and 2) its Military. The persons who will feel most directly threatened by the Ethical State will be the bureaucrats of the Communist parties. They will do everything in their power to destroy any Ethical State.

Until this time only Communism has been a "positive" world force for unifying the human race by promising security in the absence of freedom. The United States has been impotent in the ideological battle with Communism because it has had nothing positive to offer. It seemed only to promise the freedom for predatory exploitation by capitalism to persons who were already dying of starvation. This promise has been an utter failure politically. The Ethical State will completely preempt the ideological appeal of Communism by promising all men even greater security than the Communists, all in the presence of freedom and purpose. This new state of affairs will terrify the Communist bureaucrats.

The terror will be instilled not so much from fear of losing the ideological war among the uncommitted nations of the world as from fear of having their own people "contaminated" by the ideals of the Ethical State. Once some of their own highly-aware generalists, such as Sakharov, begin to become fully aware of the potentialities of an Ethical State, the ethics of life may spread throughout the entire Communist society until the Communist bureaucrats are driven from power by their own Protagonists. For this reason the Communist bureaucrats will try to stifle the Ethical State in its cradle. They will even take desperate risks toward this end. In order to survive, the Ethical State must be militarily so strong that even the threat of attack by a Communist power would be suicidal. Only in overwhelming strength will there be security from the convulsive reactions of the Communist bureaucrats striving to preserve their security and power by avoiding negative feedback. The success of the Ethical State within its own house should put tremendous internal pressure on the bureaucrats and ideologues to mutate the Communist society into an Ethical State. The Ethical State can also give moral support to the Players within the Communist countries to persevere against the corrupt political bureaucracies. Expansion to non-Communist countries, however, is another matter.

The expansion of the Ethical State should be mainly a peaceful endeavor brought about by the Protagonists of each country. The Ethical State should give moral and financial support to ethical persons everywhere so that they may engender an Ethical State in their own country and then join in voluntary association with the other Ethical States. Countries which have reached such a high state of entropy that they cannot produce a critical mass of Protagonists should be left alone, so long as they do not threaten the Ethical State militarily or by environmental pollution. If they do so threaten, the Ethical State should defend itself militarily. Once a nation or any person has become a part of the Ethical State, all persons should be given equal rights and should be considered full citizens. Whatever their origins, persons need only perform at an appropriately high level on the LTA tests to run for any public office. All who wish it can vote. All citizens are entitled to the full benefits of the Ethical State.

The Ethical State should wage a world-wide education program to teach the citizens of all countries the ethics of life. The Ethical State should do everything in its power to foment world revolution with the aim of bringing all men into a single Ethical State, but it should never force free men to become citizens of the Ethical State. For this purpose the Ethical State should maintain a place of exile and should not forcibly interfere in the internal affairs of free nations unless it is being directly threatened by them.

The place of exile will enable all men who do not share the principles of the Ethical State to develop their own independent civilization. Because of the random nature of the cosmic force, it is possible that the Ethical State might make a serious developmental mistake. In this case, human evolution might still be continued by those in exile. The Ethical State would also be able to learn from the civilization of those in exile until all men become united in the Moral Society.

Difficulties

As was mentioned earlier, the greatest difficulties encountered in expanding the Ethical State will be the intransigence of the entrenched Communist bureaucracies. Linguistic and cultural differences will also cause difficulties. However, these difficulties can be overcome by broad toleration of diversity and by developing an eclectic culture within the Ethical State. Eventually a single, common language should emerge which incorporates the best from all languages. English is already a step in this direction.

Another obstacle to the expansion of the Ethical State will be presented by organized religion in general and the Catholic Church in particular. The Catholic Church, like the Communist Party which it so closely resembles, is usually terrified of feedback. All ideologies attempt to isolate their members in ideological cocoons of self-satisfied ignorance. The religions can be expected to oppose vigorously the "ungodly" educational system and purposes of the Ethical State. The Catholic Church will oppose any type of birth control which is used to limit the population, even when the absence of a eugenics program bodes certain disaster for the entire human race. The opposition of the churches can only be overcome by educating the masses so that the absurdities of all ideology become manifest and the people feel they have the inner strength to stand alone in a world of uncertainty without the soporific comfort of ideological delusions.

In the final analysis, religious ideology like all ideology is a fragile, illusionary support for those who cannot face up to their own ignorance and the uncertainties of life processes which they can neither predict nor control. An Ethical State is incompatible with all ideology but it should allow people to overcome their ideological delusions by themselves. The only weapon it should use against ideology is education. Highly-aware persons who play the Game of Life will automatically avoid the illusions of religion and other ideologies.

The religious opposition to the Ethical State may have its most effective expression through the Jesuit Order. The Jesuits are a Society quite analogous to the Protagonists. They started out in the sixteenth century as a group of highly aware, selfless, disciplined men, determined to unify the world in a single ethical society which they conceived as a Catholic totalitarian state. They were, until the early part of the seventeenth century, one of the most vital, intellectual forces in the world. During this period, they infiltrated the governments of China, Japan, Russia, Poland, Spain, France and many other countries. The Jesuits were eventually destroyed through bureaucratization because they had an ideological base and limited feedback. The Jesuits of yesterday, like the Communists of today, propounded the ethic that the end justifies the means; in the process they themselves became unethical. They were inevitably persecuted and expelled in each country in which they had achieved power. Finally, the convulsions of the impending French Revolution and the fear they engendered in the Catholic Church itself caused the Jesuits to be completely disbanded by the Pope in the late eighteenth century. They became reorganized again in the mid-nineteenth century, but they were only a shadow of the former vital Society which had been on the verge of world domination. Today the Jesuits are in many ways a pathetic group of men still striving admirably for awareness and world union but blinded by ideological delusions. They are impeded in accomplishing their obejctives by their own self-imposed entropy through lack of feedback. The Jesuits are a living example of how ideology and bureaucracy can corrupt a basically ethical society. The Protagonists should heed their negative example.

The Jesuits are still the most effective international religious bureaucracy, they may significantly impede the expansion of the Ethical State. If the Jesuits could give up their ideology, many of them would be highly effective Protagonists, as they have most of the ethical qualities. Teilhard de Chardin, a Jesuit priest, is the most tragic example of a brilliant ethical mind attempting to expand man's total awareness yet tortured and eventually made largely ineffective by the self-imposed delusions of religious ideology.

Another obstacle to the expansion of the Ethical State will be nationalism and/or ethnocentrism. These will manifest themselves in two ways: 1) the more chauvinistic citizens of the Ethical State will be reluctant to absorb "aliens" into their midst and to assume responsibility for their welfare;* 2) nationalistic and ethnocentric persons from the smaller nations will not wish to be absorbed by another people. This latter problem will be compounded by the fact that innate TAP is almost certainly not equally distributed among all human groups. Indeed, it would be astonishing if any genetically-determined characteristic were identically distributed in genetically-isolated groups. However, no ethnic or racial group has a monopoly on genius or morality. Similarly no ethnic or racial group is totally devoid of stupidity or immorality. The full

* "Welfare" is used in the ethical sense of expanding awareness.

gamut of ethical potential probably exists within all human groups, even if it may not be identically distributed.

Some leaders of the smaller nations will be reluctant to enter a competitive situation in which they are not likely to fare as well as their new competitors. These obstacles can only be overcome by a rigorously fair treatment of all minorities in the TAP and LTA tests, and by appealing to the unifying principles of a subsidized universal educational system which is individualized and scientific. Persons must be more concerned with their absolute awareness than with their relative awareness. Awareness must eventually be seen as an end in itself and not as a form of personal competition. The competition in an Ethical State is only an ethical means for maintaining feedback; it is not an ultimate end but only an intermediate end. When all men are moral, competition will probably not be necessary.

All men must realize that the totality of man is more important than any sub-set of men. Ethnocentrism is another form of ideology and, like all ideology, is mainly divisive and can only increase the entropy of the human race. It unites a small segment of humanity at the cost of isolating it from the rest. In the United States as well as other countries both the Black and the White racists must learn to accept persons on the basis of their individual merit and not on a priori expected behavior associated with the group from which they come.

Hopefully the unifying educational objectives of the Ethical State will tend to make persons forget their parochial worries and to become a part of a movement greater than any single nation. Every man will eventually wish to partake in the exploration of space and the creation of the Moral Society. The drive toward the Moral Society should in time, be stronger than any nationalism or petty ethnocentrism. The Ethical State will unite all ethical persons by giving them a common purpose to which each can contribute and of which each can partake.

The Ethical State will give men what no political system in history has offered—freedom, security and purpose beyond one's personal life, all at the same time. The need for awareness is as basic to man as his instinct for self-preservation. The fulfillment of this need is the basis of human joy.

The internal structure of the Ethical State, where 1) everyone is a full citizen and 2) the competition for responsibility is on the basis of objective TAP and LTA tests, will tend to ameliorate the divisiveness of more parochial interests. The senatorial and mayoral system will assure that every region is equally represented on the basis of population.

Yet not all identifiable groups will fare equally well in the constant competition and creative tension of an Ethical State. Some of these groups will certainly feel discriminated against and under-represented. The Ethical State can only try to assuage their fears by a scrupulous adherence to ethical principles and by getting all persons more involved in expanding awareness than in catering to their own primitive emotions. Persons who have little confidence in their intellectual abilities should not despair at the competition in the Ethical State because ethical behavior is the highest form of awareness and all persons probably have the innate capacity to become ethical and moral.

CONTINGENCY

Considering all the obstacles which can impede the creation of an Ethical State, it is prudent to have a contingency plan. The contingency plan should be put into effect if it ever appears that the United States has reached irreversible entropy. There are indications* that unless purposeful action is taken soon, the United States and the Soviet Union will annihilate each other and in the process most of the human race.

The contingency plan itself should consist primarily in 1) preserving as much of humanity as possible and 2) implementing an Ethical State among the survivors. Since the evidence is now overwhelming that the Soviet Union intends to use thousands of cobalt bombs on American cities a nuclear war will almost certainly make the Northern Hemisphere uninhabitable. Because the radioactive fallout would be diffused very slowly into the Southern Hemisphere, there is a slight chance, however, that humanity might still survive there. Eventually the fallout would probably make the Southern Hemisphere as uninhabitable as the Northern Hemisphere, but there might be time to save large segments of humanity.

* Recall Chapter 5.

The Southern Hemisphere is populated by some of the most primitive people in the world. None of the nations in this part of the world have critical ethical mass at this time. Indeed virtually all of the nations in the Southern Hemisphere have unethical though not necessarily immoral societies. Only a highly intelligent nation can be immoral.

The most ethical major nations in the Southern Hemisphere seem to be Argentina, Australia, Chile and New Zealand. This is evidenced by the educational levels of the populations and their general output in the Sciences and the Arts. Other major nations, such as Brazil and South Africa, are unethical. South Africa is a repressive police state. Brazil has an entrenched military dictatorship. Argentina may also go the same way as Brazil. Rhodesia has gone the way of South Africa and will probably become just as repressive. There are nations in the Southern Hemisphere which seem on the borderline between being ethical and unethical societies, such as Peru and Uruguay. The borderline nations as well as most of the ethical nations, however, are firmly in the grip of leftist ideology which in time should lead to irreversible entropy. Therefore, most of the nations in the Southern Hemisphere have no hope of becoming Ethical States without outside catalysis. However, if the Northern Hemisphere is destroyed the situation in the Southern Hemisphere would change radically. The nations there would no longer be able to avoid negative feedback, neither would they continue to be exploited by the nations of the Northern Hemisphere.

The Exploitation of Nations

Within its own sphere of influence the Soviet Union deliberately and ruthlessly exploits its satellites—Czechoslovakia, Hungary, Poland, East Germany, etc. The United States also exploits the non-Communist nations but this occurs in a subtle, non-deliberate manner.

The United States practices post-industrial colonialism in which intellect is drained from the less advanced nations and invention is exported to be manufactured by cheaper labor in the exploited nations. Since World War II no nation outside of Russia and the United States has had the critical mass of ethical persons to innovate significantly. The United States, because of its great wealth and freedom, has been for a quarter-century the principal scientific innovator in the world. C. P. Snow has estimated that the United States has been responsible for eighty percent of all human progress since the end of World War II. However, at best this is only superficially true.

The principal influx of genius into the United States came with the refugees from Nazism beginning in the 1930's. Before this the United States had produced many outstanding inventors of mechanical and electrical devices but virtually no theoretical discoveries. The marriage of the concrete mechanical genius of America with the abstract theoretical genius of Europe produced a synergistic effect which led to the great post-World War II innovative period in American history. The United States has maintained this momentum partially by feeding parasitically on the best minds from virtually every free nation in the world. This is not done maliciously or even deliberately but occurs automatically through simple economics.

Within the non-Communist world only the United States has the critical mass of laboratory facilities, teachers and research funds to give any scientist or engineer virtually unlimited opportunities to develop his intellectual potential in an atmosphere of freedom and comfort. Therefore, the most creative scientists from all the non-Communist countries tend to come to the United States to study and to work. The high standard of living and the educational opportunities eventually seduce them permanently. This causes the infamous "brain-drain" on all non-Communist countries.

The "brain-drain" takes the best minds out of other countries. This causes the exploited countries to become increasingly unethical. The United States in the meantime, through its bureaucratic and hedonistic decline, is producing an ever-decreasing percentage of the scientists and technologists from its own native-born population. The foreign students become an ever-increasing percent..ge of the student body in all the graduate centers for scientific and technical studies. Some graduate departments even have a majority of foreign students! The native-born Americans study mostly humanities and social science ideology. In this way the United States has been draining the intellectual potential of other countries and giving very little in return, except patent licences and manufacturing franchises of innovations which have been produced in part by the immigrants from the exploited countries.

This phenomenon amounts to the bureaucratization of science on a world scale. It is decreasing feedback within the scientific community and ruining other nations in the most pernicious manner by making them unethical. This process is coming to an end because the United States is finding it politically expedient to cut research funds in favor of military and other bureaucratic spending. Only an immoral leadership would deliberately sacrifice education for political expediency. However, the damage to other nations has already been done.

The Last Chance

The mutual destruction of the Soviet Union and the United States should re-establish feedback into the still-ethical nations of the Southern Hemisphere. They would no longer be able to depend on American technology and their best minds would no longer be flocking to the United States. If at this time there exists a critical mass of Protagonists within these nations it should then be possible to establish an Ethical State in one or more of them. The Ethical State in these nations could then direct the energies of the revitalized nations toward providing shelters and other technological means for saving as much of humanity as possible until the fall-out in the Southern Hemisphere subsides sufficiently to allow human life to survive in a more natural state.

The contingency plan, therefore, involves establishing societies of Protagonists as soon as possible in the Southern Hemisphere. These societies will probably not have critical mass and they will be largely ineffectual until after the nuclear holocaust. At this time the unavoidable negative feedback of nuclear annihilation might attract more persons to the Protagonists and they might take over one or more nations which could be mutated into an Ethical State. This is a very slim hope for the human race but it seems to be the only hope left if the United States has indeed reached irreversible entropy.

The best hope for the human race and the Southern Hemisphere is, of course, that an Ethical State may be established in the United States in the near future. It would be the policy of the Ethical State to expand awareness for *all* mankind. This would imply that the only foreign aid given would be educational; the establishment of competitive research centers and universities in other countries would be encouraged. This would be in the best interests of any Ethical State because it would 1) increase feedback and 2) make other nations more ethical, thereby bringing about the World Ethical State and diminishing the probabilities of war. Therefore, at this time the Protagonists should concentrate their energies on creating an Ethical State within the United States.

This policy should never be completely abandoned even when it seems almost certain that the United States has become an immoral society. So long as there is any hope at all an effort should be made to establish an Ethical State in North America.

HOPE

Hope may diminish but it is never zero. It is unethical to give up hope because it is unethical to be certain. There will be many obstacles to be overcome in engendering the first Ethical State and then expanding it to include all of humanity. The strategies outlined here only give the general over-all pattern of how to begin. Specific problems will require specific solutions which can best be worked out *ad hoc* through the use of ethical principles and scientific method. The basic strategy for an Ethical State is based not on logical method but on the fact that an Ethical State probably is the *only* hope for the survival of the human race. The Ethical State should succeed because man does not seem to have any alternative. He must succeed in creating an Ethical State or all hope for himself and his progeny will probably be lost forever. The commitment of the most highly-aware generalists of a nation to the creation of an Ethical State is a strategy which should succeed because it is in keeping with the basic evolutionary patterns that have *always* assured long-term victory to the more-aware competitor. But it is the hope inherent in the Ethical State which should fire the imagination of the world and drive it to create the Moral Society.

In the creation of the Moral Society, under maximum creative tension, man will find what has always driven him to try to be a part of something greater than himself. The illusions of ideology have been a perverse manifestation of this basic need. In creating the Moral Society man will do more than find the security and happiness which have always eluded him. The Moral Society will for the first time in history make each man complete by making him an integral, necessary part of an intelligence far greater than his own. Only an Ethical State can lead man toward the Moral Society and only the Moral Society can lead man to total awareness. The Ethical State will succeed because it must. There is no other way.

PART FOUR

summation

Nothing is impossible; there are ways that lead to everything, and if we had sufficient will we should always have sufficient means. It is often merely for an excuse that we say things are impossible.

—La Rochefoucauld

In this summary of the preceding material, an effort is made to tie all the speculation, observation and proposed experimentation together into a single coherent pattern. This is done directly in Chapter 8 and indirectly in the Epilogue. Since this is a summation of uncertainties, it itself is uncertain and may be in error. Every description, hypothesis, theory and strategy in this book may be in error. With this reservation in mind, the prime ethic of life is summarized in the following statement:

Each person must do his best to maximize total awareness.

All ethical behavior can be logically and scientifically derived from this ethic. In trying to follow the prime ethic, each person must keep in mind that 1) it is unethical to be certain; 2) it is ethical to doubt; 3) inaction is unethical; and 4) unethical means never produce ethical ends. The understanding of the prime ethic is facilitated by observing that:

1 The universe is probably infinite.
2 The total awareness in the universe is probably constantly increasing.
3 Entropy probably only increases when awareness decreases.

These three conjectured laws are the evolutionary counterparts of the three laws of thermodynamics which state that energy cannot be created or destroyed and that entropy must always increase. The conjectured laws imply that local increases in entropy do not affect the over-all evolution of awareness in an infinite universe. Therefore, the continued evolution or entropic extinction of humanity is unimportant in the greater scheme of things. Man's evolution is either important to himself or it is important to no one. Each species is responsible for its own evolution. For this reason every ethical person must devote all his energies to joining with other ethical men in the creation of an Ethical State. If this is not done, then humanity has already reached irreversible entropy.

8
SUMMING
UP

This book has been an attempt to develop a simple, coherent, scientific model of the universe which is consistent with all that we know. The two salient evils which have been identified are bureaucratization and ideology. These evils will destroy the human race in the near future unless man can overcome them through ethics, scientific method and a determined effort to play the Game of Life.

Ideology destroys personal morality. Bureaucracy destroys social morality. Both types of morality are essential for maintaining ethical behavior within the human race. An unethical species is doomed to extinction.

It is not only possible but highly probable that a joining of Protagonists in the United States would bring about an Ethical State, and eventually lead to the creation of the Moral Society. Throughout evolutionary history the more aware have inevitably triumphed over the less aware no matter how strong or numerous the latter appeared to be. The only serious problem that remains is motivating ethical persons in our society to become Protagonists. Here lies the only true threat to humanity. It is not so much the evil of the immoral men which will destroy humanity. It is the apathy and inaction of the ethical persons of the world which will make man's entropy irreversible. Inaction is always unethical. The motivation for ethical action can only come from direct perception of the evolutionary patterns.

DIRECT PERCEPTION

Pierre Teilhard de Chardin spent most of his life trying to help mankind directly perceive the evolutionary patterns of the Noosphere. The Noosphere represented his more limited and ideological view of the Moral Society. During his life, he was thwarted by the Catholic bureaucracy and his own ideology. The Catholic Church censored his most significant work. After his death in 1955, his secular friends arranged for publication of his books.

Teilhard's greatest work, *The Phenomenon of Man*, is a book of such beauty and power that it alone should have moved men to the study and reflection which leads to direct perception of the evolutionary patterns. However, very few people appear to have been moved by it. The combination of poetry, mysticism and science in Teilhard's book is confusing to the specialized scientists as well as to the scientific illiterates. It may be that Teilhard, a scientific generalist, unconsciously addressed himself *solely* to scientific generalists. In so doing, he greatly limited his audience and decreased his effectiveness in many ways. The concept of the Moral Society is so radical that most people have difficulty accepting it even after Teilhard has carefully developed the theoretical basis for it. Unfortunately the attempt by Teilhard to make his great work compatible with Catholic dogma detracted from the power of his arguments. Teilhard did not couch his arguments in a plan for rational action. He points the way and identifies the goal but does not tell us how to get there. Purpose without method cannot be sustained.

Teilhard does not discuss bureaucracy or ideology, but he does discuss faith. Faith, as discussed by Teilhard, is not a belief in a cause and effect relationship for which there is no scientific evidence, but it is equivalent to hope. Faith is the hope that our desires may somehow be fulfilled without knowing precisely how this will happen. In order to perceive directly the evolutionary patterns of the Moral Society, it is necessary to have faith that morality can ultimately triumph over entrenched and aggressive immorality. However, this is a belief which is supported by all of history and it need not be based on ideology.

No plan is practical unless it is believable. A scientifically consistent plan will not work if no one believes it will work. To believe that a plan will work implies that at least a few people have sufficient faith (in Teilhard's sense) to try to make it work. To bring about an Ethical State, it is only necessary that some persons do *not* accept the propositions that 1) bureaucracy and ideology are inevitable; 2) it is "natural" to prefer happiness above awareness; and 3) we have already reached irreversible entropy and the continued decay of humanity is inevitable.

The desires for awareness and the union with other men are even more basic to man than his desires for happiness and security. Only man among all the animals will sacrifice his life for awareness and freedom. With only a little reflection we can see that true happiness and security can only be brought about indirectly by the direct pursuit of total awareness through brotherhood and personal freedom. Only the highly aware can know joy.

The Ethical State does not seek to change man's nature but to let his true nature flourish. The Ethical State is Utopian but every single successful political idea in history began as a Utopian idea which most men considered unrealistic. This was the case with Judaism, Confucianism, Buddhism, Christianity, the Democratic secular state and Communism. These seemingly impractical Utopian dreams succeeded only insofar as they were indirectly inspired by and consistent with the evolutionary force. They failed only when they became corrupted by bureaucracy and/or ideology.

The Ethical State may *appear* elitist, but every society in history *has* been elitist. Today every nation is controlled by an elite of legal-minded, power-seeking bureaucrats. Only the Ethical State offers true equality of opportunity by 1) complete universality of suffrage, 2) completely subsidized, individualized education for all persons and 3) a non-bureaucratic, individualized competition for responsibility on the basis of objectively-measured ability.

The Ethical State is a movement directly inspired by the evolutionary force and recognizes at its inception the dangers of bureaucracy and
ideology. It is unique in being a political system founded on doubt and
not on belief. The will to doubt is the basis of science. There is no logical
reason why the Ethical State should not be the most successful politico-
philosophical movement in history. There is no logical reason why men
cannot evolve forever toward total awareness. There are no insurmountable obstacles in the way of man directly perceiving and accepting the
patterns of his own evolution and transforming himself into the Moral
Society.

Man need take but one more step to create the Moral Society. The
step must be deliberate. The step is the final test before human evolution becomes irreversible. Only an Ethical State can become the Moral
Society.

We have seen that the only common denominator in evolution is an
ever-increasing total awareness. By and large, the older the species, the
less aware it is. *Homo sapiens* is the youngest major species on Earth
(about 50,000 years old). The cockroach is among the oldest (about
250,000,000 years old). Matter is the oldest phylum of all. The less specialized (i.e., the less bureaucratized) a species, the longer it can survive.
Homo sapiens is a recent generalized species. The cockroach is an ancient generalized species. However, survival by itself is meaningless. Only
through a constant, deliberate expansion of awareness can life be made
meaningful. Only by deliberately playing the Game of Life can man
achieve continued purpose, freedom, security, happiness and survival.
Otherwise he can, at best, go the way of the cockroach.

Man has reached a point of such extreme biological complexity that
significant further complexity and the consequent great increase in
awareness can only occur by joining. There is little evidence that the
human brain has evolved significantly since the time of Cro-Magnon
man. The geniuses of today are no more clever than the geniuses of
yesterday. Einstein, Newton and Archimedes are all of the same mold.
There has been little if any individual progress.

Progress today is reflected mainly in the cultural evolution of our
species. Natural selection serves mainly to alter the *relative* frequency of
highly-aware versus unaware persons. There probably has been no sig-

nificant increase in the *absolute* innate potential for maximum total awareness (TAP) of individual persons for thousands of years. *Homo sapiens* has become increasingly aware primarily because science and technology have enabled man to preserve and extend to many the awareness of one. In other words, the evolution of awareness since the time of Cro-Magnon man has been due *almost entirely* to an increase in transferable knowledge and the quality and quantity of our machines.* *Homo moralensis* will be a consequence of psychosocial evolution not biological evolution. Indeed our bodies are decaying as we become ever more dependent on machines. Yet our awareness is constantly increasing.

There has been an enormous increase in the absolute number of human beings together with a slight increase in the relative frequency of persons with a high innate potential for total awareness. The latter gains, however, are now being totally dissipated by a bureaucratized civilization in which the reproduction of parasitical human beings† is deliberately subsidized by the political bureaucracies as a means of consolidating their power. The advance of a captive science and technology will in time make it possible for an entrenched political bureaucracy to achieve absolute control of the population and breed an ever-greater percentage of parasitical human beings as a means of achieving complete power over all men. The decent political bureaucrats may even believe that they are being altruistic and humanitarian in the process. This will result in an increasingly degenerate society sustained by machines developed by an ever-dwindling number of scientists and engineers. Eventually there will be only parasitical human beings completely dependent on self-improving machines they can no longer understand or control.

The Soviet Union is becoming an immoral society with irreversible entropy. The United States is becoming an unethical society. The Revolt Against Reason has the power not to take over a nation but only to entrench a repressive police state of the Right. This will produce irreversible entropy in the United States. Modern technology has made it im-

---

* Recall that any manufactured tool or device that changes one form of energy into another is a machine. Therefore, language, clothing, houses and computers are all machines.

† Recall that parasitical human beings are persons who consume resources and produce pollution but do absolutely nothing to increase man's total awareness during the rest of their lives.

possible to overthrow a determined police state from within. A "democratic" police state with majority support and complete control of the Military is virtually invulnerable to revolution. In this and only in this lies the danger of the Revolt Against Reason.

Of course, the human element in the *gestalt* of men, machines, and knowledge forming modern society is much more likely to become extinct through nuclear annihilation or pollution before total decay sets in. Survival and continued progress is dependent on men directly perceiving the patterns of evolution and the true nature of their own society as well as having the desire to evolve toward total awareness. The essential concept to be perceived in the over-all pattern is the fact that men, machines, and knowledge are *together* a single entity we call "humanity." Each one without the other is valueless. Together they make up the total awareness of humanity. If any one of the three elements were totally destroyed, humanity would quickly become extinct. Therefore, it is just as important to continue to expand knowledge and improve our machines as it is to preserve the human element. The preservation and expansion of human beings solely to make them happy can only increase the total entropy of humanity. Only the expansion of *total* awareness is ethical. Only it can lead to the irreversible evolution of the Moral Society.

THE MORAL SOCIETY

The Moral Society represents a logical extension of the current form of humanity. The Moral Society is a joining of human beings—all of whom are moral. The joining will be made possible by machines, knowledge, and morality. Science and technology will be used to amplify and unite the individual components of intelligence of many men into a single collective intelligence greater than the sum of its parts.

The last random joining of single cells into the metazoa led to the highest known intelligence we call "man." The deliberate, free joining of highly aware men will lead to the collective intelligence of the Moral Society. The Moral Society will continue to evolve by fanning out, testing, and joining. It will evolve toward the Moral Society of all joined

Moral Societies—the ultimate, infinite Moral Society of pure thought. The Moral Society will evolve toward total awareness which is an infinite goal.

Mind is an effect which can affect itself. Therefore it can evolve toward pure thought and total awareness by becoming less an effect of the body and more an effect of itself. This process has been going on for thousands of years as man's body has deteriorated until he is completely dependent on machines and collective human knowledge.

Man has, unconsciously, been creating the Moral Society by creating analogues and amplifiers of the components of his own intelligence. This has occurred under the constant tension and random testing of the evolutionary force. In a similar fashion, the evolutionary force drove the first primitive metazoa toward the collective intelligence of man. Man's intelligence results from the billions of individuals cells making up his body. Man's individual intelligence is, therefore, like all intelligence, really a collective intelligence. The Moral Society will be to man as man is to a cell; however, the ultimate Moral Society is infinite. It can only be reached at infinity. We can evolve toward it, always getting closer but never reaching it. It is infinitely greater in relation to the first Moral Society than man is to the first metazoan.

The critical evolutionary difference between the Moral Society and all other life forms is that the Moral Society is fully conscious of its own evolution and it deliberately controls it instead of submitting blindly to the random testing of the evolutionary force. Man is mutating into the Moral Society by becoming aware of his own evolution. This process can only be completed deliberately within an Ethical State. *When all men are fully aware of the evolutionary patterns and are unified with the sole purpose of increasing their collective total awareness, the Moral Society will have begun.*

The Moral Society will, at first, be as little superior to the Ethical State as the first metazoan was to an unjoined group of cells. However, once men begin to unify their individual intelligence for the sole purpose of amplifying their collective intelligence, the Moral Society will begin to develop rapidly. The development of the collective intelligence of the Moral Society should mirror the development of man's individual intelligence, since all evolution repeats its former patterns.

The first metazoa only amplified the Effectors of the individual cells by making them collectively larger and stronger than a single cell, somewhat in the same way that an army is larger and stronger than an individual soldier. Eventually the cells of the metazoan began to give up an ever increasing part of their individuality by specializing. Specialization has always been a way in which individuals lose their freedom by becoming narrowly aware as opposed to broadly aware. First, collective Connectors and Memory began to develop in the metazoa. Ultimately collective Sensors and the brain were simultaneously developed. Within the brain, collective Logic, Memory, Imagination and Will were to evolve until they became man.

Man has similarly, in his psychosocial evolution, first developed artificial amplifiers of Effectors (e.g., tools), then of Connectors and Memory (e.g., language and writing), then of Sensors (e.g., telescopes). He has continued to develop new and better machines for amplifying the components of his intelligence until today he is on the verge of creating the body of the Moral Society.

The components of the body of the Moral Society will evolve from communications networks, electro-mechanical servo-mechanisms and sensors, computers, synthetic cells and other machines. The Ethical State will represent the embryonic collective Will and Imagination of the Moral Society. Ultimately the Moral Society will be a single entity in which all men, knowledge and machines have become unified. At that time all the components of intelligence will have become so greatly amplified that the Moral Society will have the same relationship to man as man has to a group of unjoined cells. But man will never have to give up his individuality. He will never have to specialize. The specialized functions will be done by machines. The machine has always made man free by allowing him to remain unspecialized and individualized. It will continue to do so within the Moral Society. He will remain an indvidual while still a part of a greater whole. The body of the Moral Society may someday be made entirely of specialized machines, but the mind of the Moral Society will be composed of free, unspecialized men who are moral generalists. The life force of the Moral Society will be morality— the conscious desire for ever greater total awareness for itself and for others.

The Moral Society, like all organisms, will evolve gradually from a fragmented humanity to a single, far greater entity. There will be no sudden radical changes in structure. Such was the pattern which led from cell to man. Such was the pattern which led from matter to the cell. Such should be the pattern of the Moral Society evolving toward infinite total awareness. The Moral Society will make man ever more free by making him ever more aware. Only the freedom of man will make the Moral Society possible. Only through the Moral Society will man be able to become ever more free. Freedom and awareness are each a cause and effect of the other.

FEASIBILITY

The technical feasibility of the Moral Society is clear. The pattern of man's ever-increasing ability to predict and control his total environment indicates that the body of the Moral Society is feasible and that most of it already exists or is readily created. It only remains to extend the scientific method fully to the psychosocial environment in order to create the mind, i.e., soul, of the Moral Society. Only in this way can mankind be made moral. Only moral men can create the mind of the Moral Society.

The collective mind of the Moral Society will be created from the individual minds of a humanity freely and ethically united by art, science, technology, and a common purpose. The essential components of the mind are the essential components of intelligence plus ethics. By "essential" is meant those components that produce awareness. We are already beginning to understand Memory. It appears that once the molecular structure of Memory is deciphered, it will be possible to pool all the important Information of the entire human race in such a way that each person has all the important Information of every other person.

It seems that Will and Imagination are amplified by voluntary, close cooperation between highly-aware persons with a common purpose. The education programs of the Ethical State will augment this process by 1) making all persons highly aware and 2) by the creation of direct, artificial Connectors between individual minds. The latter will be an extension of the artificial Connector we call language. This will represent a

natural extension of the work currently being done in biophysical neurophysiology and mathematical psychology. Once the Information, Imagination and Will of many persons have been pooled, then the collective
mind of the Moral Society will begin to develop. Its development will be
enhanced by the amplification of Memory and Logic through the development of super-computers with sub-microscopic components. The entire
process will be further enhanced through the rapidly-growing technology
of artificial Sensors and Effectors. It will all be made possible by the moral
field of humanity.

The ever-increasing collective awareness of the Moral Society will
then be used to accelerate its own evolution. Once the Moral Society is
engendered, it will evolve at an ever-increasing rate toward infinity. The
technical feasibility of the Moral Society is, therefore, assured. Its creation may take hundreds of years or it may be possible in fifty years. The
time is highly uncertain, but not the technical feasibility. The only serious impediment to the creation of the Moral Society is the currently
increasing high state of entropy within the human race.

ENTROPY

Man is currently in a state of acute entropic decline as a consequence
of bureaucratization and ideology. This manifests itself in the democracies through the Revolt Against Reason, hedonism, specialization, scientific illiteracy, and most of all through the immorality of the leadership.
In the totalitarian states it manifests itself through the unethical stifling
of freedom by self-serving, corrupt, ideological bureaucracies dominated
by indecent men. The suppression of freedom through ideology and bureaucracy leads inevitably to the extinction of awareness by making all
men unethical. This occurred in Islam and has almost occurred in Iberia.
The world is becoming unethical. The United States is becoming an
unethical society. The Soviet Union is becoming an immoral society.
Immoral societies have irreversible entropy.

The only defense that the human race has against entropy is education, but education is in the same entropic decline as the rest of society.
The educational system is bureaucratized and the psychosocial sciences

are impeded by the ideologically-based establishment of the social "scientists." The only hope for overcoming the entropy which will inevitably destroy the human race is an Ethical State. An Ethical State is only possible if the entropy of mankind has not increased beyond the point of no return.

Just as entropy has a point of no return, so does awareness. Once awareness increases to a certain level, it becomes a self-catalyzing reaction that cannot be reversed. This level of awareness is probably represented by a fairly primitive Moral Society which is becoming fully aware of the evolutionary patterns. Once a Moral Society is aware of what it must do to expand its awareness continuously, it cannot help but continuously expand its awareness at its maximum rate. It then no longer has to worry about the testing of other Moral Societies. It will *always* grow in awareness and its entropy will *always* decrease.

In order to create the Moral Society and raise it to the level of total awareness from which there is no return, it is essential that man begin the Ethical State now and then begin the expansion of total awareness at his maximum rate. It is questionable whether the point of no return in entropy has yet been reached. In the near future it will almost certainly be reached unless the entire structure of society has been radically changed and man has started an Ethical State. This will occur only if there still exists a critical mass of moral men and ethical children.

WHAT MUST BE DONE

If man is to continue to evolve toward total awareness then there are certain essential steps which must be taken. The first and most essential step is the joining of the Protagonists, the deliberate players of the Game of Life. *It is the duty of all ethical persons to concentrate all their energy on the creation of an Ethical State. They must do this whatever the cost may be to them and their loved ones. If this is not done humanity is doomed.*

Each moral man perceives the evolutionary patterns in his own way. Historically this perception has been at the unconscious level. Such was probably the case with Moses, Confucius, Buddha, Socrates, and Jesus.

The first deliberate attempt at conscious perception of the evolutionary patterns was probably made by Spinoza. After Spinoza, other thinkers made similar attempts. Most notable among these were Goethe, Darwin, Marx and Teilhard de Chardin. These five men were all of radically different temperament and ideological persuasion. Only Spinoza seems to have been devoid of any conscious ideology, but he had to work with primitive science and logic. Yet, if we were to extract ethical principles from the writings of these men, we would arrive at an amazingly consistent code of ethics—the Game of Life. Therefore, moral men may not agree on cause and effect relationships but they are likely to agree on basic ethics. It is this propensity to agree on basic ethical principles which should be used to join all ethical persons in a society of deliberate players of the Game of Life.

The Protagonists must unite in a close-knit society. They must seek each other out as best they can, join, organize and direct all their energies toward the creation of an Ethical State. Once they are organized they must overcome the political bureaucracies and take over the government by ethical means.

All bureaucracies exist because of a lack of feedback. Any bureaucracy will be destroyed by reintroducing unavoidable feedback into the organization. The political bureaucrats who dominate the world cannot survive in the light of truth. The truth about the way the world is and the way it is likely to become must be taught to all men. Toward this end the Protagonists must start schools, write, and teach all men as best they can.

One way of accomplishing this objective would be to start schools which teach all the sciences and ethics as a single, integrated subject unified by the general theory of evolution. This is an essential function which is not being done by the educational bureaucracy and for which considerable public support may be expected. The schools by simply teaching the truth will reveal the nature of the bureaucratic corruption which must be stopped before it destroys mankind.

The major objective must be to drive the political bureaucrats from office and to elect highly ethical leaders. Toward this end the Protagonists must concentrate wealth by whatever ethical means are possible. The easiest means of concentrating wealth will be through inventions, creations, and the production of technology which increases awareness. Some of the Protagonists and their supporters may also contribute their personal wealth toward this objective.

All the accumulated wealth must then be used to elect ethical men to public office and drive the immoral leaders from power. This may be done within the regular party context in some cases, but it will probably be better strategy to form a completely new political party dedicated to eradication of political corruption by ethical means. This might be called the *Ethical Party*.

The Ethical Party, hopefully, could be used to redirect the presently destructive and largely unethical activities of the Revolt Against Reason into ethical channels. The children must be made to see that unethical means never achieve ethical ends. In a free, democratic society such as the United States political power can be obtained ethically only at the polls. The failure of the Revolt Against Reason is due entirely to use of unethical means. The young revolutionaries are entrenching the very forces they seek to destroy. They must see that ethical behavior can triumph over immorality; it *always* has in the past.

In conclusion the main actions to be taken are:

1 Organization of the Protagonists as an embryonic Ethical State.
2 Withdraw all support from the bureaucracies.
3 Establish feedback within the nations of the world by educational means.*
4 Formation of a political force for electing ethical men to office.
5 Implementation of an ethical constitution similar in principle to that of the Ethical State in Chapter 6.
6 Expansion of the Ethical State to include all of mankind.
7 The creation of the Moral Society.

At first, activities should be concentrated in the United States. If the United States indicates that it has reached irreversible entropy and cannot be mutated into an Ethical State, then as a contingency plan the Protagonists must concentrate their efforts in the most ethical nations of the Southern Hemisphere. These nations may have a chance of continu-

* The Science Education Extension of Potomac, Maryland, represents a modest step in this direction.

ing human evolution after the Soviet Union and the United States destroy the Northern Hemisphere.

THE FUTURE OF MAN

If man wills it, he has an infinite future. First the Protagonists will join; then they will overcome the political bureaucracies and implement an Ethical State. There will be great turmoil but for the first time in history the deliberate expansion of man's total awareness will have begun. The citizens of the Ethical State will begin a rapid increase in total awareness. Simultaneously the Ethical State will expand and absorb other nations. Eventually the majority of mankind will be deliberate players of the Game of Life. Humanity will be moral.

The collective awareness of the Moral Society will begin to take form. This will make individual persons more highly aware and they in turn will catalyze the further creation of the Moral Society. Men will wish to be a part of the Moral Society because it increases their *individual awareness*. Eventually the individual components of intelligence of all men will become a part of the Moral Society. Their personalities will forever be a part of the infinitely-expanding total awareness of humanity.

Life lost its pseudo-immortality when cells joined to become metazoa. Life will become truly immortal when man joins to become the Moral Society. Only in the Moral Society will the individual awareness of each person who joins it continue to grow and expand forever as the Moral Society transcends time, space and matter. It is not likely that any person living today will become a part of the Moral Society. We who live today have a finite future and our individual awareness will cease with our lives. We live on only in the awareness that we engender in others and in our children. Only our children are likely to evolve forever toward total awareness in the Moral Society. It is for them that we must create an Ethical State.

EPILOGUE

The Lens Grinder

There lived a man of ethics
All he said offended
His writings were forbidden
He lived by grinding lenses

The grinding destroyed his body
The living became dying
The dying could be ended
Only by compromise and lying

He declined the living
And chose the grinding
It is better to die by seeing
Than to live by dying

His life made men see
His death was not empty
His ethics live in me
His awareness—part of infinity

J. D. G.
March 1970

GLOSSARY

Amoral Only sub-human beings are amoral. To be amoral is to be unaware of the Game of Life at both the unconscious and conscious levels. Amoral beings are only pieces, never players, in the Game of Life. An amoral species is doomed to extinction. Only a moral species can continue to evolve without mutating physically.

Art A process which uses entertainment to expand awareness. This is usually done symbolically through unconscious stimulation of the mind. Art is similar in its social function to dreaming. Art reflects the awareness of a culture.

Asymptotically A word which refers to a process by which something is always getting closer to something else but never reaches it.

Awareness The property of mind which subsumes the ability to predict and control the total environment—physical, biological and psychosocial. The notion of "awareness" also subsumes the notion of "ethical behavior." It is possible for an ethical person to be more aware than a more intelligent person who is less ethical. For example, Spinoza was more ethical but less intelligent than Leibniz. However, only when ethics and intelligence are combined can the person be creative. Creativity is the highest form of awareness. The creation of *The Ethics* by Spinoza reflected a higher awareness than any of Leibniz' creations in the physical environment. *The Ethics* gave mankind the first completely rational code of behavior; the highest form of creation is when we create our own behavior instead of merely responding to physical and biological stimuli.

Belief A belief is a state of mind in which someone imagines something to be true. In science there are no beliefs but only probabilities of certain relationships holding under certain circumstances. In science there is never certainty. Only ideologies propound certainties.

Biosphere The envelope of life which surrounds the Earth. It includes all life forms on water, land, or in the air. The biosphere is the precursor to the Noosphere.

Bisexual Refers to a condition in which a person is equally disposed to companionship from either sex. The companionship may be for any purpose and not necessarily solely for sexual gratification. (See heterosexual and homosexual.)

Bureaucracy Refers to an organization with a built-in mechanism for reducing feedback. Bureaucracy is the evolutionary analogue of specialization and is the major source of entropy within the human race.

Certainty Refers to a mental state in which there exists no doubt about the validity of a cause and effect relationship. Apparently the only thing we can be certain about are our own thoughts, never their causes. This is the case even with thoughts produced by drugs or disease. Error arises only when from our own thoughts we infer a cause and

effect relationship between other events in the total environment. It is unethical to be certain.

Chaos Total disorder. Where nothing has meaning or purpose and all is random. The lowest level of awareness. A patternless nothingness.

Child A child is a transitory being bridging the gap between amorality and morality. Children are always ethical for at least a while. When children become unethical, they may become immoral adults. Immoral adults can only have power by controlling children. Children are pliable and can just as easily become moral or immoral adults. An unethical society turns most of its children into immoral adults. An immoral society turns all of its children into immoral adults. The converse is true for moral and ethical societies. Man has been a child for most of his existence. *Homo sapiens* seems to be the first species of man with the capacity to produce moral adults. "Child" as here used is an ethical descriptor and not a chronological indicator. "Young child" is used to describe "children" in the more conventional sense.

Communism A socialistic system with a rigid, unscientific, bureaucratic basis derived from Marxist and Leninist ideology.

Conscious Refers to that state of mind in which we are aware of our own awareness. This is opposed to our unconscious. Creativity seems to necessitate a synthesis between the conscious and the unconscious mind.

Connectors Channels through which Information flows from one component of intelligence to another. In our bodies Connectors are represented by nerves.

Conservative Refers to any attitude which is intolerant of change. This characteristic exists on a continuum with adamant opposition to any change at one extreme and complete tolerance for any change at the other. (See liberal.)

Control The deliberate causal formation of a predicted set of events. Control is essential to awareness. Without control an entity is deprived of feedback and becomes incapable of correct prediction.

Cosmic Force The "cosmic force" is a collective term for the joint operation of all natural laws. The cosmic force has two major components—evolution and entropy. All is an effect of the cosmic force. The cosmic force is random, mindless and infinite in temporal and spatial extension.

Cosmic Moral Society The Moral Society which results from the joining of two or more distinct Moral Societies with independent origins on different planets.

Creation The deliberate organization of energy, matter, life and/or mind into new patterns which increase awareness. The patterns may only be new to the creator; they are not necessarily original. Creation is the joint result of intelligence and ethics. All ethical persons are to some degree creative. Moral persons are extremely creative; they are the ones who create new, coherent models of the universe and engender new societies. Immoral persons can never create; they only destroy.

Critical Mass The point at which the density and quantity of a substance is such that completely new effects take place. For example, a critical mass of plutonium will cause nuclear fission to occur. A critical mass of ethical men is necessary to create an Ethical State. A critical mass of moral men is sufficient to engender an Ethical State and to make evolution irreversible.

Cyborg (Cybernetic organism) A man who incorporates a machine as an integral part of his structure. May be pictured as a robot with a man inside it who completely controls the robot and uses it to amplify and simulate his individual powers.

Death The state of maximum entropy for life. It is the state where the awareness produced by life sinks to the level of matter. The preponderance of scientific evidence indicates that for all life forms death represents total extinction of awareness.

Decency A person is decent when he will not deliberately enhance his welfare at the expense of another person's

welfare. A decent person is ethical if and only if he interprets "welfare" as synonymous with awareness. A decent person is unethical if and only if he interprets welfare as synonymous with happiness. Decent immoral persons increase entropy by destroying negative feedback for themselves and others. Indecent persons are always immoral and increase entropy by destroying other persons' awareness as well as their own as a means of increasing their own happiness.

Decline (Decay) A process by which the total collective awareness continuously decreases, while the entropy increases until the capacity to evolve disappears.

Democracy A system of representative government in which the representatives are chosen in free elections. Elections are assumed to be free if and only if all persons are guaranteed personal freedom. It is assumed, ideologically, that freedom is a necessary and sufficient condition for progress.

DNA (Deoxyribonucleic acid) A complex polymeric organic molecule in the form of a double helix. DNA molecules carry all the information for structuring all known life forms. All the information for structuring the body of a human being is contained in a few thousand DNA molecules. The DNA molecules are the blueprint from which life can be structured. DNA is built on templates of RNA.

Destruction To decrease awareness by increasing entropy. Moral persons never destroy. Immoral persons can only destroy. Children may create or destroy. The more intelligent an immoral person is, the greater will be his capacity to destroy.

Direct Perception The clear realization of a pattern in nature, analogous to the perception of our own thoughts. Illusions of certainty are sometimes mistaken for Direct Perception. Direct Perception is valid only insofar as it enables us to predict and control

Education Any process which directly increases the awareness of those exposed to it.

Effectors That component of intelligence which generates events in the total environment. Within the body, effectors are represented by our bones, muscles and connective tissues in general.

Emotion A pre-programmed pattern of behavior which is primarily instinctual, i.e., genetic, in origin. All emotions, except love, are becoming increasingly destructive, i.e., they serve only to decrease awareness instead of to expand it. Emotions other than love are only useful for survival in a primitive, Darwinian environment when there is little knowledge at hand. Love is always a constructive emotion because it catalyzes the transfer of knowledge.

Entertainment Any process which increases the happiness of some persons without necessarily increasing the awareness of any person. Entertainment which increases awareness is called "Art."

Entropy A condition of chaos as well as a force which increases the chaos in the universe. The entropic force drives mind toward matter and matter toward chaotic energy. Entropy manifests itself in mind by a decreased ability to become aware. In mankind, entropy is measured by the amount of imaginary awareness and by the effectiveness of the mechanisms for limiting feedback. Entropy feeds upon itself and is negatively correlated with awareness.

Ethical Behavior is ethical if and only if it is a strategy in the Game of Life. Therefore, only behavior which increases awareness is ethical. A person is ethical if and only if he is increasing total awareness. In other words, a person is ethical if and only if he plays the Game of Life more often than he plays the Game of Pleasure. To be ethical is to create. Ethical behavior is, therefore, synonymous with creativity; it is the highest form of awareness. Only man has exhibited ethical behavior, because only man has increased his awareness as a species. All other species only increase awareness by mutating into new species. Virtually all human beings are ethical during their childhood. Persons only become unethical by being subjected to the pressures of an unethical society and entropy.

Ethical State An Ethical State is a nation which is structured to increase total awareness. A society is ethical when most of its members are ethical. A society can only remain ethical if its leaders are moral men. A society with moral leadership and an ethical structure has irreversible awareness.

Ethics Rules of optimal behavior. It may be shown logically that behavior is optimal if and only if it is a strategy in the Game of Life. The rules of the Game of Life are, therefore, the Ethics of Life and are the only true ethics. All other forms of behavior are unethical or trivial.

Eugenics A process by which controlled reproduction is used to improve the quality of a species. (See selective and uniform birth control.)

Evil Refers to any action or thing which decreases awareness.

Evolution (See entropy.) A condition of awareness as well as a force which drives everything in the universe toward greater awareness and complexity. Evolution is the opposite of entropy. The evolutionary force drives matter toward mind and mind toward ever greater awareness. A level of evolution is measured by the degree of awareness. The greater the awareness of a being the higher it is on the evolutionary scale. Evolution is a law of nature and not a coherent plan. Evolution has a direction of ever greater awareness and certain properties; however, it is basically a random process because it always coexists with entropy. The higher a being is on the evolutionary scale the less subject it is to entropy. Therefore, evolution catalyzes itself.

Extended Family A family which includes persons not our parents, children, spouse or siblings. The extended family evolves from the immediate family to the clan, to the tribe, to the nation, to the empire, to the Ethical State, to the Moral Society. (See family.)

Faith The hope that our desires will be fulfilled without knowing precisely how this will happen.

Family A group of beings tied together by mutual love. (See immediate and extended family.)

Fanning Out Part of the process of evolution by which members of a phylum speciate by acquiring different specialties until they can no longer interbreed and have increasingly less in common.

Feedback Refers to the perception of the consequences of our actions. Positive feedback refers to perception of successes, i.e., when the total environment was in fact predicted and controlled. Negative feedback refers to perception of our mistakes, i.e., to attempts at prediction and control which failed.

Freedom Refers to a state in which we can do and say as we please so long as we do not in the process interfere with the right of another person to do and say as he pleases. When there is a conflict, a compromise is reached which maximizes the freedom for both persons.

Game A set of rules of how to behave in order to win a specified stake. The stake may be symbolic or tangible. A game has no purpose beyond itself. All men play games either consciously or unconsciously. Every game is either a variation on the Game of Life or a variation on the Game of Pleasure. For any given person, the same game may be a variation on the Game of Life at one time and a variation on the Game of Pleasure at another time.

Game of Life A game in which the stakes are ever-expanding awareness. The Game of Life is the pivotal point between good and evil, life and death. The Game of Life is the basis of all evolution. To play the Game of Life is to increase awareness. To deliberately play the Game of Life is to increase awareness as best we can for the rest of our life.

Game of Pleasure A game which serves only to increase happiness, never awareness. Persons who play the Game of Pleasure are the major source of entropy for the human race. Players of the Game of Pleasure make themselves

and others increasingly unethical until they become immoral.

Generalist (See specialist.) A generalist is a person who is aware of the total environment in approximately equal degrees. He has tried to learn in approximately equal amounts all of human knowledge. He attempts to maintain sphericity by not developing great depth in one area while he is still ignorant of another area. It is possible for a generalist to have more depth in every area than a specialist.

Genotype The genetic make-up of an organism which interacts with the external environment to produce the overt phenotype.

Good Refers to any action or thing which increases awareness.

Great That is great which significantly expands the awareness of others. This applies to art, science or men. Greatness implies extremely important social morality.

Happiness The state of mind which results from being in the process of fulfilling our desires. The intensity of happiness is directly proportional to the strength of our desires and the rate at which we fulfill them. In the absence of desire there is neither happiness nor unhappiness.

Hedonism A sense of values which gives the highest value to pleasure and happiness. Hedonism represents the pursuit of happiness to the exclusion of awareness. A hedonist seeks to maximize his happiness above all else. The pursuit of happiness without awareness leads only to death.

Heritability A statistical notion based on the theory of analysis of variance. It is expressed by a number between zero and one. A heritability of zero indicates that the phenotypic differences between statistically differentiable groups are not due to genotypic differences, but are determined solely by the environment of the organism. A heritability of one indicates that the environmental differences between the groups in question produce no significant differences with respect to a specified trait; all differences concerning the trait are assumed to be due to genetic differences.

Heterosexual Refers to a condition in which a person prefers the companionship of the opposite sex. This does not preclude the desire for companionship or sexual gratification from the same sex. Most persons appear to be heterosexual. Homosexuals and bisexuals, as a group, appear to be more deficient in social morality than heterosexuals. There are, of course, many individual exceptions.

Homo moralensis Moral man. The latest development in *Homo sapiens* represented by men who deliberately play the Game of Life.

Homo progressivus Progressive man. A term used by Teilhard de Chardin to connote men who perceive and value human progress and have faith in mankind's future.

Homo sapiens The species of man which has been dominant for about 50,000 years. Cro-Magnon was a *Homo sapiens*; Neanderthal was not, although they could probably interbreed, as can lions and tigers.

Homosexual Refers to a condition in which a person prefers the company of his own sex. Homosexuality is a statistical concept which is difficult to assess. It can only be inferred by overt behavior which leads persons *voluntarily* to choose the company of their own sex. A person who experiences sexual gratification with persons of his own sex is not necessarily homosexual, but may be bisexual or heterosexual.

Ideology An ideology is an interdependent set of ideological beliefs. An ideological belief is a belief in a cause and effect relationship which is not based on scientific evidence. All superstitions are ideological beliefs. All religions are ideologies. Marxism and most of what is called "social science" are ideologies.

Imaginary Awareness Refers to an illusion of awareness which has no basis in reality. It can occur by imagining a model of cause and effect relationships which cannot be substantiated scientifically. Most imaginary awareness results from accepting the imagined model of someone else as true when it is in fact false. Skepticism is the best defense against imaginary awareness. Systematic, creative skepticism is the basis of scientific method.

Imagination That component of intelligence which generates Information independent of the Sensors. Imagined events are used to complete the pattern of sensed events so that there are no inconsistencies. The effectors test the validity of the completed pattern by generating new events until all sensed events are consistent. This is how awareness grows. Imagination has never been localized as have the other components of intelligence. It seems to be associated with the cortex in some way. The more ethical a person is, the more imaginative he seems to be. It may be that Imagination is produced in part by the moral field of the Cosmic Moral Society and that receptivity to this field depends on ethics.

Immediate Family A family limited to our parents, children, spouse and siblings. (See family.)

Immoral A person is immoral if and only if he deliberately declines the challenge of the Game of Life and consciously chooses to play the Game of Pleasure. An immoral person only plays the Game of Pleasure. Persons become immoral by becoming increasingly unethical until all their actions are strategies in the Game of Pleasure. An immoral person never plays the Game of Life again; he has irreversible entropy. Persons are made immoral by an unethical society. Only highly intelligent persons can be immoral. Most unethical persons are children, not immoral adults.

Immoral Community The Immoral Community is that group of persons who seek power without awareness. When these persons are decent, they seek to make others happy. When they are indecent, they seek only to make themselves happy. The Immoral Community is represented by the "Establishment" in every country. It consists of politicians, priests, Marxists, some social "scientists," and others. The Immoral Community serves only to increase the total entropy of the human race.

Immoral Society An immoral society is a society in which all adults are immoral and all children are made unethical. An immoral society has irreversible entropy. Russia is probably becoming an immoral society. The U.S. is on the verge of becoming an unethical society.

Important Refers to any activity which significantly affects awareness either positively or negatively.

Industry A collective term for any organization which serves to produce any goods and services other than entertainment and education.

Information The symbolic representation of events and their relationships. Information is an essential component in the structure of intelligence. An entity devoid of all Information would have no intelligence. All the Information in our bodies, except instinct, is produced by the Sensors or by the Imagination.

Intelligence The ability to predict and control the total environment—physical, biological and psychosocial. Intelligence is a structure with discrete components, namely, Will, Memory, Logic, Imagination, Sensors, Effectors, Connectors and Information. Each of the components is essential to intelligence. All the components, except for Information, seem to have a largely hereditary basis.

Investigator Any person who systematically seeks new knowledge on any subject(s).

Joining Part of the process of evolution by which entities which have reached a threshold of awareness organize themselves into a more complex entity such that the new collective awareness is greater than the sum of the parts. (e.g., Atoms represent a joining of elementary particles; molecules represent a joining of atoms; cells represent a joining of molecules; man represents a joining of cells; the Moral Society represents a joining of man.)

Joy A condition of extreme happiness. Joy is happiness without anxiety; it is a happiness which we have no fear of

ever losing. It seems that only the deliberate expansion of awareness for ourselves and others produces joy.

Knowledge A critical mass of information which creates direct perception where before none existed. Our knowledge is a function of our innate intelligence and our environment. The geometry of our knowledge (i.e., a spherical or an ellipsoidal surface) is dependent on ethics. Information becomes knowledge only when it is a component of intelligence. Knowledge subsumes creativity.

Leftist Refers to a belief that behavior is determined primarily by environment and not heredity. This belief exists on a continuum. The extreme leftist believes that heredity plays no role in shaping behavior and that environment is all important. The extreme rightist believes the opposite. (See rightist.)

Liberal Refers to any attitude which is tolerant of change. This characteristic exists on a continuum with the extreme conservative at one extreme and the extreme liberal at the other. (See conservative.)

Life That effect of matter which produces an awareness of non-self and causes awareness to expand and grow until it produces awareness of awareness. At this time mind begins to develop rapidly until it ceases to be an effect of life and becomes an effect of itself. (See mind.)

Logic That component of intelligence which determines when different quanta of information and/or knowledge are inconsistent. Logic is a filter which tells the Will which events are inconsistent in order that new events may be generated until all events are consistent. All events are consistent if and only if a person is totally aware. Therefore, all events are never consistent. A person who sees inconsistent events as consistent is either psychotic, ideological or both. Logic appears to be a function of parts of the cortex.

Love A state of mind where the welfare of another person is sufficiently important to us that we are willing to sacrifice some of our welfare in order to enhance his. Love is "natural" when "welfare" is synonymous with "awareness." Love is "perverse" when "welfare" is synonymous with "happiness."

LTA (Level of Total Awareness) A condition of total awareness which may be estimated by statistically sampling a person's knowledge in each dimension of noospace and by testing his ability to integrate the knowledge to produce coherent, multi-disciplinary models. Tests such as the Army General Technical and the Graduate Record Examination are crude attempts to develop scientific LTA tests. The latter tests are essential to the creation of an Ethical State. The validity of an LTA test is measured by how well it predicts a person's current ability to predict and control his total environment.

Machine A manufactured device which converts one form of energy into another. Language, clothing, computers, houses, tools, and organizations are examples of machines. The machine is the basis of human evolution. Since the advent of *Homo sapiens* human evolution has depended almost entirely on the development of ever better machines.

Mankind (Man, humanity, the human race, etc.) The family of ethical beings, which began about four million years ago. It is represented by *Homo sapiens* today. It may become *Homo moralensis* in the future.

Memory That component of intelligence which stores Information in addressable units. The address is determined in part by the nature of the information and its relationship to other information. In our own bodies Memory is a process by which molecules are altered in our brain by sensed or imagined Information.

Metazoa Multicellular animals as opposed to Protozoa, which are unicellular. Sponges, insects, fish and man are all metazoa.

Military A collective term for any organization which serves to impose the will of any authority by force.

Mind That effect of life which is aware in general and aware of self in particular. The evolution of mind goes from 1) awareness of self to 2) awareness of others to 3) awareness of awareness (the beginning of ethical behavior) to 4) awareness of ethics (the beginning of morality). There is no sharp distinction between matter and life or energy and matter, therefore the concept of mind may extend back through the evolutionary scale to chaotic energy, with matter representing awareness of self because it maintains integrity of form. Therefore, mind while certainly an effect of life may also be an effect of matter. Our minds and the perceptions therein are the only thing about which we can be certain.

Minimax Strategy A plan for minimizing our risks by obtaining the best of the worst in a game. In the Game of Life the worst is entropy, therefore, the minimax strategy is also the uniformly optimal strategy which maximizes our awareness while minimizing our entropy. In the Game of Pleasure the worst is unhappiness. The best of the worst is extinction. Death is, therefore, the minimax strategy in the Game of Pleasure. Following the rules of the Game of Life is a uniformly optimal strategy in both the Game of Life and the Game of Pleasure. (See uniformly optimal.)

Moral A person is moral if and only if he deliberately and consciously plays the Game of Life. A moral person never plays the Game of Pleasure again after becoming moral. Moral persons always increase total awareness. Morality is the highest form of ethical behavior. Moral persons are, in general, highly creative; they never destroy. (See personal and social morality.)

Moral Community The Moral Community is that group of persons who are primarily concerned with expanding awareness. The Moral Community consists of artists, scientists and technologists. A technologist is anyone concerned with producing goods and services which increase awareness. Physicians, farmers, teachers, laborers and mechanics are all examples of technologists. The Moral Community represents the true workers of the world who are exploited by the Immoral Community.

Music The purest art. It is devoid of conscious meaning and operates entirely at the unconscious level to communicate the awareness of a culture.

Nature-Nurture Problem The problem of determining whether differences between groups or individuals are due to heredity (nature) or environment (nurture).

Noospace The abstract space of mind where each dimension represents an orthogonal area of knowledge. For convenience, noospace may be seen in three dimensions—the physical, biological, and psychosocial. In reality, noospace probably has infinitely many orthogonal dimensions. Only by relating each dimension of noospace to all other dimensions can awareness be maximized. Knowledge can be specialized, but awareness is total.

Noosphere (nö-oś-fēr) n. [<Gr. *noos*, mind, and *sphaira*, a body whose surface always has all its points equidistant from a single point], the envelope of collective human mind which surrounds the Earth. A word first used by Pierre Teilhard de Chardin to describe some aspects of the Moral Society. (See biosphere.)

Optimal Refers to the extremal of a desired effect. Something is optimal when it is the best and there is nothing better. Optimality is not necessarily a unique property. In a game there may be many optimal strategies. When a person behaves optimally it means that he has done the best he could. It does not mean that someone else might not have done better.

Organization A group of persons tied together by a set of common objectives and rules. All organizations have the propensity for being turned into bureaucracies if they are deprived of feedback. All bureaucracies are organizations, but not all organizations are bureaucracies.

Orthogonal At right angles. When events or actions are orthogonal, then each can occur without necessarily affecting the other. However,

orthogonal events are not necessarily independent.

Parasite (parasitical human being) Any entity which produces pollution and consumes resources without in any way expanding awareness.

Perception That property of mind which integrates sensed information into a meaningful whole so that knowledge results.

Personal Morality Refers to the deliberate desire to increase one's own personal awareness. Personal morality must coexist with social morality or it will atrophy. Without social morality personal morality may become perverted into a desire solely for personal power. All moral persons have both components of morality, but not necessarily in equal amounts.

Personal Power Control over the environment used solely as a means of creating personal security.

Perverse Refers to any action which seeks to increase happiness in such a way that awareness is not increased. A pervert is any person who systematically increases his own happiness without increasing anyone's awareness, including his own.

Phenotype The external appearence of an organism in terms of its morphology and overt behavior. (See genotype.)

Phylum A group of life forms characterized by unique properties which make them distinct from all other life forms. E.g., arthropods are characterized by jointed legs and a chitinous exoskeleton; chordates by the notochord; and ethical beings, including man, by awareness of their own awareness.

Power The ability to control the environment.

Prediction Imagining an event correctly before it is directly perceived. Prediction is essential to awareness. Without the ability to predict an entity could not see the patterns which tie its perceptions together; it would have neither a past nor a future but would exist only in the present in a state of continuous destruction.

Probability Refers to the degree of confidence that a person has that a cause and effect relationship is true. Zero probability implies that the person is certain that the relationship is false. A probability of one implies that the person is certain that the relationship is true. An ethical person always places a probability greater than zero, but less than one on the validity of all cause and effect relationships outside The progress of the human race is in-total awareness within the universe.

Progress The process of ever-expanding of the existence of his own thoughts. dicated by man's increasing ability to predict and control the total environment. This progress is least evident in the psychosocial environment, but even here it occurs. Only immorality can stop human progress.

Protagonist When used without adjectives and capitalized, "Protagonist" refers to a person who is a deliberate player of the Game of Life. A Protagonist plays a leading part in doing the best he can to maximize total awareness. Those who will create an Ethical State are all Protagonists.

Racism A belief that the behavior of a person can be inferred from the *a priori* expected behavioral characteristics of the racial group to which the person belongs. Racism neglects to allow for widespread individual differences within races. Science indicates that there is a wide overlap in the behavior of all races.

Random Refers to any process whose outcome cannot be predicted with certainty. Any process of which we have incomplete information is random. Nature can only be exactly predicted when we possess all knowledge, i.e., when we are totally aware of everything. For this reason, nature will always seem random to any finite being. However, the accuracy and precision of our predictions and control can increase asymptotically toward perfection. The randomness is within ourselves, not necessarily within the external universe. The cosmic force will always seem random to any finite being because entropy and evolution coexist in infinite extension and we can never

have complete knowledge of either process.

Reality That which we can 1) predict and control or 2) know that we can neither predict nor control. All perception is real but not our beliefs about the causes of the perceptions. Only true awareness is real. Only awareness that passes the test of prediction and control is true awareness.

Relevant Anything which expands total awareness is relevant. That which best serves to integrate and expand the *totality* of knowledge is the most relevant. Relevance implies something which is both important and ethical.

Religion An ideology which seeks to explain everything in the universe and stresses ideological beliefs about the soul. (See soul and ideology.)

Revolt Against Reason A phenomenon which is sweeping all the democracies. It is characterized by a rejection of scientific method and an uncritical acceptance of ideology. It seeks to destroy the structure of society, but has no specific alternative to the structure. Traditionally the Revolt Against Reason was a rightist movement which began with Rousseau and culminated in Hitler. The "Old Left" was not part of the Revolt Against Reason; the "New Left" is.

Rightist Refers to a belief that human behavior is determined more by heredity than by environment. The characteristic exists on a continuum with the extreme rightist believing that environment has no effect whatsoever on behavior. The extreme leftist believes that all behavior is determinated entirely by heredity. (See leftist.)

Robot A machine which is self-improving (i.e., self-organizing) and can predict and control its environment.

RNA (ribonucleic acid) A complex, single-stranded, polymeric, organic molecule. RNA is a constituent of all living cells. It has the capacity to store information. DNA can be built on templates of RNA. RNA can carry information between DNA molecules.

Science A method for increasing awareness which is based on the principle that all hypotheses and theories are to be held in doubt until proven true by controlled experimentation. Hypotheses and theories are held to be tentatively true only so long as they make correct predictions. Those hypotheses and theories which make the most accurate and consistently correct predictions are the "truest." In science only that which works is true.

Scientific Illiterate A person who possesses little or no scientific knowledge. This is a relative term since almost everyone has some scientific knowledge. In general, persons who have no knowledge of systematic biology, physical science, or mathematics are scientific illiterates.

Security A state of mind in which a person believes he has or can readily obtain all he thinks he needs and has no fear of losing what he already has.

Selective Birth Control A system of eugenics whereby members of a species with desirable characteristics are encouraged to reproduce as many offspring as possible. Members with undesirable characteristics are discouraged from producing any offspring. In general, the number of offspring produced by any member is directly proportional to his desirable characteristics and inversely proportional to his undesirable characteristics. This technique assumes that there are genetic differences in all important characteristics between different members of the species. The technique is used in such a way that the total population is in proper balance with available resources.

Selfless Refers to a mental state in which personal security and happiness are seen as secondary to a higher purpose. The only purpose which seems to have the potential for producing selflessness is the pursuit of total awareness as an end in itself.

Sexism An ideology analogous to racism, which ascribes behavioral characteristics to a person solely on the basis of his sex. The scientific evidence implies that although the genetic potential for various types of behavior may not be identically distributed in each sex, the full gamut of human behavior, other than the reproductive functions,

probably exists within each sex. The best way to avoid both racism and sexism is to accept each person solely on the basis of his individual merit and to avoid a *priori* judgments.

Sensors That component of intelligence through which some of the events in the total environment are represented symbolically by Information which is stored in the Memory. In the body the Sensors are visual, auditory, olfactory, kinesthetic, etc.

Socialism A socio-political system in which every person is held responsible for the welfare of every other person. The Ethical State is a socialistic system, but it does not have an ideological basis as do most of the existing systems which today call themselves "socialistic." In all current socialistic systems, "welfare" is considered synonymous with "happiness." In the Ethical State, "welfare" is synonymous with "awareness."

Social Morality Refers to the deliberate desire to increase the awareness of others. Social morality must co-exist with personal morality or it will become perverted into immoral decency, whereby the person seeks to increase solely the happiness of others. All moral persons have both components of morality, though not necessarily to the same degree.

Soul The notion of "soul" is identical to that of "mind" except that the soul is tied to supernatural cause and effect relationships. The soul, unlike the mind, is usually assumed to be immortal. Our mind insofar as it is an effect of our body almost certainly dies with our body. The notions of "soul" which are not identical to "mind" are ideologically based and have no scientific basis.

Specialist A specialist is a person who has developed depth of knowledge in one area at the cost of being ignorant in other areas. The specialist differs from the generalist not because of what he knows but because of what he does not know. It is possible for a specialist to be more intelligent and have more knowledge in every area than a generalist. When a generalist and a specialist are of comparable intelligence the generalist is always more aware. It is possible for a generalist to be more aware than a specialist even when the latter is much more intelligent than the former. If a generalist is represented by a sphere and a specialist by an ellipsoid, then their total knowledge, which is a product of their intelligence, is represented by their surface area. Their awareness is a product of *both* their intelligence and their ethics and is represented by their volume. A sphere has maximum volume for a given surface area.

Speciation Refers to the process by which a new generalized phylum starting with a single species fans out into the biosphere by having succeeding generations adapt until they can fit into one and only one ecological niche. Each adaptation represents a new species which is forever separated from its former brothers.

Statistically-Similar Intuitively, this concept refers to a condition in which two or more entities have many measureable characteristics in common and do not differ radically in any characteristics. Persons would belong to a statistically similar group if, for example, they had a common age, I.Q., health, ethnic background, education, income, etc. For a rigorous treatment of this notion see "Mahalonobis Distance Function," "Fisher Likeness Coefficient" and other techniques for statistical taxonomy in C. R. Rao's *Advanced Statistical Methods in Biometric Research*; also see Kendall and Stuart, *The Advanced Theory of Statistics*, Vol. 3.

Tachyons Hypothesized subatomic particles which always travel at speeds in excess of the speed of light. Tachyons accelerate by losing energy until they are traveling at infinite speeds when they have zero energy. Although the existence of tachyons is theoretically feasible they have not as yet been experimentally detected. However, many theoretically predicted subatomic particles were conjectured long before they were detected, e.g., mesons, positrons, and neutrinos. The general rule seems to be that any particle which theoretically fits into the over-all structure of matter will exist. Tachyons were originally postulated by Gerald Feinberg.

TAP (Total Awareness Potential) The potential that any person has for increasing his total awareness. Insofar as an LTA test can give a good indication of a person's total awareness, the validity of a TAP test is indicated by the test's ability to predict future LTA from the persons current health, age, LTA and general condition. The closest thing to a TAP test is the so-called "I.Q. test." The I.Q. test is deficient in that it does not evaluate Will and Imagination. For this reason it can only predict gross inability to cope with the total environment. This is the case when a person is seriously deficient in Logic or Memory. A combination of good Logic and Memory measured together with measures of Imagination and Will should lead to valid TAP tests.

Technology A scientific process for building, operating and/or designing machines; the application of science for control of the environment.

Total Environment Total environment includes all that can be perceived or conceived. The total environment may be divided for convenience into 1) the physical which includes all of matter and energy; 2) the biological which includes all life forms including Man; and 3) the psychosocial which includes all activities of the mind. These divisions are only a convenience which should vanish in time. Ultimately, it should be shown that matter, life and mind are all interrelated phenomena produced by a single cosmic force. In recent years, the apparent discontinuities between life and matter have been disappearing. Eventually all psychosocial phenomena will be understood in the same manner.

Trivial Refers to activity which neither increases nor decreases awareness. Trivial activity will increase entropy. In the long run, trivial activity may decrease awareness indirectly by increasing entropy to the point where awareness is no longer possible.

Truth A cause and effect relationship

is true if and only if it enables one to predict and control the environment. All models of cause and effect relationships involve error. Therefore, truth is a goal which is approached asymptotically as total awareness grows. Whoever claims to have found truth, speaks falsely; whoever pursues truth, will get ever closer to it. Only an entity who is totally aware knows truth. Even apparently tautological statements may involve semantic errors.

Unconscious Refers to that state of mind in which we are aware, but we are not aware of our own awareness. The Imagination seems to work primarily at the unconscious level (See conscious.)

Unethical Behavior is unethical if and only if it decreases awareness. All unethical behavior is a strategy in the Game of Pleasure. A person is unethical when he plays the Game of Pleasure more often than he plays the Game of Life. Unethical behavior always increases entropy.

Unethical Society A society is unethical when most of its members are unethical and it is structured to decrease awareness. Every nation is an unethical society or an incipient unethical society. Societies become unethical through bureaucracy, ideology and immoral leadership.

Uniform Birth Control A system of eugenics by which the quality of a species is increased by deliberately keeping the population down to a level where all members of the species are assured adequate resources. This is done by limiting the number of offspring each member can produce uniformly for all members. This technique is based on the assumption that there are no important differences in genetic structure between any members of the species.

Uniformly Optimal Strategy A uniformly optimal strategy is a plan for minimizing our risks while simultaneously maximizing expected gains. Following the rules of the Game of Life is a uniformly optimal strategy in both the Game of Pleasure and the Game of Life. (See minimax.)

Will That component of intelligence which directs the flow of Information to the other components. Will is a vector quantity with a direction and a magnitude. The direction determines what type of knowledge will be acquired; the magnitude determines the resolve to acquire the knowledge. The Imagination and the Effectors generate events which provide a critical mass of Information until knowledge exists. Under the direction of the Will all the components of intelligence operate to expand awareness continuously. Will in our bodies appears to be an effect of cells in the depths of the brain and is unrelated to the cortex. The Will operates at both the conscious and unconscious levels.

BIBLIOGRAPHY

The following bibliography includes some references which provide useful background for directly perceiving the patterns of evolution. Entries with the symbol * refer to footnoted references given previously in the text. Entries followed by a (1) are elementary books which require some degree of rigorous thinking. Entries followed by a (2) are still of a relatively elementary nature, but require some preparation in college-level mathematics and/or science. Entries followed by a (3) are more advanced treatises and texts. Entries which are not followed by a number are easily-understood accounts which do not require rigorous thinking.

All technical references are at the undergraduate level, but some, such as Feller's *Probability* and Courant's *Calculus*, can be quite deep.

The reader is referred to the works of Isaac Asimov for easily-understood, non-rigorous treatments on virtually all important scientific topics. The books by Asimov give considerable breadth, but little depth; Asimov's books are good for motivating further study and for giving a sense of relevancy to anyone seeking to become a generalist.

What has preceded in this book is a distillation of the following references and/or other experiences. An attempt was made to reduce the knowledge to the same elementary level as in Asimov's books. A more rigorous treatment is being prepared.

ALEKSANDROV, KOLMOGOROV, and LAVRENT'EV, *Mathematics: Its Contents, Methods and Meaning.* (2)
ANDRADA, E. N. da C., et al., *Evolution of Man.* (1)
ARBIB, M. A., *Brains, Machines and Mathematics.* (1)
ASIMOV, I., *Understanding Physics* (3 vols.); *The Intelligent Man's Guide to Science; the Universe from Flat Earth to Quasar; The Human Brain; The Genetic Code; The World of Carbon; The World of Nitrogen,* etc.
ASTIN, A. W., "Undergraduate Achievement and University Excellence," *Science,* August 16, 1968; pp. 661–667.*
ASTRACHAN, A., "Soviet Scientists Demand Freedom for Geneticist," *Washington Post,* June 6, 1970, p. 1.

BARNES, H. E., *An Intellectual and Cultural History of the Western World.*
BEADLE, G. and M., *The Language of Life.* (1)
BEASLEY, W. G., *Modern History of Japan.*
BELMAN, R. E. and DREYFUS, S. S., *Applied Dynamic Programming.* (3)
BERGMANN, P. A., *The Riddle of Gravitation.*
BERGSON, H., *Creative Evolution.*
BERNE, E., *Games People Play.**
BISHOP, ELDER and HEATH, "Intracranial Self-Stimulation in Man," *Science* 140, 1963, pp. 394–396.*
BLUM, H. F., *Evolution: Time's Arrow.* (2)
BOAS, F., *Race, Language and Culture.*
BOFFEY, P. M., "Japan (I): On the Threshold of Big Science?" *Science,* Jan. 2, 1970; "Japan (II): University Turmoil is Reflected in Research," *Science,* Jan. 9, 1970.
BORN, M., *Einstein's Theory of Relativity;* (2) *Natural Philosophy of Cause and Chance;* (2) and *Experiment and Theory in Physics.* (2)
BONHOEFFER, D., *Ethics and Letters and Papers From Prison.*
BRADLEY, D. G., *Guide to the World's Religions.*
BROWNE, V., *The World's Great Scriptures.*
BROW, W. A., *The Church: Catholic and Protestant.*

BULLOCK, A., Hitler: A Study in Tyranny.
BUTLER, J. A. V., Progress in Biophysics and Biophysical Chemistry. (3)
CALVIN, M., Chemical Evolution. (2)
CAMUS, A., The Myth of Sisyphus* and The Rebel.*
CHAMBERLIN, W. H., The Russian Revolution, 1917–1921.
CARR, H. W., Leibniz.
CASON, J., Essential Principles of Organic Chemistry. (2)
CHASE, S., The Proper Study of Mankind.
HU, CHIANG-TU, China: Its People, Its Society, Its Culture.
CHURCHILL, W. S., A History of the English Speaking Peoples, and The Second World War.
CLARK, K., Civilisation.
COLEMAN, J. S., et al., Equality of Educational Opportunity, U.S. Department of Health, Education and Welfare, Office of Education, July 1966.
COHEN, M. R. and NAGEL, E., An Introduction to Logic and Scientific Method.* (1)
CONANT, J. B., The Chemistry of Organic Compounds. (2)
COURANT, R., Differential and Integral Calculus. (2) Highly Recommended.
COURANT, R. and HILBERT, D., Methods of Mathematical Physics (3), Highly Recommended.
COURANT, R. and ROBBINS, H., What is Mathematics? (1) Highly Recommended.
CRAGY, K., The Call of the Minaret.
CREEL, H. G., Chinese Thought from Confucius to Mao Tse-tung. Highly Recommended.
CUBER, J. F., Sociology: A Synopsis of Principles.

d'ABRO, A., The Evolution of Scientific Thought.
DANIELS, F. and ALBERTY, R. A., Physical Chemistry. (2)
DARWIN, C., The Origin of Species; and The Descent of Man.
DHALLA, M. N., The History of Zoroastrianism.
de JOUVENEL, A., On Power.
DELGADO, J., Physical Control of the Mind: Toward a Psychocivilized Society.*
DEUTSCHER, I., Stalin: A Political Biography.
de VAUCOULEURS, G., "The Case for a Hierarchical Cosmology," Science, Feb. 27, 1970. (1)
DOBZHANSKY, T., Heredity and the Nature of Man; and Mankind Evolving.
DuPRAW, E. J., Cell and Molecular Biology. (3)

EINSTEIN, A., Out of My Later Years.
ELIOT, A. M. and RAY, C., Biology.

FANN, K. T., Ludwig Wittgenstein: The Man and His Philosophy.
FEINBERG, G., The Prometheus Project; "Particles that Go Faster than Light," Scientific American, Feb. 1970.
FELLER, W., Probability Theory, Vol. I (1), Vol. II (3) Highly Recommended.

FERGUSON, T. S., *Mathematical Statistics: A Decision Theory Approach.* (3)
FEYNMAN, R. P., et al., *The Feynman Lectures on Physics.* (3 vols.) (1) Highly Recommended.
FIESER, L. F. and FIESER, M., *Advanced Organic Chemistry.* (3)
FISHER, R. A., *Genetical Theory of Natural Selection.* (3)
FITZGERALD, C. P., *China: A Short Cultural History.*
FREUD, S., *A General Introduction to Modern Psychoanalysis; Moses and Monotheism, The Basic Writings,* (Modern Library); and *New Lectures on Psychoanalysis.*
FULLOP-MILLER, R., *The Jesuits.*

GAMOW, G., *Creation of the Universe.*
GAMOW, G. and CLEVELAND, J. M., *Physics Foundations and Frontiers.*
GELFAND, I. M. and FOMIN, S. V., *Calculus of Variations.* (3)
GOETHE, W., *Faust.*
GOLDMAN, S., *Information Theory.* (3)
GOSS, C. M., *Gray's Anatomy of the Human Body.* (2)
GREENBERG, D. S., "Israel: Research and Education," *Science,* Apr. 24, 1970.
GRINSPOON, L., "Marijuana," *Scientific American,* December 1969.*
GROSSMAN, S. P., *Physiological Psychology.* (3)
GUILFORD, J. P., *The Nature of Human Intelligence.* (1) Highly Recommended.

HAMILTON, MADISON, JAY; *The Federalist Papers.*
HAMPSHIRE, S., *Spinoza.*
HANDLER, P. (Editor), *Biology and the Future of Man.* (1) Highly Recommended.
HAWKINS, J. K., *Circuit Design of Digital Computers.* (3)
HEGEL, G., *The Philosophy of History.*
HEGNER, R. W. and STILES, M. A., *College Zoology.* (1)
HILDEBRAND, J. H. and POWELL, R. E., *Principles of Chemistry.* (1)
HILGARD, E. R., *Introduction to Psychology.*
HOFFER, E., *The True Believer.*
HOYLE, F., *Frontiers of Astronomy; Astronomy;* and *The Nature of the Universe.*
HUIZINGA, J., *Homo Ludens.**
HUME, R. E., *The World's Living Religions: A Historical Sketch.*
HUXLEY, J., *Religion Without Revelation.*

JAMES, E. V., *Comparative Religion.*
JAMES, W., *Varieties of Religious Experience.*
JENSEN, A. R., "How Much Can We Raise I.Q.?" *Harvard Educational Review,* Reprint Series No. 2: Environment, Heredity and Intelligence, 1969.* (2) Highly Recommended.
JENSEN, H., "Soviet Dissenter Speaks Out," *Washington Post,* May 17, 1970, page 1.
JEPSEN, SIMPSON, and MAYR, *Genetics, Paleontology and Evolution.* Highly Recommended.
JUNG, C. G., *Collected Works.*

JUNG, C. G. and PAULI, W., Interpretation of Nature and Psyche.

KALES, A., Sleep: Physiology and Pathology.*
KANT, E., Critique of Pure Reason. (1)
KARLIN, S., Mathematical Methods and Theory in Games, Programming and Economics. (3)
KENDALL, M. G. and STUART, A., The Advanced Theory of Statistics, Vols. I, II, III. (3) Highly Recommended.
KENNAN, G. F., Russia and the West under Lenin and Stalin.
KIMBLE, G. A., Hilgard and Marquis' Conditioning and Learning.
KITTEL, C., Thermal Physics. (3)
KOESTLER, A., The Lotus and the Robot; The Ghost in the Machine; Act of Creation.
KOHLER, W., Gestalt Psychology.
KOFFKA, K., Principles of Gestalt Psychology. (1)
KULLBACH, S., Information Theory and Statistics. (3)

LA BARRE, W., The Human Animal.
LANDAU, L. D. and LIFSHITZ, E., Mechanics. (3)
LEARY, T., Psychedelic Experience.
LEIBNIZ, G., The Monadology and Other Philosophical Writings, (Robt. Latta, Oxford); New Essays Concerning Human Understanding; and Philosophical Papers and Writings, (2 Vols., Chicago Univ.).
LEIGHTON, R. B., Principles of Modern Physics. (2) Highly Recommended.
LENIN, V. I., The State and Revolution; Imperialism: The Highest Stage of Capitalism; and Materialism and Empirio—Criticism.
LEVINS, R., Evolution in Changing Environment.
LIDDELL HART, B. H., Strategy.
LIPPMAN, W., Essays in Public Philosophy.
LIPSON, G. P. and LIPSON, H., Optical Physics. (3)
LOTKA, A. J., Elements of Mathematical Biology. (2)
LUCE, D. R., Developments in Mathematical Psychology. (2)
LUCE, D. R. and RAIFFA, H., Games and Decisions. (1)

MACHIAVELLI, N., The Prince.
MAIMONIDES, M., The Guide for the Perplexed.
MAO TSE-TUNG, Quotations from Chairman Mao Tse-Tung; On Revolution and War; and Selected Works.
MARCH, J. G. and SIMON, H. A., Organizations.
MARCUSE, H., The One Dimensional Man; Essay on Liberation.
MARX, K., Capital, Manifesto and Other Writings, (Modern Library). (1)
MASSETT, L., "Marijuana and Behavior," Science News, February 7, 1970.
McGINNISS, J., The Selling of the President.
McNEILL, W. H., The Rise of the West.
MELGES, F. T., et. al., "Marijuana and Temporal Disintegration," Science, May 29, 1970; pp. 1118–1120.
MILNE, L. J. and MILNE, M. M., The Biotic World and Man. (1)
MINSKY, M., Semantic Information Processing. (1)
MOOD, A., Introduction to the Theory of Statistics. (3) Highly Recommended.

MOORE, G. E., *Principia Ethica; and Some Main Problems in Philosophy.*
MOORE, J. A., *Principles of Zoology.* (1)
NEMHAUSER, G. L., *Introduction to Dynamic Programming.* (3)
NEWMAN, J. R., *The World of Mathematics,* (4 vols.). Highly Recommended.
NEWTON, R. G., "Particles That Travel Faster than Light," *Science,* March 20, 1970. (1)
NIETZSCHE, F., *Also Sprach Zarathustra.*
NIKHILANANDA, S., *The Essence of Hinduism.*
NORTHROP, F. S. C., *Alfred North Whitehead; An Anthology.*

OLDS and MILNER, "Positive Reinforcement Produced by Electrical Stimulation of Septal Area and Other Regions in the Rat Brain," *J. Comp. Physiol-Psychol,* 47, 1954, pp. 419–427.
O'NEILL, B., *Elementary Differential Geometry.* (3)
ORTEGA Y GASSET, J., *Obras Completas.* (Particularly Volume 8.)

PADOVER, S. K., *Thomas Jefferson on Democracy.*
PAVLOV, I. P., *Selected Works.* (2)
PICKTHALL, M., *The Meaning of the Glorious Koran.*
PLATT, J. R., *The Step to Man; "What We Must Do,"* *Science,* Nov. 28, 1969.
POLYA, G., *Patterns of Plausible Inference,* (2); and *Induction and Analogy in Mathematics.* (2)
PRIBRAM, K. H., *Brain and Behavior,* (4 vols.). (2)
PROGOFF, I., *Jung's Psychology and Its Social Meaning.*

QUARTON, MELNECHUCK, SCHMITT, *The Neurosciences.* (3)

RASHEVSKY, N., *Mathematical Foundations of Biology.* (2)
RAUCH, GEORGE VON, *A History of Soviet Russia.*
REISER, O. L., *The Integration of Human Knowledge.* (1) Highly Recommended.
RICHARDSON, R. S., *Astronomy in Action.* (1)
ROSENBLUETH, A., *Mind and Brain.* (1)
ROTH, C., *History of the Jewish People.*
RUSSELL, B., *A History of Western Philosophy,* Highly Recommended; *The Philosophy of Leibniz; Power;* and *Dictionary of Mind, Matter and Morals.*

SACKMAN, H., *Computers, System Science, and Evolving Society.* (1)
SAKHAROV, A. D., "Thoughts on Progress, Peaceful Co-Existence and Intellectual Freedom," *New York Times,* Jul. 22, 1968, pp. 1, 14–16; "Letter to Brezhnev," *Newsweek,* April 13, 1970. All Highly Recommended.
SANSOM, G. B., *Japan; A Short Cultural History; The Western World and Japan.*
SARTRE, J. P., *Being and Nothingness.*
SAXON, D. S., *Elementary Quantum Mechanics.* (3)
SCHLICK, M., *Problems of Ethics.* (1)
SCHROEDINGER, E. C., *Science, Theory and Man; and What is Life.*
SCHWEITZER, A., *An Anthology; J. S. Bach; Goethe: Five Studies; Philosophy of Civilization; Teaching of Reverence for Life.*

SEMAT, H., Introduction to Nuclear and Atomic Physics. (2)
SHKLOVSKII, I. S. and SAGAN, C., Intelligent Life in the Universe.
SIMPSON, G., The Major Features of Evolution. Highly Recommended.
SIMPSON, G., et. al., Life: An Introduction to Biology.
SNOW, C. P., The Two Cultures and a Second Look (Mentor).
SOKOLNIKOFF, I. S. and REDHEFFER, R. M., Mathematics for Physicists and Modern Engineering. (3)
SOLOMON, H., Mathematical Thinking in the Measurement of Behavior. (2)
SOMMERVILLE, D. M. Y., The Geometry of N Dimensions, (3); Non-Euclidean Geometry. (3)
SPENGLER, O., The Decline of the West.
SPINOZA, B. de, Works of Spinoza, Vols. I and II, (Dover), Highly Recommended.
STERN, C., Human Genetics, 2nd Ed. (1) Highly Recommended.
STERNGLASS, E. J., "The Death of All Children," Esquire, Sept. 1969; and "Infant Mortality and Nuclear Tests," Bulletin of the Atomic Scientists, April 1969.
STRUVE, O., Stellar Evolution. (3)
SULLIVAN, W., "Kapitsa for U.S.-Soviet Convergence," New York Times, Oct. 9, 1969.
SUZUKI, D. T., Essays in Zen Buddhism.

TAYLOR, A. E., Elements of Metaphysics. (1)
TAYLOR, R., Metaphysics. (1)
TEILHARD de CHARDIN, P., The Phenomenon of Man,* Highly Recommended; The Future of Man; Letters from a Traveller; The Divine Milieu; Hymn of the Universe; and The Appearance of Man.
THODAY, J. M. and GIBSON, J. B., "Environmental and Genetical Contributions to Class Differences," Science, Feb. 1970, pp. 990–992.*
TITIEV, M., Science of Man.
TOYNBEE, A., A Study of History.
TROTSKY, L., A History of the Russian Revolution.
TRUMAN, OTTO and TOWLE, Modern Biology. (1)

ULETT, G. A., and GOODRICH, D. W., A Synopsis of Modern Psychology.

VAN DER HAAG, E., The Jewish Mystique.
VON NEUMANN, J., Theory of Self Reproducing Automata (3); The Computer and the Brain.
VULIKH, B. Z., Introduction to Functional Analysis. (3)

WADLE, K., Differential Geometry. (2)
WATSON, J. D., Molecular Biology of the Gene. (2)
WATTS, A., The Way of Zen.
WEICHERT, C. M., Anatomy of the Chordates. (1)
WEIL, ZINBERG, and NELSON, "The Clinical and Psychological Effects of Marijuana," Science, December 13, 1968; pp. 1234–1242.*
WEIZMANN, C., Trial and Error.
WELLS, H. G., An Outline of History.
WEST, E. S. and TODD, W. R., Textbook of Biochemistry. (3)

WHITEHEAD, A. N., *Science and the Modern World*, (1); *Process and Reality*, (1); *Adventures of Ideas*, (1); and *Dialogues*.
WHYTE, L. L., *The Next Development in Man*.
WHYTE, W. H., *The Organization Man*.
WIENER, N., *The Human Use of Human Beings*, (1); *God and Golem Inc.*; and *Cybernetics*. (3)
WITTGENSTEIN, L., *Tractatus Logico-Philosophicus*, (3); *A Lecture on Ethics*, (3); *Philosophical Investigations*, (3); *Zettel*, (3). All highly Recommended.
WOLFE, B. D., *Three Who Made a Revolution* (*Lenin, Trotsky and Stalin*).

THE BIBLE (King James Version).

"Marijuana and Performance," *Science News*, February 21, 1970.*

INDEX